Interventions with Bereaved Children

of related interest

Talking with Children and Young People about Death and Dying
A Workbook
Mary Turner, illustrated by Bob Thomas
ISBN 1 85302 563 1

Helping Children to Manage Loss
Positive Approaches for Renewal and Growth
Brenda Mallon
ISBN 1 85302 605 0

The Forgotten Mourners
Sister Margaret Pennells and Susan C. Smith
ISBN 1 85302 264 0

Grief in Children
Atle Dyregrov
ISBN 1 85302 113 X

Group Work with Children and Adolescents
A Handbook
Edited by Kedar Nath Dwivedi
ISBN 1 85302 157 1

Good Grief 1
Exploring, Feelings, Loss and Death
with Under Elevens second edition
Barbara Ward and Associates
ISBN 1 85302 324 8

Good Grief 2
Exploring Feelings, Loss and Death
with Over Elevens and Adults second edition
Barbara Ward and Associates
ISBN 1 85302 340 X

Interventions with Bereaved Children

Edited by
Susan C Smith and Sister Margaret Pennells

Foreword by Professor William Yule

Jessica Kingsley Publishers
London and Bristol, Pennsylvania

First published in the United Kingdom in 1995 by
Jessica Kingsley Publishers Ltd
116 Pentonville Road
London N1 9JB, England
and
1900 Frost Road, Suite 101
Bristol, PA 19007, U S A

Second impression 1998

Library of Congress Cataloging in Publication Data
A CIP catalogue record for this book is available from the Library of Congress

British Library Cataloguing in Publication Data
A CIP catalogue record for this book is available from the British Library

ISBN 1 85302 285 3

Printed and Bound in Great Britain by
Athenaeum Press, Gateshead, Tyne and Wear

Contents

Foreword

In recent years, I have been approached by neighbours, colleagues and profes-sionals asking my advice as to what to tell a young child when one of their parents has died, often unexpectedly. My first reaction is usually to ask whether the child has been involved in the funeral, and this often provokes slightly embarrassed and alarmed reactions. In general, my advice is very direct: the child has a right to know all they want to about the death; they have the right to say goodbye to their parent in whatever way they want; they should be given the opportunity to participate as fully as they want in any mourning rituals or funeral – even to not participate. All too often, grieving relatives want to spare the child from further hurt and feel that avoiding difficult issues is somehow for the best. The sensitive accounts in this present volume are strong testimony to the fact that children do experience loss; it hurts them as much as it hurts adults, and they need to be able to express their loss in a safe environment.

In my early work with school refusers, I noted that many children who were unexpectedly refusing to attend school after previous exemplary attendance had experienced the loss of a relative, a close friend, or even a family pet. While the text books of the day told that there was an increase in the prevalence of school refusal shortly after transfer to secondary school (and there is), the implication was that the transfer led to the breakdown (and it can). But I was struck by how many children around 10–11 years were reaching a stage where they began to understand more maturely that death was both universal and irreversible. Of course, there are wide individual differences with some children as young as four years appreciating these truths. But the relationship between bereavement and school refusal had been obscured by the coincidental change of school.

So when I was undertaking further research into fears and school refusal, I added in items about fears of death of father and death of mother to the standard fear survey schedule. Interestingly, these items had not been included in the American version and so earlier studies correctly reported that fear of being hit by a car and fear of suffocating were the commonest fears in childhood. But fear of death of father and of mother were each endorsed by 75 per cent of children, making them by far the most common fears yet asked about. There is a message here for researchers and clinicians alike. Unless you ask children what is troubling them, you may never learn it!

When the Herald of Free Enterprise capsized outside Zeebrugge in March 1987, I was asked to assess and help the child survivors and their families. The earliest group I ran demonstrated to me just how much children who have survived a common traumatic experience can gain from sharing their reactions and, more important, their coping strategies. These lessons were put to good use a year and a half later when I was involved in group work with adolescents who survived the sinking of the cruise ship, Jupiter, on the anniversary of the Aberfan disaster. It was, therefore very poignant to read John Shears' account of how he, as headteacher of one of the schools involved in the Jupiter disaster, managed the crisis and his own reactions to it.

This text brings together the practical experiences of a wide range of workers in helping children who have been bereaved. There are moving and sensitive accounts of interventions that clearly had beneficial effects for the children concerned. There are many practical suggestions for activities that can be used with children to help them share what they are most troubled by. There are a number of important themes: first, there are wide individual differences in how children view and experience death, so while the 'stages' are useful guides, always check what each child understands; second, the suggestions given must be adapted to the needs of the individual, family or group. This is not a cook book for grief work. Third, some thought has to be given to the needs and support systems for the workers involved. Working with bereaved children can be challenging, rewarding but also draining.

The editors have done children, and other professionals, a great service in bringing this material together in this readable, accessible and helpful volume.

William Yule
University of London
Institute of Psychiatry

Preface

The aim of this book is to provide its readers with a useful resource guide to practical interventions with bereaved children. Our research and numerous contacts with people has shown us that much is being done with bereaved children across the country and indeed across the world. We feel the time is right to produce a book which gathers together the experience and knowledge of many professionals in the field of childhood grief.

When we began our bereavement groups in 1988 a book of this nature would have been a useful resource. However, at that time there seemed to be little written about children and grief, and even less about interventions with them. This resulted in our using our own initiative and devising a groupwork programme modelled on groups for children who had been sexually abused, and based on the stages of grief. Feedback from the children involved in our first bereavement groups seemed to suggest that this model was viable and, encouraged by this, we developed and refined the programme further.

As we felt our experience had been a valuable one we decided it was important to document it to encourage others working in this area. As a result we wrote 'Holding Back The Nightmares' (1990) 'Bereavement Groups for Children' (1990) and 'Bereavement & Adolescents – A groupwork approach' (1992).

Alongside this we had also produced a Video Training Package (1991) which won the Social Work Today Award for that year and resulted in a degree of media attention both locally and nationally. Copies of the videos have been sold all over the United Kingdom and to other countries including New Zealand, Cyprus, Greece and Holland.

As our work became more widely known, we were asked to assist with the production of several television and radio programmes concerned with children and bereavement. In the last few years this has resulted in our being consulted by many professionals (locally, nationally and internationally) seeking information on grieving children and how to work with them, particularly in a groupwork setting. We believe that there are now many groups being established upon our model. Increasingly, we have been asked to provide training sessions/workshops on groupwork with bereaved children. This reflects the growing interest and awareness of issues surrounding loss and bereavement in childhood. It culminated in our writing our first book, *The Forgotten Mourners*, (1995).

During all of this time we have seen the growth of literature and training material on the theoretical aspects of childhood grief. However, we are still constantly being asked for the practical tools for helping children through grief. For some time we have been aware of a number of professionals in various settings using creative methods in their work. We asked them to join us in producing this book. We felt we should encompass the three main methods of working with bereaved children: Individual, Family and Groupwork. We also wanted to include a section on some of the interesting work being conducted in America, and felt that it was important to cover specialist areas such as working with those who have learning difficulties, those affected by HIV and responses to specific disasters. We would like to have included more on working within schools and in multi-cultural settings; we hope this can be remedied in the future.

This is not a definitive work; there will be many readers who feel they are working equally creatively and originally in different ways. Perhaps their work will stimulate a second volume! The quality and standard of good practice in this book will be evident throughout the chapters. A great deal of time and effort has gone into the preparation and evaluation of these interventions and we feel that they have contributed to the decrease of childhood traumas resulting from bereavement.

We wish to thank all the contributors for their hard work in writing their chapters and sharing their ideas; we have no doubt that these ideas will be of value to many other interested professionals. Our thanks also extend to Shirley Parker for her secretarial support, to our colleagues for their enthusiasm about our work; to our co-workers, who have given us fresh ideas and helped us to refine old ones; to the parents, carers and young people who have taught us so much and inspired us to continue.

Finally, special thanks also go to Sue's family and Margaret's community for bearing with us during the writing of the book and supplying us with endless cups of coffee and chocolate biscuits!

Margaret Pennells and Susan Smith
December 1994

References

Kitchener, S. and Pennells, M. (1990) 'Bereavement groups for children.' *Bereavement Care 9*, 3, 30–31.

Pennells, M. and Kitchener, S. (1990) 'Holding back the nightmares.' *Social Work Today 21*, 25, 14–15.

Pennells, M., Smith, S. and Poppleton, R. (1992) 'Bereavement and adolescents – a groupwork approach.' *Newsletter of the Association of Child Psychology and Psychiatry 14*, 4, 173–8.

Pennells, M. and Smith, S. (1995) *The Forgotten Mourners*. London: Jessica Kingsley Publishers.

Video Training Pack (1991) 1. 'That Morning I Went to School' 2. 'Childhood Grief'. Available from: Child and Family Consultation Service, 8 Notre Dame Mews, Northampton, NN1 2BG.

The Grieving Child
From Grief to Belief

Susan Smith and Margaret Pennells

What does it take to recognize that children can suffer as a result of a significant loss? For us, as workers, it was receiving several referrals in one week, of children who were exhibiting emotional and behavioural problems, and for whom there was a clear link of having also experienced a bereavement in the recent past. For society, we feel that the recognition has developed out of the cumulative effects of several disasters. We have witnessed and been forced to deal with the effects of tragedies such as The Bradford Stadium fire, the sinking of the Herald of Free Enterprise, the Lockerbie Air Crash and, more recently, the Gulf War and Hagley School mini-bus crash. However, we could go even further back to the Aberfan disaster in 1966 when 116 children and 28 adults were killed when their school was engulfed by a coal slip.

Most of us, as professionals and indeed as members of the general public, will have been moved by some aspect of these events and can begin to get in touch with the devastating effects they can have upon our lives. They have also caused us to reflect upon the effects on those involved, especially the children. The media has played a large role in this process in two distinct ways. First, it has brought more national and international events into our living rooms, thereby exposing more of us, including children, to visions of horror and exploitation as well as the after effects of disaster and war. We cannot escape this form of awareness raising which in many ways has also helped us appreciate children's needs when they are faced with issues of death.

Second, the intrusive nature of the media invades private grief and creates fears in vulnerable young people. The media reports on the Gulf War provides a prime example of the impact of this invasion. Several local children of Army families who had seen television news reports of events in the Middle East began to develop fantasies and experience nightmares about what had happened to their fathers. They had already begun to imagine that Daddy may be dead or horribly injured. This highlighted the likelihood that professionals may be faced with a large number of children whose fathers had died, and also the clear need to deal with issues arising from anticipatory grief.

Since the 1980s a debate has emerged about Post Traumatic Stress Disorder (PTSD) in adults (Thompson 1989) and some research has also been carried out on the effects of PTSD in children who have been sexually or physically abused (Deblinger 1989). This showed that children under stress exhibit the symptoms associated with PTSD. Professor William Yule (1989) concluded that children as young as eight years can suffer from PTSD and that they present in almost identical form to that presented by adults. Yule has noted common reactions such as sleep disturbance, separation and concentration difficulties, memory problems, intrusive thoughts, and problems in communicating feelings. Complementary to these findings, professionals who have been working with ordinarily bereaved children (i.e. those not affected by disaster) have noted similar reactions (Dyregrov 1991; Couldrick 1991; Duffy 1991).

Although in society a dispute remains as to whether children do grieve, we are now seeing a movement towards the belief that children indeed do so. A re-examination of psychological theories shows that children exhibit anxious behaviour in loss situations. Bowbly (1979) developed his theory of attachment and loss after observing institutionalized children showing separation anxiety. He felt that the breaking of the affectional bond formed in infancy can be disturbing, producing protest behaviour. These behaviours can also be observed in grieving children. Melanie Klein's work (1960) on splitting and para-noid/schizoid positions postulated that children react to incomplete or badly managed separation from the mother and that this could lead to mental health problems in adulthood. These theories help us understand that from infancy children react to separation and loss and that the management of these situations has implications for future emotional development.

Studies of adult psychiatric patients have confirmed that a bereavement in early childhood can have a damaging effect. Rutter (1966) reported that adult attenders at his psychiatric clinic were more likely to have suffered a bereave-ment as children than the normal population. Freudian theories (Brown 1961) have also taught us that the repression of painful and disturbing experiences can result in neurosis in later life. Thus it is important for children who experience a loss or traumatic event to have the opportunity to express their grief and work through unresolved feelings and issues in order to prevent the possibility of later psychopathology.

Some confusion in the debate on childhood grief may arise from the fact that children show their grief differently from adults. Studies such as Erikson's (1965) help us understand how a child's psychosocial development may influence their handling of a bereavement at a particular developmental stage.

It is felt that from birth up to approximately six months, children need to experience security and consistency of care. When separated from their care giver or when they are bereaved, they can react by showing irritability and erratic eating, sleeping and crying patterns (Duffy 1991). Between six months and two years, children begin to understand object constancy. Adults play games of hide and seek or peek-a-boo to show that objects or people can go out of sight but can return. A child will search for the lost object or absent care giver showing signs of separation anxiety. This behaviour will also occur if the child is bereaved at this stage of development, though they may also become withdrawn, apathetic and lose interest in food toys and outings (Bending 1993).

From the age of two to five years a child's developing intellectual skills allow them a degree of independence. However, children are still unable to grasp the permanence of a separation and if the care giver is absent they will exhibit behaviours aimed at restoration. A child will cry, cling or show anger at the separation through tantrums or destructive behaviour (Couldrick 1991). Experiencing the death of a significant person at this stage may undermine the child's security and sense of the reliability of the world. They will need constant reassurance and repeated explanations in order to make sense of the situation. The child's first experience of death at this age may be through the loss of a pet. However, they may not understand that this is permanent, thinking that their pet can return.

During the years between five and nine a child is becoming more social and has a greater intellectual capacity. This is the age of magical thinking, reinforced by fairy stories where wishes can come true. Bereaved children may feel they are responsible for the death because they had wished it to happen in an angry moment. The social impact of a bereavement at this stage is an additional burden; the child has to cope with the reactions of peers, school and the wider social environment.

In pre-adolescence (9–12 years) children have an increased cognitive capacity which enables them to develop an awareness of the finality of death – that death is common to all living things, that it is final, universal and inevitable. This can lead to recognizing the possibility of their own death which can be frightening, and may induce psychosomatic symptoms in an attempt to draw attention to their distress. However, at this age, children often deny their loss and simply 'get on with life.' (Pennells and Smith 1995).

During adolescence the grief reaction begins to approximate that of adulthood. However, the adolescent's grieving may be further compounded by their characteristically rapid physical and emotional development. At this age young people are seeking independence from adults and are often rebelling against them. A bereavement at this time could result in increased dependence on surviving relatives, possibly leading to confusing and conflicting emotions. Some adolescents have reported feeling suicidal (Vander Wyden 1991) and some have made attempts to end their own life. Powerful feelings can cause them to question the meaning of life and create a need to explore the issues of life after death, the occult and ritualistic behaviour.

These stages are only guidelines as children and young people may not fit neatly into these categories. It is our experience that in some cases a bereavement in childhood advances the child's understanding of death and its consequences. The child may therefore exhibit features that occur in another stage, regardless of age. Having accepted that children do grieve regardless of their age or developmental level, it appears to us that children's reactions to loss fall into three main categories.

Behavioural and Emotional

Children and adolescents may express negative feelings about their bereavement through violence and aggression towards other children or adults. Younger children may express angry feelings through their play, smashing toys or tearing books. These reactions may lead to the child being labelled as anti-social or disruptive. It is important that professionals are alert to the fact that this behaviour is often an expression of grief and conflicting emotions.

Children should be encouraged to express their negative feelings in a way that is acceptable and safe. Some ways of encouraging this expression are expanded on throughout the book. Younger children frequently tend to express their worries and anxieties through bed wetting and sleep disturbance. They should be given the opportunity to explore these problems and provided with the reassurance and security which they need to help resolve their difficulties.

In adolescence behaviour is often evidenced through mood swings and periods of depression (Pennells, Smith and Poppleton 1992) and, as it can be difficult for adults to separate out normal adolescent behaviour from grief reaction, a degree of sensitivity and patience is required.

Somatic Reactions

Some children experience health and physical problems following a bereavement. These include complaints of headache, stomach ache and general feelings of being unwell and on occasions may imitate the symptoms of the deceased. Persistent ill health can lead a child to worry about the possibility of their own death and that of others around them. Eating disturbance is another common feature. Over anxious children may experience periods of anorexia or may use food as a compensation for the loss.

School Based Problems

This area represents a major difficulty for bereaved children as on returning to school they are unsure who has been told, what has been said and how their peer group will react. In some cases this can lead to school phobia. Children with whom we have worked have reported being teased and taunted by others and being hurt by unsympathetic remarks made by teachers or pupils. A great difficulty is concentration which inevitably decreases in response to the myriad problems the child is trying to deal with. Conversely, we should be alert to over achievement as a child may be denying their grief and channelling their energies into school work.

The feelings and reactions children experience when faced with a death are many and varied and will of course reflect their cultural background (Black 1991). We need to acknowledge that a family's customs and lifestyle will be echoed in the child's responses. It is important that workers have many methods of intervention at their disposal in order to deal with the variation of responses to bereavement which arise from differences in individual and cultural heritage. We hope this book will be evidence of our belief in children's grief, that it will provide some useful methods to meet the needs of grieving children, and that it will act as an impetus for other creative ideas.

References

Bending, M (1993) *Caring for Bereaved Children.* Richmond, Surrey: CRUSE – Bereavement Care.

Black, J. (Spring 1991) 'Death and Bereavement: The Customs of Hindus, Sikhs and Moslems' *Bereavement Care 10,* 1, 6–8.

Bowlby, J. (1979) *The Making and Breaking of Affectionate Bonds.* London: Tavistock.

Brown, J.A.C. (1961) *Freud and the Post-Freudians.* Harmondsworth: Pelican Books.

Couldrick, A. (1991) *Grief and Bereavement. Understanding Children.* Oxford: Sobell Publications.

Deblinger, E. (1989) 'Post-traumatic stress in sexually abused, physically abused and non-abused children.' *Child Abuse and Neglect 13,* 403–8.

Duffy, W. (1991) *The Bereaved Child.* Ongar: The National Society

Dyregrov, A. (1991) *Grief in Children: A Handbook for Adults.* London: Jessica Kingsley Publishers.

Erikson, E. (1965) *Children and Society.* Harmondsworth: Penguin.

Klein, M. (1960) *Our Adult World and its Roots in Infancy.* London: Tavistock.

Pennells, M., Smith, S., and Poppleton, R. (July 1992) 'Bereavement and adolescents – a groupwork approach.' *Newsletter of the Association for Child Psychology and Psychiatry 14,* 4, 173–8.

Pennells, M. and Smith, S. (1995) *The Forgotten Mourners.* London: Jessica Kingsley Publishers.

Rutter, M. (1966) *Children of Sick Parents.* Oxford: Oxford University Press (Maudsley Monograph XVI).

Thompson, C. (1989) 'Post-traumatic stress disorder.' *Psychiatry in Practice,* Summer, 17–18.

Vander Wyden, P. (1991) *Butterflies. Talking with children about Death...and Life Eternal.* Texas: Tabor Publishers.

Yule, W. (1989) 'The effects of disasters on children.' *Newsletter of the Association for Child Psychology and Psychiatry 11,* 6, 3–6.

Part One

Individual Work

CHAPTER 1

Communicating with Children Through Play

Peta Hemmings

Introduction

A bereaved child has knowledge beyond her years. She[1] knows how fragile the world is and her childhood becomes partly coloured with the sadness of loss. Her knowledge of death can be a burden and a source of great anxiety as she knows that nothing can be taken for granted any longer. The world has become a fearful and dangerous place. This cluster of new sensitivities, if left unaddressed, will lead to the child becoming inhibited and consequently unable to embrace the work of mourning.

Every bereaved child may potentially arrive at this bleak outcome and it is our role as professionals working with children to break that cycle and help the child regain the joy and spontaneity of her childhood. We achieve this by helping the child explore her experience and knowledge of death and set these in a wider context. This process creates a more balanced perspective on the world, lessens the anxious burden of her knowledge and gives back some of the control that is lost when catastrophe strikes. The ability to exert a degree of control over events reduces anxiety and so the child becomes freer and can be supported and encouraged to start her mourning.

Mourning a major bereavement is a personal process with no set formula or absolute ending. It is not a finite process but a lifelong adjustment to a world without the deceased person. Through mourning the child experiences the

---

1   Although in this chapter I refer to the bereaved child as 'she', this is purely for convenience and does not denote or imply any specific gender characteristics in the content or the text.

meaning of the loss for *them* and learns to *live* with their bereavement. The resolution of bereavement lies in the child being able to maintain an awareness of its emotional impact, without those emotions either overwhelming her ability to make and maintain new attachments, or stopping her from enjoying the spontaneity and discoveries which are the essence of childhood.

Adult bereavement counselling relies largely upon the spoken word, but for children language is a dangerous and treacherous medium. Words are unreliable allies, cluttered with subtleties and double meanings. Play is a more natural language and contains all the vocabulary needed for effective communication. The challenge for people working with children within this work is to discover which types of play are best for which children.

In this chapter I will describe a model of work I have developed based upon the principles of Attachment Theory. I will discuss how I establish a therapeutic relationship with children and explore some of the ways in which, with children's trust and patience, I have learnt how to communicate with some of them.

Establishing a Working Friendship

As workers we often receive referrals identifying one child in a bereaved family as in need of professional help. There is a tendency to accept the judgement of the referral and respond to it without considering alternative approaches. Before embarking upon work with a family it is essential to conduct a thorough assessment of the family's situation. This may entail the worker making a number of visits in order to compile a full picture of the family's resources and history but it is time well spent as it often reveals hidden resources at a time when grief-stricken parents feel de-skilled and demoralized.

Sometimes it is possible for parents, supported by the worker, to help their child themselves and, for two main reasons, this is by far the best way to manage a child's problems. First, it promotes for the child an image of the parent as someone who is sensitive to their needs and able to help them through their distress. Second, it affords the family greater privacy at a critical time. Terminal illness, death and bereavement can be very public affairs and the newly bereaved family needs time to draw itself together and establish a new order. However, if my assessment shows that this is not possible, and that it would not be reasonable to allow the child to wait until it were, then, in accordance with my model of work, I would offer the child some sessions of play-work. The way in which the offer is made needs careful consideration.

Children are given little choice about many things in their lives and this is often quite appropriate; however, I firmly believe that bereaved children need to be given some choice about how their bereavement should be managed. Terminal illness and bereavement remove our sense of being in control: illness may progress relentlessly, but it is often not a predictable pattern of events. The time following the death does not usually bring any greater sense of inner calm, as the thoughts and emotions that accompany bereavement constitute another personal storm. The randomness that characterizes these experiences needs to be counterbalanced. Giving the child some effective control within the therapeutic relationship, right from the start, sets the pattern of shared partnership within the work. This notion of partnership is an intrinsic part of the model of work I follow and is part of every aspect of the relationship.

The way in which I introduce the notion of play-work to the child exemplifies the principle of partnership. She is asked by someone, other than the worker, if she would like to accept the *offer* of play-work, rather than be told it is going to happen *to* her. If she agrees to it, then the worker needs to arrange a meeting with her where she feels most comfortable. This could be at home, at school or in the park, so that she can see for herself what is on offer before she commits herself to play sessions.

This approach emphasizes the respect the worker has for the child and is a fundamental element in the working relationship.

Creating the Secure Play Environment

Creating the right sort of environment for the work is essential and requires preparation. There are four key elements in this process; the physical setting, the play materials, a clear statement about the working friendship and the social worker as a resource for the child.

The Physical Setting

There are a number of practical ways in which the physical setting is created. If the sessions are to be held in a room then there is a need to consider its furnishings and decoration. Furniture should be comfortable and attractive, with a variety of chairs, bean bags and scatter cushions. These last two items can be used within play or to cuddle up with during stories. The room should be well lit and warm with posters and children's paintings which help to create a child-centred atmosphere.

It is important that the room is private, not overlooked by other buildings or in the middle of a busy, noisy area. The quality of play is affected if people are seen walking past the window or telephones are constantly ringing nearby.

Although I have considered the play setting as a room, from time to time sessions can be held on the beach, at a playground, walking through a wood or going swimming. The important elements are the conversation between the child and worker and the pleasure the child can take in being with someone who is trustworthy and genuinely listens.

The Play Materials

Toys, games and other play materials are all part of creating an attractive setting. Children revel in the discovery of new toys and can be invited and encouraged to explore toys by the way in which they are displayed. Dolls, monsters and puppets can be presented in colourful baskets with some spilling out onto the floor ready to be used. A spread of coloured paper of different weights, scissors, glue, ribbons, sticky shapes and glitter. Dressing-up clothes, plasticene and playdough, Lego/Duplo, bubbles and balloons, board-games and playing cards. A selection of books, some which they may already know and some specially chosen for the purpose of your work. All of these are recognizable, attractive materials for the child and should be accessible so she can browse through them and choose what to look at and use. By being able to explore in this way the child discovers a little more about you because of what you have to offer in this practical way.

Preparing the room and the materials enables both the social worker and the child to feel more at ease in a potentially sensitive situation. The toys should be presented in a similar way at each session because the predictability of the room's layout is an important factor in promoting a secure play environment. Security comes from feeling able to rely on some thing or someone being constant and predictable regardless of what else is happening in the world. Illness and bereavement profoundly undermine our sense of security; therefore, to be most effective, the playroom and the worker need to maintain a constant image for the child and so come to represent a haven of stability in a changing world.

It is as a consequence of this need that the child will come to count on the play materials being there at every session, whether she chooses to play with them or not. There have been occasions when I have been gently reprimanded by a child because I forgot to put out the hospital basket, a certain book, or some other item. Even though she may never have used the book, she liked to know it was always there. This clearly shows how important it is to present a stable set of materials within the play room and not assume to know what the child wants to use.

The Contract

The third element centres on the creation of an agreement between the social worker and the child about what are the parameters of the relationship; in effect, its character and purpose. This can be done verbally and explained to the child but, as this needs to be done at the outset, when the child is possibly more anxious and less able to assimilate information, there is a likelihood that the information might be misheard or misremembered. This may lead to problems later on; it is therefore advisable to draw up a more concrete agreement, a contract with the child. Even if the child is pre-literate, or partially literate, the principle of a contract stills holds good because the words can be read to them. I design it to present as an attractive document with a series of pictures that describe the nature of the relationship on offer. It is something which has been created especially for the child and is available at every session, so that the terms can be reviewed and renegotiated if necessary.

Drawing up a contract defines the boundaries of the relationship from the first session. The contract states the number of sessions agreed to and how long each one will last. The child needs to be reminded at each session how many she has had to date and how many are left. It is important to draw attention to this because the separation implicit in ending the relationship echoes the separation experienced within bereavement. The termination of the working friendship must be managed actively and sensitively from the first session onwards to avoid causing additional distress to the child. This is discussed more fully at the end of this section.

The rules about behaviour are stated clearly too. Although it is hoped the child will develop a freeness within her play, this freedom needs to be couched within certain limits, otherwise she will become anxious at the lack of boundaries and feel insecure. The contract addresses this issue by defining what is acceptable behaviour in the playroom. The agreement is that the child can use the toys, furniture and worker in any way she wants, providing neither person is hurt. The playroom is a special place where special rules apply. For example, I would allow a child to jump on the chairs and throw the cushions around in the playroom, but in allowing this latitude, I would ensure the child understands that these are special rules that do not apply outside of the playroom. It would not help her if she were to go home and carry on in the same way there, saying that I had said it was all right!

The next element of the contract refers to confidentiality. The child needs to know that whatever is said or done during the sessions is private to you both and will not be repeated to others. There is only one exception to this, which needs to be stated clearly. The child needs to know that if she discloses physical or sexual abuse then the worker must let others know, in order to protect her from further harm. This exception does not weaken confidentiality but confirms to the child that you care about her safety and well-being, both within the room and in other areas of her life.

The final element is that of continuing availability. Although it has been agreed that there will be a limited number of sessions, it is understood that, even when we have finished, I remain available to the child *should she initiate contact*. After the last session I write to the child and give her my office address and number. If she does get in touch and asks to see me again, then I arrange that, providing the parent agrees that it would be helpful. Many children keep in touch years after I have stopped seeing them, sending Christmas cards or pictures they have drawn. One little girl wrote to me four years after our last session to show me that now she was seven years old, she could do joined-up writing! These contacts are always delightful and reflect the significance which the relationship has for these children, long after the actual death. We can be important people at a critical time in a child's life and children know the value of such help in times of crisis.

The Social Worker as a Resource

The fourth part in creating a secure play environment is what we personally have to offer. It is unrealistic for us to think that we can be all things to all children. Although this is a job, we are nevertheless human beings first and practitioners second. We need to consider and nurture ourselves as people in order to be able to offer ourselves as a resource to the child. It is essential that we receive personal and professional support and learn to recognize our strengths and vulnerabilities within the work. Only by maintaining this watchful, caring stance over ourselves can we remain a reliable resource for the child.

Examples of Some Play Techniques

Having briefly considered some aspects of the preparatory stage, I will now describe some of the play techniques which I have developed.

All About Me[1]

All About Me resulted from some work conducted several years ago with a nine-year-old girl, Michelle, whose mother had recently died. An outline of the family's situation and the way in which the work with Michelle developed, seem the best way to describe the practice and the principles behind All About Me.

Before her mother's death Michelle had been a popular girl who was doing well at school. A few weeks after the bereavement she was having problems at school, getting into scraps in the playground, was withdrawn in class and very quiet at home. Her father knew something was wrong and he recognized the need for some professional help because he was too weighed down with his own sadness to be able to support his daughter at that time.

Michelle welcomed the idea of having play sessions and readily joined in with the games and activities I provided. She talked about her mother and the months of illness they had lived through together. Like many children who live with illness, she could recite a long list of medications her mother had taken, complicated names which tripped off her tongue because they had been so much a part of her life for such a long time. She was very articulate and yet, when we came to think about emotions she became tongue-tied and would deflect the conversation away to something safer.

---

1   *All About Me* is available from Barnardo's, Tanners Lane, Barkingside, Ilford, Essex IG6 1QG. Tel.: 0181–550–8822.

The weeks passed as did the play sessions and still no progress was made in helping Michelle to think about her feelings and what they meant to her. She was still having problems at school and her mood in class was relatively unchanged. I had tried everything I could think of to unlock this part of her and nothing was working. It was with some desperation that I eventually decided to devise a game to help this conversation, a game which eventually developed into *All About Me*.

All About Me embodies the principles of my work with children. It encourages appropriate sharing between the child and worker, and gives the child control over just how much she reveals at any one time. Through the process of the game, the child makes discoveries about herself and others and this is, in part, what mourning is about. It is a journey of discovery. The mourner contemplates the significance of the relationship which has been lost and what that means to those who are left behind, both now and in time to come. It is not a journey that a child can make on her own, she needs guidance and support, as we all do. *All About Me* provides that within its structure and the way it is used.

All About Me is a board game and is, therefore, instantly recognizable. The board is decorated with a path that twists through a colourful jungle scene, illustrated with animals and birds. There is little effort required to understand the rules because, like all board games, it revolves around taking turns to throw the die and move the pieces. Having moved their playing piece, each player takes a card from the top of a prepared pack and responds to the statement written there, saying as much or as little as they want. There are over 120 cards to choose from, each one having a different design. The statements cover a wide range of issues which can be categorized in the following way.

Some are relatively safe cards which say such things as, 'My favourite clothes are…' and 'My lucky number is…'. These help the child to relax and enjoy the fun of the activity. The next set starts to explore feelings and the ways in which they are expressed. These cards carry statements such as, 'I feel happy when…', and 'When I'm angry I like to…'. Other sets of cards explore such topics as school, family relationships, fears, fantasies and wishes.

Although these can be very serious issues for a child, the game is designed to give the child control over the depth of the conversation and allows her to stay within the bounds of what feels comfortable at the time. There is no pressure or obligation on either person to say more than they want.

The worker's role is to help the child think about her emotions by showing that they are not alone with feelings of anger, fear or sadness and that grown-ups cry, get frustrated and feel confused sometimes, just like children. It is the act of sharing which makes the difference. When we realize that we are not alone with our feelings, it becomes safer to share them and so come to understand their source and impact. Knowledge is power and the acquisition of greater personal knowledge through insight is part of the process of regaining control over the inner emotional world.

By establishing this sharing in our conversation, Michelle was able to explore the dangerous areas of her emotional life and come to understand her feelings better. For example, like many bereaved children, Michelle *felt* she had been abandoned by her mother even though she *knew* her mother had died because of her illness. Abandonment generates feelings of anger and yet it is very uncomfortable for us to hold feelings of anger towards the dead person. Children need to understand that feeling angry does not mean they love the dead person less; in fact, quite the reverse. It reflects the depth of their love because of the hurt the death causes them, and this is what Michelle was feeling. Her anger towards her mother was so intense and inexpressible that the energy it generated caused her either to explode from time to time, thereby getting into fights at school, or hold it in and feel depressed and unconnected with the world. Through exploring her anger and its meaning, we were able to devise a way of managing its explosive, physical tension, without that creating secondary problems.

In order to help with this we devised the following management technique, using my knowledge of Michelle and the resources which I knew were readily available to her. Michelle lived by the sea and nearby there was a shingle beach with a plentiful supply of stones. A few yards off the beach there was a group of rocks and, when Michelle recognized the tension was building up, she would go down to the beach and hurl stones at the rocks and into the waves, flinging the anger out of her and into the water. Only by gaining insight into her anger was she able to release it in this way, because she understood the meaning of her stone-throwing. It was effective for her because of her insight. Without insight such action is a pointless pursuit as it only addresses the physical effects and not their cause.

Using *All About Me*, within the boundaries of a secure and trusting relationship, allowed Michelle to explore dangerous emotions, safe in the knowledge that she was with someone who could hold them and help her find some solution. She went on to do further work in our sessions, exploring troubling and painful aspects of her life and bereavement and, in doing so, demonstrated great courage. Today, Michelle is a vivacious and sensitive teenager who enjoys life and, together with her father, remembers her mother with a warm, deep affection.

Where are Our Feelings?

Children are perhaps more aware than adults that emotions are not just experienced in our heads or hearts, but are spread throughout our bodies. Anyone who has seen a frustrated two-year-old will recognize how the child feels and expresses their rage and impotence with every fibre of their being. The emotion is felt and communicated in clenched muscles, rigid and thrashing limbs, screams, bellows and tears. This is not a controlled, cerebral experience for the child or, for that matter, for the parent. Although maturity brings with it a degree of self-control, intense emotions are rarely head and heart matters. It is also true that one emotion can be experienced in different ways, depending upon its intensity or the prevailing mood at the time. Consequently, our emotional life becomes a subtle mixture of internal processes which, in turn, are influenced by what we are allowed to express.

Social pressures constrain our emotional expression from a very early age and children receive many messages about how they ought to be. Bereaved children are particularly vulnerable to such commandments. Loving, well-meaning adults will often prescribe the bereaved child's emotional life by saying such things as '...be good', '...look after Mummy' and preface specific requested behaviours with '...because you're a big girl now'. All these statements silence the child and suppress her true inner state. The child is explicitly and implicitly told to consider adults' needs before her own and, because the bereaved child's sense of security is profoundly affected by her experience of loss, she is understandably reluctant to compromise her personal safety further and so toes the line.

It is also true that a young, bereaved child feels different from her peers. Her experience of death and her knowledge of bereavement sets her apart from her friends who are too young to know about such things. Their ability to empathize is limited by their developmental immaturity. The peer group contributes to our self-image but this aspect of the bereaved child's self-image cannot be supported by their friends and needs to be explored in other social settings. (This is perhaps one of the strongest arguments for establishing bereavement groups for young children because it is through such groups that the child can develop an appropriate peer group for their bereavement.) As a consequence of feeling different, the child creates masks for their emotions in the outside world. Children can become adept at masking, but it's at a price and the price is that their inner life becomes disjointed and they come to lack spontaneity.

Body Mapping

There are many ways in which we can help a child reconnect with her emotions. The following, which I call Body Mapping, is one which can be used with children of any age. The materials needed are rolls of wallpaper and a wide range of art materials, such as crayons, pencils, charcoal, felt-tipped pens, fun fur, cotton wool, paper and paper shapes, sequins, glitter, buttons, shells, pasta shapes, wool, string; in fact anything that can be glued to paper. Although it can be great fun, because of the bodily contact involved, this is an exercise which should only be used with a child when the working relationship is firmly established and there is mutual ease and confidence.

The child chooses a colour for herself and lies down on the paper while you draw around her, carefully avoiding those extra ticklish areas! If it would help to ease things then perhaps the child might like to draw round you first and test both your trust in them and where you might be ticklish. (N.B. It is important to be aware of the child's personal history and carefully consider the appropriateness of this exercise with a child who has been sexually or physically abused. Her body boundary has already been compromised and this exercise may present her with echoes of those traumatic experiences.) If the child is unsure about the whole body drawing then it is possible to use only a head and shoulders outline, or even just the hands.

When the outline is completed, present the child with a short list of feelings (e.g. sad, happy, angry, excited, lost, lonely, loved) and ask her to choose one. Using all the different art materials, explore the feeling's colour and texture and where she feels it in her body. Children readily understand about whole-body emotions and respond to this exercise with pleasure. Providing a wide range of materials implicitly encourages the child to think about her feelings in great detail, to see them as three-dimensional entities which need creative combinations of materials in order to describe them accurately.

While the child is choosing the materials, cutting out and sticking each emotion onto her body, a conversation about what she is doing and why can easily develop. Small prompts to the child such as 'That's an interesting shape. I wonder why you have chosen that', and 'What a lovely colour/piece of ribbon/ button you have there. I wonder where it is going to go.' do not demand a response, but allow her to say something if she wants to. The activity provides a vehicle for the conversation and for the child to begin the internal processes that will help to give her greater personal insight.

All the activities I have included in this chapter function on a number of levels, but they are without value unless they are enjoyable too. The work would be a dry affair if there were no fun in it. At the end of this exercise the child has a wonderful collage and has probably enjoyed themselves into the bargain. What could be better, for both of you?

Paper-Plate Faces
Another exercise, for use with children of all ages, is mask making. The child can be asked to think about how her face looks when she is happy and to create that face on a paper plate, using a variety of materials (e.g. wool or shredded tissue-paper for hair, felt, paper-shapes, glitter). When she has done her happy face, ask her what is the opposite of happy, so she can choose the emotion which is most troubling at that time and draw that feeling on another plate. The two plates can then be stuck back-to-back.

During this process the child is encouraged to think about the feelings she is making on the plate and how, where, when and with whom she is able to express them. She can be asked what causes her sometimes to feel one emotion and yet have to hide it and pretend to be feeling something else. This is something which happens regularly to bereaved children and the pretence causes a lot of stress. The next two exercises explore this theme further.

Whom Can I Trust?

It is very important that a bereaved child quickly learns that she is much more vulnerable to hurt than before her loss and needs to protect herself more than before. She is an easy target for other children and it is sadly true that most bereaved children will, at one time or another, have their feelings hurt by the careless or deliberate remarks of others. In addition, adults may tell them to be 'strong' and 'good' for the surviving parent. This request conveys a message to the child that she should be quiet about her distress and not upset her parent. Consequently, in losing one parent through death, the child comes to feel as though she is orphaned. The surviving parent is distanced from the child by the depth of their grief and made less available to her because of how other people think she should behave. At the very time when the child needs *more* reassurance, love and understanding, she is told to want less. It is no wonder then that the bereaved child perceives the world as a confusing and fragile place.

The Snowstorm

The child's global view of the world and the people in it is an extremely complex area. One toy which I have found useful for approaching some of the issues is a snowstorm. It may seem as though this is a very simple toy for such a complicated topic, but it is often true that the simplest tools do the job most effectively.

The glass dome usually has a little scene inside it, with an animal or person. The child is told that the glass bubble represents the world, it is a safe place to be for the person inside. They know where everything is and feel very comfortable in their world. They have a happy, predictable life until one day when disaster strikes. The child is asked to think of something awful that could happen to bring a disaster into this safe world. Whatever she chooses tips the world upside down and everything whirls around inside, like the storm of uncertainty that has whirled around her. She is asked how it feels to be the person inside the bubble, what are they thinking, feeling and what is happening around them?

It takes a long time for this storm to subside and for all the little snowflakes to settle to the ground. Eventually, when it seems as though everything has gone back to where it was before, the child is told that, although it may look like that from the outside, the person on the inside of the bubble knows only too well, that nothing is the same, or ever could be again. She is asked to think of how that might be for her if she were inside the bubble and this was her disaster.

I also show the child that, once this has happened to someone, for a while they feel that the slightest knock can send those snowflakes swirling around again. By showing that we understand something of what she is experiencing, the child feels less alone with her feelings and more able to think about them with the person who has shown themselves to be sensitive.

Trust Circles

The acts of thinking and sharing bereavement-related feelings and thoughts are the essence of mourning. The problem for the bereaved child is that other, non-bereaved children cannot be part of that conversation. The bereaved child has experienced events and intense emotions which many of her peers cannot begin to imagine. The child needs to be able to think about her memories, thoughts and feelings and learn to share them appropriately. She needs to know who is going to understand and respect her feelings. She needs trustworthy people who are going to be sensitive to her, people who will believe her when she says she's worried and will give her the extra reassurance and affection she needs. Knowing who those people are is difficult for the child because it requires a mature insight into human nature. Insight is a quality which is beyond the developmental ability of a young child: she is still learning about people through experience and can only make intuitive judgements.

It is possible, however, to help the child develop a greater awareness of the personal qualities in people around them. The exercise for this is one I call, Trust Circles. On a large sheet of paper, I draw a small circle in the centre and ask the child to think of that circle as being herself and decorate it accordingly. Some children write their name in it, others use stickers or sequins, or draw and colour a shape.

Another circle is then drawn close to and around that one. The child is asked to think about which people she can say anything to at any time and know that she will be understood. These people are placed in this second circle. Another concentric circle is then drawn, slightly wider than the first, and this is for those people to whom she can say some things at any time. A third circle is for those people to whom she can say some things only at some times. In this way the child learns that there are layers of friends and that she needs to be selective about who she trusts with what.

This exercise, although very simple, has three important features. First, it creates a concrete representation of significant people in the child's world and encourages her to think about their individual strengths and values. Second, it allows this train of thought to be continued in subsequent sessions and for the changing nature of relationships to be reviewed and revised in terms of where people are in the circles. Third, it provides an interesting insight into the child's growing awareness of her need to have extra safe people and encourages her to think before she shares her innermost thoughts, so that she is sharing them with someone who will know their worth.

This exercise is not a means of teaching cynicism to the innocent. It is a way in which the child can begin to appreciate that she is vulnerable to hurt and needs to protect herself.

Fantasy or Reality

When someone we love dies it is a reality we struggle to resist. Through mourning we come gradually to accept that reality and explore the meaning of the loss of that person in order to develop a new relationship with them. This is the central feature of the process. Therefore, the aim or resolution of mourning is not to create an emotionally safe distance between the living and the dead, but a different and new closeness. This closeness should not inhibit or interfere with the bereaved person's ability to form or maintain attachments to others. Mourning, when viewed as a continuing state of adjusted attachment to the dead person, takes on a developmental element for the child.

As the child matures, so her ability to appreciate the significance and personal meaning of this life-event alters. Consequently, her bereavement needs to be reviewed. It is, therefore, wholly inappropriate to expect children to 'get over' or 'through' early childhood loss because, to a lesser or greater extent, it is part of who they are and is not affected by irrelevant time limits.

Starting the process of mourning depends upon accepting the reality of the loss. The mourner needs to believe that the dead person is gone forever and cannot be retrieved. Only then can the work start.

The next task is to explore the nature of the relationship which has been lost. This can be a monumental task. All human relationships are imperfect and a matter of compromise. Successful mourning requires contemplation of the whole person. When the bereaved person considers the dead person's short-comings, or the difficulties there were in the relationship, feelings of betrayal and treachery are generated. The dead cannot defend themselves against our criticisms, even if they are unspoken. Children and adults alike have great difficulty with this. This aspect of accepting the reality of the loss can feel like an attack on the loved one, an attack which loyalty resists and here lies the root of the dilemma.

It is not the worker's role to flood the child with the reality of the person, but to support and encourage her to develop a reasonable view of who it is that has died. It is only by developing a realistic view that she can mourn all that has been lost.

One of the ways in which I have approached this sensitive subject is by using a picture of old fashioned weighing scales, the sort that have two balancing pans. The first stage to this exercise is for the child to think about herself and to list all the things she enjoys about herself and place them in one of the pans. Then she considers the things about herself which she would like to change or which cause her difficulties, and these are placed in the other pan. The instruction is carefully phrased in this way to avoid using the words 'good' and 'bad' because of the value judgements implicit in both terms.

The child is then asked to think of all the ways in which the dead person both pleased her and showed their enjoyment of her. She then writes or draws symbols of those qualities in one of the pans and spends time thinking of those positive aspects, giving examples and remembering shared activities. She is then asked to think of times when things did not turn out as she would have liked, or when it was more difficult to be with the dead person. The positive memories help the child to tolerate the more difficult ones which are placed in the other pan.

This is an exercise which may need to be done gradually, over a number of sessions. It is advisable to pace this work gently to avoid overwhelming the child with the intensity of pleasant or troubling memories. The aim of this exercise is to construct a reasonably balanced view of the dead person. It is then that the child can know who she has lost and mourn the reality, not the fantasy of an idealized person.

Conclusion

In this chapter I have given a brief description of the principles which underpin my practice and the ways in which those principles are manifested in the structure of the work setting and relationship. Although the sessions are limited by number and time, the relationship established there can be continued beyond that contract and so is in keeping with the timetable of the model of mourning outlined.

The play techniques have been described in terms of their appropriateness for addressing particular issues, but they have also been selected because of their adaptability. Their applications are only limited by creative imagination. *All About Me* is an excellent example of this: designed for one bereaved child, it has gone on to be produced for sale and has been used with distressed children in a wide variety of situations. It is a very adaptable medium because it is based on an understanding of children and the principles of partnership and appropriate sharing.

On a more personal note, I would like to add that I greatly enjoy my work with children and hope that this chapter communicates some of my pleasure in the work. I also hope that it serves to support and encourage others who are working with bereaved children and their families.

Suggested Reading

Bowlby, J. (1979) *The Making and Breaking of Affectional Bonds.* London: Tavistock Publications.

Bowlby, J. (1987) *Attachment and Loss, Volume II. Separation: Anxiety and Anger.* London: Pelican Books.

Bowlby, J. (1985) *Attachment and Loss, Volume III. Loss: Sadness and Depression.* London: Pelican Books.

Bowlby, J. (1988) *A Secure Base: Clinical applications of attachment theory.* London: Tavistock/Routledge.

Cattanach, A. (1994) *Play Therapy: Where the Sky Meets the Underworld.* London: Jessica Kingsley Publishers.

Jewett, C. (1984) *Helping Children Cope With Separation and Loss.* London: B.T. Batsford Ltd.

Oaklander, V. (1987) *Windows to Our Children.* Utah, USA: Real People Press.

Raphael, B. (1984) *The Anatomy of Bereavement.* London: Hutchinson.

Redgrave, K. (1987) *Child's Play.* London: Boys' and Girls' Welfare Society.

Winnicott, D.W. (1990) *Playing and Reality.* London: Tavistock Publications.

Winnicott, D.W. (1980) *The Piggle.* Harmondsworth: Penguin.

CHAPTER 2

Direct Work Techniques with the Siblings of Children Dying from Cancer

Maureen Hitcham

Introduction

Inside every child there is a story waiting to be told, but when that story involves difficult issues such as death and dying it is neither easy to tell nor is it easy to listen to.

When I first began working with children who have cancer and their families, I realized very quickly how I had underestimated the impact an illness like this can have on the healthy brothers and sisters in the family. Most of us cannot begin to imagine what it is like to be told, 'your child is dying'. The impact of such unwanted, often unexpected news is both overwhelming and devastating. Parents who have faced this recall vividly their feelings of helplessness and hopelessness – it is a time of great vulnerability. Not surprisingly the psychosocial literature produced over the past 25 years suggests that healthy siblings may be especially vulnerable to the stress created in the family. Families can only cope with a limited amount of stress at any one time; consequently, parents often appear to lack the energy or desire to identify and respond to anyone other than the sick child. So many times I have listened to shocked and anxious parents describe their healthy children as 'Oh they are fine, they are with my parents'. Such arrangements we know are only 'fine' in the short term.

Children like their world to be safe and predictable. They enjoy routine and dislike disruption, but growing up is a painful process. There is much that frustrates, frightens and confuses them. They have to struggle to understand the reactions of the adults around them and they experience repeated feelings of uncertainty and lack of confidence. Experience has taught me that no matter how secure, loving or attentive a family is the diagnosis of a chronic life-threatening childhood illness destroys family life as it used to be and in consequence the healthy siblings experience many further sources of distress. There is the initial turmoil of diagnosis, separation from loved ones during treatment and the inevitable chaos and unpredictability, leaving them bereft of normal family life.

One study concludes, 'the presence of a critically ill child in a family leads to unintentional "neglect" of the healthy siblings and to a lack of communication between them and their parents' (Rosen 1988). The losses associated with living in a family where there is a life-threatening illness create an atmosphere of bereavement in which families adapt and learn to function. Consequently, the children in these families are often 'bereaved' long before they ever experience an actual death. The healthy siblings, it would seem, are in a 'no win situation'. It is certainly understandable why all the parents' attention is focused on the sick child when they are very ill, but studies have shown that even when the child recovers, 'parental concern shifts to other non disease related matters and the siblings are again left without support' (Spinetta 1981).

This can create a variety of responses and feelings. Many experience overwhelming sadness, jealousy, anger, resentment and fear. They feel 'left out' or second best; some become withdrawn and irritable, others openly aggressive and hostile. They are reacting to the losses and tragedies that suddenly invade their once secure and loving families. These are perfectly reasonable responses to unique and difficult situations, but adults often find it difficult to accept these responses. They see them as inappropriate and consequently label them as naughty, attention seeking or wilful. Age is no excuse, because they make up different labels according to the child's age and or stage of development, understanding their behaviour in terms of 'the terrible twos' then, as they grow older, 'defiance'. Adults often dismiss the needs of bereaved children, seeing their use of resilience and defining it as insensitivity and or intellectual immaturity, thus absolving themselves from doing anything. One bereaved parent said

> 'I still can't get over how as parents you just expect them to cope and unwittingly give them the message not to intrude and just to get on with their own lives. If only I could have my time again I'd explain much more right from the beginning bringing it into normal everyday conversation.'

Intervention with all family members is vital if we are to combat such potentially damaging feelings and create an environment in which they can begin to share and explore these thoughts and experiences openly.

As a preventive measure this must begin at diagnosis. As one study concludes, 'siblings should be seen as an integral part of a whole family approach to treatment and acknowledged as important participants in the family's life throughout the illness' (Koocher and O'Malley 1981) and, I would argue, death.

At an early stage in the illness, professionals must in a gentle, non-threatening way, remind parents of the emotional needs of their healthy children and provide opportunities for each member of the family to express an opinion as to how the illness has affected or might affect them and what could be done to improve the situation. Such action may prevent or ameliorate many of the siblings' problems and avoid the development of closed, restrictive and over protective family systems which deny children the opportunity to share their very changeable feelings.

Techniques for Working with Siblings

Direct work is only one of a number of methods and approaches used to facilitate open communication with children and their families. In sharing the paper tools and techniques that I have found particularly helpful in my direct work with children, it is not my intention to suggest the ideas are taken literally or followed mechanically. Take what appeals to you and dismiss the rest. Adapt what you take to suit you as an individual then go on to experience the world as it is seen through the eyes of the child. The techniques described have been developed and adapted over an eighteen year period whilst working with damaged and traumatized children, but with a little imagination they have adapted very well for use in grief work. The techniques described all evoke very strong emotional responses and therefore it is essential that workers have a good awareness of self. We need to be aware of our own feelings about death both as an abstract notion and, perhaps more important, as a personal reality. We must also accept that this is an emotional area of work and it is normal and appropriate to respond emotionally. One thing is certain, the use of direct work techniques and being able to stay alongside the child who experiences pain and anguish will inevitably create a strong attachment. It is therefore essential that we fully understand the implications for the child and are familiar with current attachment theories before embarking on this type of work.

Once the child is confident they can rely on your availability and responsiveness, they will experience feelings of security which will encourage them to value and want to maintain the relationship; in other words they will become attached. Attachment behaviour can be described as 'behaviour that results in a person attaining or maintaining proximity to some other clearly identified individual who is conceived as better able to cope with the world. It is most obvious whenever the person is frightened, fatigued or sick' (Bowlby 1988). Acknowledging that the child is likely to view the relationship with the worker as special and or very important, we have a responsibility to explain clearly and honestly the nature of the therapeutic relationship at the outset. We must also give some consideration to the impact of ending such a working relationship with young children. The most frightening situation for a child is one in which they need or expect the relationship to continue, then suddenly find that it is over with no preparation. Such an experience could constitute yet another loss in their lives. The resulting anger and anxiety will be greater in children who have suffered repeated loss.[1]

The Therapeutic Relationship

My purpose in working individually with children is to create for them an atmosphere of trust and security where they can begin to share and explore their feelings in a safe, non-threatening environment. This work is never undertaken in isolation from what is happening in the family. Regular contact is maintained and always with the child present. Having established that I am the most appropriate person to work with the child I go on to negotiate a contract first with the parents and then with the child. My aim in negotiating a contract with parents is to make them feel that they are still 'in control', because there is nothing like a chronic life-threatening illness and or death of a child to make parents feel their lives are totally out of their control. For months or even years life may have centred around the illness and its treatment yet despite the fact they have done everything they can to fight the disease they have not been able to prevent the sick child from dying. As if this were not enough to have to cope with, many now find themselves unable to handle or understand their healthy child's reaction. These situations need very careful management by professionals as it is all too easy to reinforce feelings of inadequacy and helplessness.

Before meeting with the child I feel it is important that parents understand

(1) why I am there

(2) what I am going to do

(3) how and where I am going to do it

(4) what is likely to happen to the information and material produced.

I believe this basic information is the right of every parent and find that such an open approach means they are usually less anxious, more confident and more likely to accept that whatever the child shares within the therapeutic relationship is in confidence and will not be divulged without the child's permission.

---

1   See *Contract* Section in Chapter 1

Getting to Know You

When I meet a child for the first time I use a sentence completion questionnaire. This is used in the belief that children often have a number of concerns or worries in the forefront of their minds which they either consciously choose not to talk about or do not know how to begin to talk about them. Asking them to respond to the questions by saying the first thing that comes into their minds usually results in some excellent clues as to the important and significant issues for them at that particular time. The child completes this on the first and last session to highlight significant issues and evaluate progress. This is not a test, there are no right or wrong answers, it is merely a tool to help them discover more about themselves and to give me a greater understanding of their difficulties – from there the therapeutic process evolves. A typical questionnaire for siblings might include some or all of the following depending on individual circumstances:

> I like . . . .
>
> I am the kind of person . . . .
>
> My mother . . . .
>
> I think fathers . . . .
>
> When I first found out my sister had leukaemia . . . .
>
> My friends said . . . .
>
> This is what happened when I went to school . . . .
>
> I worry . . . .
>
> It seems difficult . . . .
>
> Cancer means . . . .
>
> Our family. . . . .

This is an excellent method of reviewing and evaluating your work with a child. Completing it on the first and last session means that together you are able to look at those areas where there has been growth and identify those areas where the child has become 'stuck' or where there may have been some deterioration. It is a very effective way of assessing and planning what future work, if any, needs to be undertaken.

One young girl used the sentence completion questionnaire successfully to highlight the issues she needed help with. They were:

Session One	Six Weeks Later
I am the kind of person...	
'who keeps things to themselves and don't talk about them.'	'who likes to help other people.'
People always say I...	
'don't show my feelings.'	blank, couldn't think of an answer.
My mother...	
'annoys me when she talks about Michael.'	'is a very caring person.'
It seems difficult...	
'to talk about Michael.'	'to start a conversation about Michael.'
I worry...	
'whether Michael is all right.'	'if I haven't done my homework.'
It's...	
'hard for me to talk about Michael.'	'easier to talk about Michael.'
Say I'm sorry...	
'I would like to say Sorry for everything I've done to Michael.'	'There is nothing to say Sorry for.'

This paper tool demonstrates very clearly the degree of change one can achieve in a relatively short period of time. Some of the following techniques may help to bring about such changes.

Techniques

The Feelings Factory

Children are capable of having feelings that come from a place so deep down inside that they find it impossible to put them into words, not talking even when they need or want to. One child called Nicola said she wanted to be able to talk about her dead brother and what had happened to him but she did not know how! I reminded her of a booklet, 'Jenny has Leukaemia' (Nicholson and Thompson 1984) used to help children understand about the illness and how it affects the body. Using little figures to represent the red cells, white cells and platelets (Figure 2.1) one can describe what happens when the blood factory stops working properly and begins to make too many sickly white cells so there is not enough room for the red cells and platelets to grow (Figure 2.2).

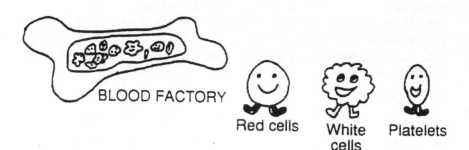

Figure 2.1 The Blood Factory

Figure 2.2 When you have leukaemia it means the Blood Factory isn't working properly

Being comfortable with the concept of the Blood Factory, I then introduce the idea of another factory in the body called the Feelings Factory (Figure 2.3), which lives inside your heart and, when it is working properly, produces a balance of good and bad feelings.

Figure 2.3 The Feelings Factory

At this point I usually suggest we both make a list of all the feelings we can think of under the headings Good and Bad Feelings. The use of Feelings Cards which can be spread out often helps this process

Good Feelings   **Bad Feelings**

Happy   Sad

Excited   Confused

Loved   Frightened

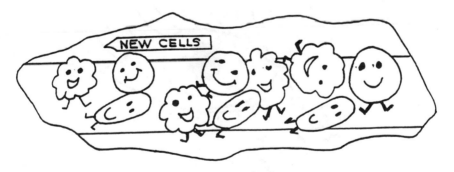

Figure 2.4

If the feelings factory stops working properly, it produces too many bad feelings, then there is not enough room for the good feelings to grow. Like the blood factory we need to get this factory working properly again. I always tell children that the treatment of both factories is painful!

In order to repair the blood factory and destroy the sickly white cells the doctors use chemotherapy and radiotherapy and because they make you feel ill and frightened you also need lots of loving and caring (Figure 2.5).

NEW CELLS

Figure 2.5

In order to repair the feelings factory we need to find ways of getting rid of the bad feelings to make room for the good feelings to grow. Nicola produced the following piece of work in this session:

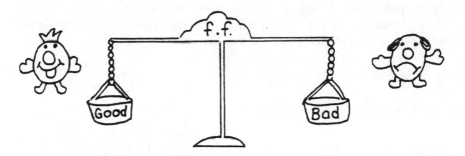

Figure 2.6 'When the factory is working properly it produces a balance of good and bad feelings.'

Figure 2.7 'But when it goes wrong it starts to produce too many bad feelings leaving no room for any good feelings to grow.'

Figure 2.8 'In order to get rid of all these unwanted bad feelings and make room for the good ones we can cry then the bad feelings will come out in our tears...'

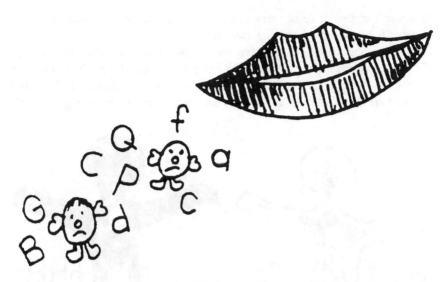

Figure 2.9 '…or talk then the bad feelings will come out in our words…'

Figure 2.10 '…or write and draw then the bad feelings go down on paper where they are less powerful.'

'The doctor told me about the blood factory and how it works but a special friend told me about the feelings factory. She helped me put my balance right again.'

As a result of this piece of work Nicola was able to move on and identify a range of feelings and related experiences.

It is possible to take this a step further by describing how the Feelings Factory transports feelings all over the body, depositing them in various parts. By colour coding feelings, children are not only able to identify feelings but show where they feel them as ten-year-old Emma demonstrates (Figure 2.11).

Figure 2.11

> 'Before Louise went away I was very happy. My happiness showed on the outside. Any bad feelings I was able to keep inside. I was a little bit anxious but I do not know why. I was also a little bit jealous of Rebecca because she was getting all the attention. Rebecca also made me feel a bit angry, little sisters often get you into trouble. I was also feeling guilty because I hurt Rebecca and sometimes told lies. I was never frightened because I had Louise. I hardly felt any sadness just a tiny bit right inside. I had a happy heart.
>
> After Louise left I felt sad all over and could not stop crying because I had lost my best friend. I had no-one to play with and keep me warm. Just seeing her smile made me feel warm inside. At school I felt very sad because I missed her so. School reminds me of Louise. My heart is broken and sad. I have lots of fears. Sometimes I lock myself in my bedroom. I just want to shut myself away from the world.'

Knowing that his seven-year-old sister had only a short time to live Gary, aged eleven years wrote

'I felt sad in my heart. Fear was a lump in my throat.
In my head I felt guilty, I thought it was my fault. I
was so angry, the anger was coming out of my head,
my eyes, everywhere.'

Linking these feelings with events, smells, sounds and touching can be a useful
and enjoyable way of providing the child with an understanding of their cause
and effect as these ten-year-olds show.

Happiness is: the smell of...sweets
the sound of...money jingling in my pocket
thinking of...getting ready to go to America
touching...someone you love.

Being scared is: the smell of...the hospital
the sound of...an ambulance siren
thinking of...being left alone
touching...needles

Life Story Books and Video Diaries have proved very successful in helping
children understand their worlds and where they fit in relation to the family,
the illness, the hospital and medical personnel. In a Life Story Book these
feelings are recorded, verbally unexpressed, but then safely retained in the life
book to be used over and over again as and when they are ready – verbal
communication often follows very quickly and with surprising fluency as the
following examples show:

Figure 2.12

After producing this drawing a young teenage girl spoke for the first time of her fear that Jane, her older sister, might die. She had previously been unable to share this with other members of her family but after writing about it in her life story book allowed them all to read it.

Figure 2.13

Eight-year-old Sam began to experience recurring nightmares but would not talk about them. After producing this drawing she wrote of her fear of separation. It shows Sam desperately trying to find her way through the maze to be reunited with her brother and her mother. She wrote,

> 'I used to have nightmares about Mam being lost in the maze and I couldn't find her. My Social Worker helped me to talk about this and understand it. Now I let my mam go home to get a good night's sleep because I know she will come back quickly if I needed her.'

After asking this seven-year-old to draw his feelings factory, he went on to share the following:

> I felt frightened
> alone
> No-one told me anything
> Mam and Dad were sad and quiet
> I did not know what was wrong with Bobby

He got more presents
No-one thought about me
Lots of phone calls and visits all for Bobby
I had to stay at Grandma's
I did not know he was going to die!

Figure 2.14

Robert, aged seven years, drew a picture of his family then described his sick brother as

'Martin is angry at me, but he should be happy because Mum takes more care of him.'

Loving and Caring Water Play

This technique is used to explain symbolically to siblings and parents the concept of one particular defence mechanism – that is, bottling up feelings – and to provide a starting point for releasing those feelings. For this you will need jugs of coloured water to represent each parent and a small glass to represent each child in the family.

Water is poured into the glasses to represent the amount of loving and caring given by the parents and how this can change in the face of a life-threatening illness. The changing levels of water symbolize the processes of diminishing and replenishment that take place. Clingfilm is placed over a near empty glass to demonstrate how we protect ourselves with a 'suffering skin' when levels get frighteningly low. The result is no more loving and caring can be lost [invert glass] but subsequent attempts by parents to give more loving and caring fail as the water cannot penetrate the clingfilm. The child must then consider making holes in the suffering skin if communication and relationships are to improve. This technique is demonstrated in the video *Somewhere Over the Rainbow* (Hitcham 1993).

After the death of a sibling many youngsters refuse or are unable to show any emotion and in consequence can present as cold, distant, uncaring and indifferent. The 'I won't let anyone get close to me again' resolution is very common after a death. The pain is so unbearable that it is natural and understandable for children to believe that it would be impossible to tolerate such a level of pain and distress again. They believe that by not loving or not getting close to others, they will somehow protect themselves from further pain and suffering. However, all that happens is that they deny themselves the joy of loving and being loved. A complicated defence mechanism such as this can be very difficult for children to grasp. The loving and caring water technique simplifies it and may help build bridges and open up new levels of communication between family members.

The Candle Technique

This involves a piece of imagery that can be particularly helpful in dealing with 'unfinished business' or all the things we wish we had said or done and those we wish we had not. Often a child's greatest wish is to be able to spend time with their dead sibling.

They are convinced that if they could do this then they would be able to get on with their lives; with the help of this technique many have done just that. For this you need a small foil tray, some plasticine to hold the candles and a candle to represent each member of the family.

Figure 2.15

The worker lights two candles and describes the flames as representing 'life' itself and that within 'life' there is 'love' (Figure 2.15). The worker holds the flames of the candles together, 'when two lives meet and fall in love, the flame gets bigger. Life is fuller and there is more room for love to grow' (Figure 2.16).

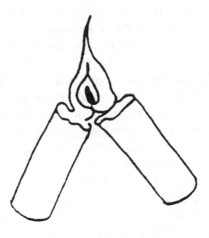

Figure 2.16

In Nicola's case I told her, 'Often children are the result of this love (lighting two more candles) when mum and dad met they fell in love, then you and Michael were born.' Holding the two flames together, the worker talks about 'when you meet someone special, they touch your life in such a way that it can never be the same again. At this point, your life becomes one so that when you separate you each take part of that big flame with you' (Figure 2.17). One candle is then blown out. 'When Michael died he took part of you with him, but part of him goes on living in you.'

Figure 2.17

Nicola talked about the mystery of heaven and said that, as a result of this technique, she could understand and accept life after death and heaven, in terms of 'that part of Michael that lives on in my heart'. Children have wonderful imaginations and readily believe that the dead can hear. They are consequently very comfortable talking to the dead, as are most adults following a bereavement. Talking aloud enables us to hear our innermost feelings. Combining the candle technique with the 'Empty Chair Technique' which is a gestalt therapy technique developed by Fritz Perls can provide the bereaved child with a comfortable way of releasing the complicated and mixed feelings they may have had about the deceased sibling. The empty chair technique 'helps convert past unresolved situations into present focused experiences' (Oaklender 1978). Youngsters often feel awkward and uncomfortable at first and so it is important to help them relax. Get them to breath deeply then tense and relax different parts of the body until they are completely at ease. Place an empty chair in front of the child and ask them to imagine that the deceased sibling with whom they have some unfinished business is seated on it. The dialogue that follows is the powerful tool that will, one hopes, move the child towards a resolution of their guilt and enable them to let go, and to reinvest the emotional energy previously tied up with the deceased sibling. In other words to get on with their lives.

Dealing with Anger

Anger is probably the most common emotional response you will come across in your work with children. Everyone gets angry. It is a very normal feeling, but before attempting to help children deal with their angry feelings you must first consider your own attitude to anger. How do you deal with your anger when it is evoked? Are you able to express it freely and appropriately without damaging others? It is not the angry feelings that are the problem but how we express them, what we do with them and whether we can accept them.

Children spend a lot of energy suppressing angry feelings and this often leads to difficult, anti-social behaviour. If we can help them deal with their anger in a way that is acceptable to the adults around them, then its discharge will often allow for the emergence of other deep seated feelings such as despair, isolation and fear. There are many ways of helping children actually experience and work through their anger but it is important that we provide them with practical methods of expressing it in a safe environment where they will not damage themselves or others.

I find it helps to take clues from the child's body language. If a child plays with his fingers, wrings his hands, clenches his fist it might help to choose a technique that focuses on the hands:-

> Clay modelling
> Beating a cushion with fists
> Throwing sponge bricks (especially good if they are wet)

Throwing stones into the sea

Throwing something at an image of the person or object they are most angry with

Tearing a drawing or picture

Scribbling

Puppets

We know that children's imaginations can be more frightening than the facts and that they will often hide their true feelings, sharing only what they think the adults around them want to hear, as Andrew demonstrates

WE BOTTLE OUR FEELINGS
AND PRETEND WE ARE OK

Figure 2.18

Sometimes children cannot cope with stories or pictures about themselves but they can act out their feelings through play and fantasy.

James was referred because of aggressive, attention-seeking behaviour. At ten years he felt he should be able to handle his feelings 'like a man'. He was clearly a very angry and unhappy young man who did not easily share his thoughts and feelings. I attempted to engage him in a variety of techniques, all to no avail. The turning point came when I introduced him to George – a bright cuddly teddy bear also known as a 'were bear'.

The following example shows how 'George' provided James with the safety and distance needed to tell his own story.

SOCIAL WORKER: 'I'd like to introduce you to my special friend George. As you can see, George looks just like lots of other teddies; he's soft and cuddly and likes to be stroked, but that's not how he feels deep down in side (*turning the head and paws inside out to reveal the fangs and claws*) inside he feels ugly and very angry so much so that when he tries to talk nicely to people all that comes out is an angry growl (*some of these bears have buttons to press which produce an angry growl*) and when he tried to get near people, he sometimes hurts them unintentionally with his sharp claws. Do you have any ideas why he might feel like this?'

JAMES: 'Well maybe he listened and heard something like his Dad had lost his job'. (*James' father had been made redundant just prior to the diagnosis of his brother's leukaemia.*)

SOCIAL WORKER: 'How did that make him feel?'

JAMES: 'Sad and frightened and he had bad thoughts.'

Figure 2.19

SOCIAL WORKER: 'What kind of bad thoughts?'

JAMES: 'Well his parents will get more bad tempered because everything piles up on top of them and they can't handle it. He probably doesn't feel safe anymore because there won't be enough money for food and things like that. Everybody else thinks things are OK but they're not really. He can't go back to normal – it's made him more cautious, not asking for much, more careful with money, a bit jealous really.'

SOCIAL WORKER: 'Does George tell anyone about these feelings and bad thoughts?'

JAMES: 'Well if he's like me, he doesn't tell anybody.'

Having made the clear link from George to himself James was then able to go on and tell his story in great detail. Later he was able to repeat this to his parents which gave them an increased insight into his problems.

A sibling's grief is frequently overshadowed by the intense reaction of the parents. In these desperate circumstances parents often want to protect their surviving children from the realities of death.

Having used direct work techniques with children for many years I know that they are best helped by adults who

(1)   share with them the truth about what is happening in their family

(2)   give them clear and age appropriate facts about the illness and death

(3)   provide them with a safe and supportive environment for their expression of feelings.

If they are denied this need for direct and honest communication then they will be forced to seek answers to questions and concepts that are often way beyond their comprehension. Remember, whatever mistakes you feel you might make in trying to help children with their grief, they are unlikely to be as damaging as if you were to try to ignore it.

Death is universal and inevitable, an unavoidable part of our heritage; therefore, bereavement has to be a natural and normal part of life. We do ourselves and our children a disservice when we constantly live in the hope that the inevitable will not happen.

References

Bowlby, J. (1988) *A Secure Base*. London: Routledge.

Hitcham, M. (1993) *Somewhere Over the Rainbow* (video and handbook). Newcastle upon Tyne: Social Work Department, Royal Victoria Infirmary (Queen Victoria Road, Newcastle upon Tyne NE1 4LP).

Koocher, G.P. and O'Malley, J.E. (1981) *The Damocles Syndrome.* New York: McGraw-Hill Book Company.

Nicholson, A. and Thompson, J. (1984) *Jenny has Leukaemia.* Newcastle: Malcolm Sargent Fund (c/o Royal Victoria Infirmary, address as for Hitcham 1992).

Oaklander, V. (1978) *Windows to Our Children.* Utah, USA: Real People Press.

Rosen, H. (1988) *Unspoken Grief.* Toronto: Lexington Books.

Spinetta, J. (1981) 'The sibling of the child with cancer.' In *Living with Childhood Cancer.* St Louis, VU: Mosby.

CHAPTER 3

Chairing the Child – A Seat of Bereavement

David A. Waskett

'My father had died and on the way to the funeral, all feeling rather sad, my youngest piped up, "Did the Daleks get Grandad?" Smiles all round!.' Terry Wogan, BBC Radio 2, 17 May 1994.

'I have two children aged three and five and after my father died they were one day with my mother when the three-year-old asked "What happened to Grandpa when he died?" Before my mother could answer her five-year-old brother answered "God came down as Superman and carried him off to heaven." "In that case" said his sister "When you die Granny and Superman comes to get you, I shall hang onto your feet."' Sarah Kennedy, BBC Radio 2, 1994.

How children view death and its aftermath is an important part of how we can begin to understand children who are undergoing some form of loss. When I came to write this chapter I thought back over thirty years to how loss came to touch and possibly affect me as a child. This thinking led me to realize that my childhood had an influence on me, which in turn has led to this piece of writing!

One thing that stands out in my mind is attending as a three-year-old Miss Mabel Monger's Dame's School – six of us in the backroom of her house. She was a devout Anglican and taught us that in the cemetery, the higher the grassy bumps on the graves, the nearer the dead person was to Heaven. Being so young, this made a profound impression on me and I remember walking home through Bagshot cemetery mentally eyeing up the height of each hump. I came to the conclusion that being of fairly low proportions the local dead were not a holy lot! Subsequent years saw me regularly watching the height, but they never seemed to grow, which only confirmed my earlier suspicions. I eventually realized that maybe Miss Monger was a little wide of the mark, but I still eye up graves – and wonder!

At an early age, I had four grandparents and two great-grandmothers. By the time I was six I only had two grandfathers. There were times when I wondered if I may have caused their deaths, I know I was a dreadful child but not that lethal. I attended none of their funerals, nor was I taken to see them in a Chapel of Rest.

My most profound loss concerned my sister Julia, always the brains of the two of us. When I was six and she was three Julia developed Encephalitis, Epilepsy and profound mental and physical handicap. I lost a playmate and my childhood. Julia is still alive, but the effects of her illness on me lasted well into my adulthood.

Whilst relatives had died, my first real involvement with death was at the age of thirteen, when my paternal grandfather died at home of lung cancer. This time I went to the funeral. He was in his coffin in the front parlour, and it was left up to me whether to go in or not. I did, and vividly remember being deterred more by the smell than how he looked. I was sad he had died and I think I felt glad I had seen him. Beyond that I appear to recall no other emotions.

The more I think back, the more I realize that I was meant to accept the events around me when a relative had died. Of the close adults in my life, not one talked to me about death or dying. It seems now as if it was tacitly assumed that I knew everything or that one did not talk to a child about such things. It all seemed very remote, death happened and life carried on.

Another Taste of Death

Two grandfathers
each different
both loved
both gone

Though still young
she has tasted grief
cried her heart dry
and loves their memory

A third death –
only a pet this time
and yet too it is missed

A pet can be replaced –
why can't we replace
grandfathers too?

T.A. Crain (1994)

For myself nobody can ever replace my favourite grandfather; when he died he left an unfillable hole.

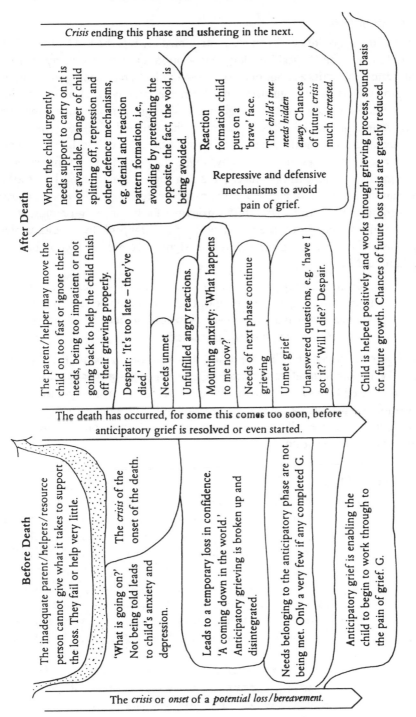

Crisis ending this phase and ushering in the next.

After Death

When the child urgently needs support to carry on it is not available. Danger of child splitting off, repression and other defence mechanisms, e.g. denial and reaction pattern formation, i.e., avoiding by pretending the opposite, the fact, the void, is being avoided.

Reaction formation child puts on a 'brave' face.

The child's true needs hidden away. Chances of future crisis much increased.

Repressive and defensive mechanisms to avoid pain of grief.

The parent/helper may move the child on too fast or ignore their needs, being too impatient or not going back to help the child finish off their grieving properly.

Despair: 'It's too late – they've died.'

Needs unmet

Unfulfilled angry reactions.

Mounting anxiety: 'What happens to me now?'

Needs of next phase continue grieving

Unmet grief

Unanswered questions, e.g. 'have I got it?' 'Will I die?' Despair.

The death has occurred, for some this comes too soon, before anticipatory grief is resolved or even started.

Before Death

The inadequate parent/helpers/resource person cannot give what it takes to support the loss. They fail or help very little.

'What is going on?' Not being told leads to child's anxiety and depression.

The *crisis* of the onset of the death.

Leads to a temporary loss in confidence. 'A coming down in the world.' Anticipatory grieving is broken up and disintegrated.

Needs belonging to the anticipatory phase are not being met. Only a very few if any completed G.

Anticipatory grief is enabling the child to begin to work through to the pain of grief. G.

The *crisis* or *onset* of a *potential loss / bereavement.*

Child is helped positively and works through grieving process, sound basis for future growth. Chances of future loss crisis are greatly reduced.

Figure 3.1 Chart of loss (by David A. Waskett, June 1994)

A Chart of Loss

One of the major influences on my professional life was the late Dr Frank Lake who founded the Clinical Theology Association. Lake created many charts to illustrate his theories and one of these, Ge8/1 ('Model representing the stunting of growth and its consequences'), has been used by myself as an outline and converted into a new chart, (see Figure 3.1). On this there are three downward arrows, from left to right. The first arrow is the potential of the loss, the second the actual loss and the third is the resolution of the crisis of loss. Life is, in many ways a series of crises and there always exists the potential for further crisis, so in some ways this chart is cyclical, for if a further loss occurs then further resolution is needed. In Figure 3.1. the model represents needs which can vary according to the phase of the child's grieving. Each minus sign represents an item of need. The appropriate resources, brought alongside by parents, professionals and others are represented as plus signs. A completed section of work is indicated by a G.

> 'The simplest form of this model must show the resource person, who is prepared to give something of themselves to the one who is in need. We must show that the one who is receiving, benefits proportionately and grows as a result of the transaction' (Lake)

In Figure 3.1 column one 'Before death' lists what can happen if the child gets little or no support before the death. Column two 'After death' shows what reactions are likely to occur to an unprepared child in an largely unsupported situation. Across the bottom of the two columns comes anticipatory grief. Here the child has received all the support needed and can move on to a satisfactory resolution over the death.

Definition of Loss

Loss is something that occurs throughout our life from the moment we are born and lose the security of our mother's womb. For the purposes of this chapter and the chart, two definitions need to be noted, one of loss and the other of anticipatory grief. The first, that of loss, is defined by Jenkins (1986). 'The disappearance of a significant object or attribute which has high physical, emotional or psychological survival value for the individual(s) concerned.'

Loss for everyone, therefore, is a unique experience and we are unable to quantify similar losses from one person to another as so many variables need to be taken into account. For a child the whole of life, and their living, is one large learning curve.

Why is it then that our society continues to ignore children's needs when a death is likely to occur or has occurred? Are we as adults afraid of getting upset if we get too close to bereaved children? Are we unable to cope with our own emotions? All too often we exclude young people and therefore leave them fearful of the future, alone and often quite insecure.

'When a death is anticipated, adults often forget to update children about the course and prognosis of the disease and children are thus badly prepared for the death, or have little understanding of what is going on'. Dyregrov (1991)

Anticipatory Grief

The whole concept of anticipatory grief can be a controversial area but it is one which is *crucial* to the child both now and in adulthood, as will be shown later in the negative chair of bereavement. Rando's (1988) definition of anticipatory grief is

'Anticipatory grief is the phenomenon encompassing the processes of mourning, coping, interaction, planning and psycho social re-organisation that is stimulated and begun, in part, in response to the awareness of the impending loss of a loved one.'

If this definition is to be taken at face value, it is important that children have the chance to begin the preparation to cope with a loss before that loss alters their life irrevocably. If anticipatory grief is not begun (see Figure 3.1) or finished it can lead to problems where all the child's worst fears can be realized in one fell swoop. At worst the child can use defence mechanisms (for example denial or reaction pattern formation) or, in the pain of exclusion, split off into depression or to a schizoid position. This clearly emphasizes the danger of not preparing a child for a loss.

It is of course assumed, when talking about anticipatory grief, that we are dealing with an illness as opposed to a sudden death where preparation is almost impossible. Today, some adults still believe that the best way for a child to get over a death is for them to be 'protected' from pain and that the path to follow is to ignore the loss or marginalize the child so much that they feel excluded. Thus, a positive pattern of how to cope with loss in adult life is denied them. Therefore, the needs of the child are denied and the chance of them having a crisis when another loss occurs are much increased.

In this I am reminded of a case seen by a bereavement volunteer I was supervising, who was visiting a woman whose father had died in the hospice. During the first session the client disclosed that as a five-year-old child she had been taken upstairs to a semi-darkened room, shown her deceased grandfather and told 'we have lost grandad'. Later in life she also experienced the cot death of one of her children and there was denial in the family that this baby boy had ever existed. On the second session she revealed that her two daughters, now aged ten and seven had asked a baby sitter if they had ever had a brother. The sitter told the mother, who it appears was furious with her two daughters for asking and forbade them ever to ask anyone ever again about it. The next session failed to take place as the worker had the door slammed in her face. In this woman's case, the experience of the three unresolved griefs lead her to denying her real feelings and by shutting the door on the worker, symbolically shut herself off from grieving. The worker had not known nor asked for the details to be shared, yet this woman appears to have been haunted by the experience of her grandfather and was repeating the process with her own children who will repeat with their children and so on down the generations. This illustrates that: 'Where previous losses have been difficult to accept and grieve, then the current loss may "re-awaken" that earlier loss and render both particularly difficult to grieve' (Lendrum and Syme 1992).

This example illustrates why a child suffering the pain of loss needs a helpful, resource person who can help the child through a relatively smooth grieving process, at the end of which it is to be hoped that the child has learnt how to cope with future losses.

The Chair of Identity

This was developed by Lake (see Figure 3.2). This chair has four legs and a seat:

> 'The seat of the chair has to have four legs of equal length fitted into it.' (Lake undated)

(1) Basic Trust... This relies on how dependable the adults are in the child's life.

(2) Autonomy...is the power to stand on one's own feet and manage independently.

(3) Initiative...is the independence in making relationships that we need to proceed with in life.

(4) Industry...implies our abilities to progress in our chosen careers.

However, in life all is not equal (see Figure 3.3) and the length of the four legs are dependant upon the quality of upbringing by our parent(s), who help to give us an identity. Figure 3.3 shows what happens when there is an identity crisis. '*Children tend to accept what their particular parents offered as a norm.*' (Lake my italics).

Examining the chair in Figures 3.2 and 3.3 I thought that these could lead to a model of children's bereavement. I therefore developed Lake's ideas to form the Chair of Positive Bereavement, the Chair of Reality and the Chair of Negative Bereavement.

The Positive Chair of Children's Bereavement

My thinking was encapsulated by asking what does a child need in order to have a successful bereavement? For me, successful bereavement is achieving the four tasks of Worden (1991):

(1) Accepting the reality of the loss.

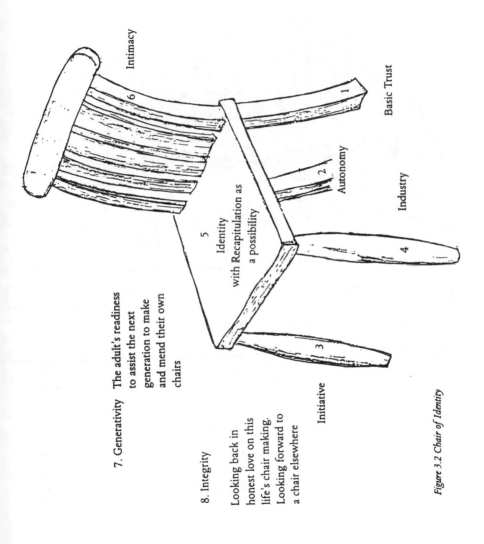

Intimacy

Basic Trust

6

1

Autonomy

2

Industry

5

Identity
with Recapitulation as
a possibility

4

3

Initiative

7. Generativity   The adult's readiness
to assist the next
generation to make
and mend their own
chairs

8. Integrity

Looking back in
honest love on this
life's chair making.
Looking forward to
a chair elsewhere

Figure 3.2 Chair of Identity

The effect of inequality in development on stability and function, thus leading to a crisis of identity

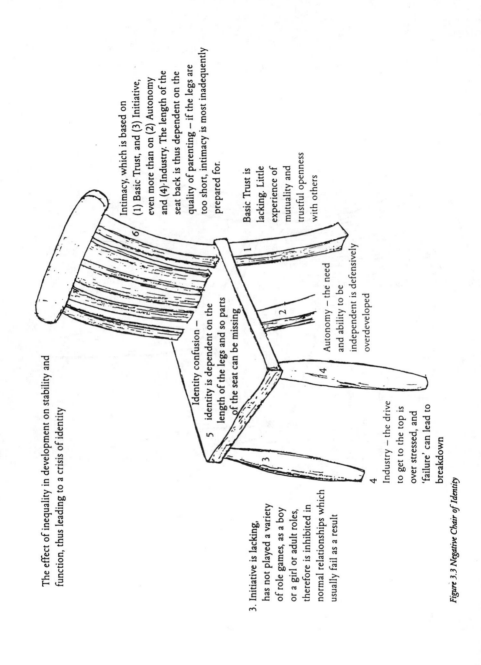

Intimacy, which is based on (1) Basic Trust, and (3) Initiative, even more than on (2) Autonomy and (4) Industry. The length of the seat back is thus dependent on the quality of parenting – if the legs are too short, intimacy is most inadequently prepared for.

Basic Trust is lacking. Little experience of mutuality and trustful openness with others

Autonomy – the need and ability to be independent is defensively overdeveloped

Identity confusion – identity is dependent on the length of the legs and so parts of the seat can be missing

3. Initiative is lacking, has not played a variety of role games, as a boy or a girl or adult roles, therefore is inhibited in normal relationships which usually fail as a result

Industry – the drive to get to the top is over stressed, and 'failure' can lead to breakdown

Figure 3.3 Negative Chair of Identity

(2) Experiencing the pain of grief.

(3) Adjusting to an environment in which the deceased is missing.

(4) To re-locate the deceased emotionally and to move on with life.

The question then remained, how do you go about this? Worden's tasks do not include any preparation for the death, so in my model it has to be assumed that we are not dealing with a sudden death. The model has to be positive. At the time I created the Positive Chair of Bereavement no thought had been given to a possible negative – what if the child is not helped? There is no doubt that the death of a person close to a child could be a devastating experience for them. It is important that the child can conceptualize abstracts and realize that death is irreversible. Certainly by the age of about nine most children understand that death is permanent. It is important that *good, precise, clear, jargon free communication* is part of helping a child grieve, and none more so than when a family bereavement is looming.

The chair I developed (see Figure 3.4) is like Lake's in as much that there is a series of phases which lead up to the whole. The chair does assume that we are dealing with a family with a fairly open system of communication – that is, adults share events and feelings with their children. It is important in this model that children are heavily involved.

In the **first leg** the child is told what is happening, explanations are given and they are consulted over their feelings about the issue. If the child asks any questions they are given honest open answers and trusted with the 'good stuff'. In other words, although the news may be bad, they are treated as equals when it comes to the sharing. A family I knew of had a grandparent diagnosed with cancer, and they made a decision that all the grandchildren should know what was happening. This enabled all family members to enjoy the time left with their dying relative. As far as could be ascertained, the grandchildren used the time left with their grandfather to the full and do not appear to have been damaged by the decision to involve them. 'They should always be told the truth and included in the family plans' Wynnejones (1985).

The **second leg** is one of participation. This is where consultation with the child is very important. Do they wish to have some form of involvement? Do they want to help out with daily living tasks, such as washing the person or even bringing them a cup of tea. Can they even cope with just seeing the person? It is important that the child is not forced to do anything he or she is not ready for. The first and second legs of the chair are important in the anticipatory grieving process, as these should prepare the child for what is to follow.

The **third leg** comes around the time of death. Here each family will have to deal with the situation as it arises. If the death is likely to be unpleasant, then inclusion could cause the child more distress, so a lot more thought may need to be undertaken before making any decision about whether to ask the child if they wish to be present. However, if the person is in a coma and will die

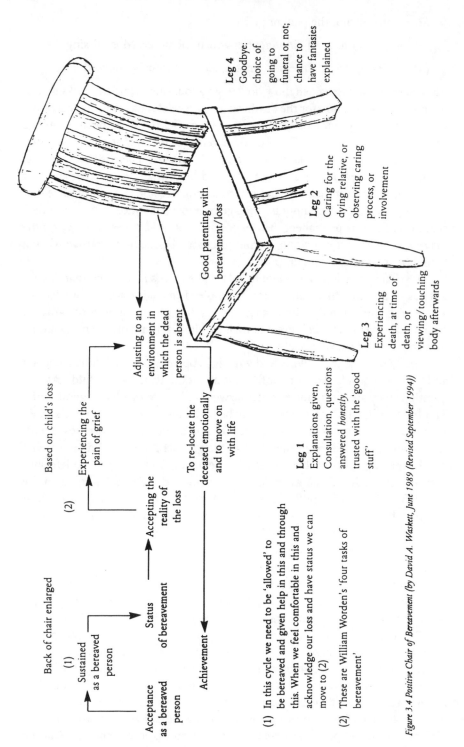

Leg 4
Goodbye:
choice of
going to
funeral or not;
chance to
have fantasies
explained

Leg 2
Caring for the
dying relative, or
observing caring
process, or
involvement

Good parenting with
bereavement/loss

Leg 3
Experiencing
death, at time of
death, or
viewing/touching
body afterwards

Adjusting to an
environment in
which the dead
person is absent

Based on child's loss

(2)

Experiencing the
pain of grief

Accepting the
reality of
the loss

To re-locate the
deceased emotionally
and to move on
with life

Leg 1
Explanations given,
Consultation, questions
answered *honestly*,
trusted with the 'good
stuff'

Back of chair enlarged

(1)

Sustained
as a bereaved
person

Status
of bereavement

Acceptance
as a bereaved
person

Achievement

(1) In this cycle we need to be 'allowed' to
be bereaved and given help in this and through
this. When we feel comfortable in this and
acknowledge our loss and have status we can
move to (2)

(2) These are William Worden's 'four tasks of
bereavement'

Figure 3.4 Positive Chair of Bereavement (by David A. Wasket, June 1989 (Revised September 1994))

peacefully, the experience may not be too traumatic for the child – if the child wishes to be there. One of my students had the case of a fourteen-year-old girl who was stroking her father's hair for some time prior to his death and a short time after death. The experience some years later appears to have assisted her. The fact that she also later spent time with her father in the Chapel of Rest may in addition have helped her through her grief.

Viewing the body after death can be very important to children; they can see the person has died. Children (and adults at times) need concrete evidence of death. If the child wishes to view the body they need to be prepared for what they will see and what they will feel if they touch. Again, the child needs the final choice. In a recent training session I was giving, a lady in her forties recounted how as a seventeen-year-old she was told she could see her dead grandmother; nobody forewarned her of how terrible the old lady looked. Not surprisingly, the teenager had nightmares for a while. She felt that if she had been warned she would have probably still seen her grandmother but would have coped more easily afterwards.

A friend recounted how she coped with her two children aged eleven and thirteen on the last morning of their father's life. The children were going out and were warned by their mother that their father would probably not be alive on their return. They went in, individually, to see him and to say goodbyes. On the children's return, they were told he had died and again the children decided to see him separately. My friend kept her husband's body at home for two days and during this time the children went in and out of the room and spent periods with their dead father. This experience does not appear to have adversely affected either child as their mother reported that they had a typical adolescence, coped well with the deaths of grandparents, went to university and moved comfortably on to adult life.

Leg four involves the all important saying goodbye, as recounted in the case of my friend and her children. The choice to go to the funeral is also very important. In today's society we have few enough grieving rites, and children who are excluded from the funeral rightly feel aggrieved as this is often their only chance for a ritual surrounding the death. My own daughters went to their first funeral, Ellena then aged five and Racheal aged three, following the death of a playmate. Explanations were given and nine years and another funeral later neither seem to have suffered from this experience: if anything they appear more comfortable with the concept of death.

If explanations are not given children can fantasize. They wonder do the bones dissolve overnight? Is the funeral conducted with the lid off the coffin? Will I see them again? My daughter, Racheal, was aged nine when her great aunt died suddenly of a heart attack. All Racheal saw was the coffin and she asked if her great aunt was really in there, as she had no evidence to believe she was. The great aunt had died many miles from home, so we were unable to visit the Chapel of Rest. It was a perfectly fair question and led me to admit I had been thinking the same thoughts but had to believe my Aunt was indeed dead.

If the four legs of the chair have been handled as well as possible in the circumstances by the child's parents (or other caring adult), this should lead to a good seat of parenting. This is where the child can sit on a secure seat with four solid legs beneath them. They can then lean onto a firm chair back and in so doing move into a cycle of grieving where the child's need to grieve is accepted. The four legs of the chair are of even length, because the child's experience of each phase has been equal. The Chair of Reality (Figure 3.5) will illustrate that this is difficult to achieve and that the legs may therefore be of different lengths.

The Chair of Reality

The concept of this chair was only recently developed by me (see Figure 3.5). The ideal is described in the Positive Chair, but, what really happens? Whilst the positive chair seems a good idea, can any family carry it all out with consistency throughout? Inevitably parts of the process may be missed out.

A hypothetical case will illustrate how The Chair of Reality has been arrived at. The scenario is one where a parent has been diagnosed as terminally ill. They share that information with the child and answer the child's questions to the best of their ability. However, emotions are a bit flat as they are all numb with shock. The child would like to cry but feels afraid in case the adults get upset by this. During the illness the child is involved fully with the care of their parent, being able to wash them and feed them, and information is given to the child in full. However, the sick parent is suddenly taken to hospital in the middle of the night and dies shortly after admission with only their spouse present. Nevertheless, the child is given the opportunity to visit their dead parent, is given full information and decides to see them. During the visit the child is alone, and all that they will say afterwards is that they kissed them, poked them to check they were dead and cried. The child is then given the choice over the funeral and decides to go, but the remaining parent finds the child's questions and fantasies hard to handle and can only answer some of them.

The child experiences relative support and can sit on a fairly solid seat of good parenting and can be sure that if they lean back the help will be there with their grieving. However, the legs are uneven. The child has had an experience of death and dying where each part of the process has been variable. Each leg is of a different length as in some parts of the process the child has been helped more than others. When the child sits on the seat and reflects on what has happened the chair will wobble.

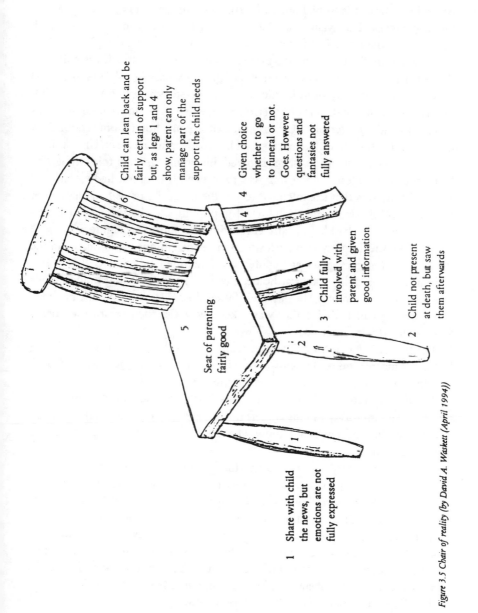

Child can lean back and be fairly certain of support but, as legs 1 and 4 show, parent can only manage part of the support the child needs

4 Given choice whether to go to funeral or not. Goes. However questions and fantasies not fully answered

3 Child fully involved with parent and given good information

2 Child not present at death, but saw them afterwards

Seat of parenting fairly good

1 Share with child the news, but emotions are not fully expressed

Figure 3.5 Chair of reality (by David A. Waskett (April 1994))

The Negative Chair of Bereavement

This is the most difficult chair as the child is excluded from the whole process (see Figure 3.6). It is to be hoped that this only occurs on rare occasions, but my experience in bereavement work indicates that children can still be excluded. This chair is the opposite of that in Figure 3.4 (The Positive Chair).

In **Leg One** the child's needs/existence are totally ignored. If the child has the temerity to ask any questions they are given excuses or told lies; the child is not trusted with any or little information. The story is told on a BBC1 TV programme of an incident in Northern Ireland when a man in a school mini-bus was shot dead by a terrorist. On his children's return home from school their mother told them that he had been killed in a road traffic accident. Unbeknown to her the next television news showed his mini-bus and told what had happened. Her eldest child, a son, was furious with her 'You lied to me'. All she could say was that she intended to tell them but the news had beaten her to it. For a child, trust and truth are all important and the first leg of Lake's Chair (Figure 3.2) had been shattered, leading to leg one of Figure 3.3.

The **Second Leg** involves exclusion, where the child is kept away from the dying person. A case, given at a conference I attended, where two girls of five and eight had a dying father at home. Every day well meaning grandparents came and took them out. The day their father died they were out at a birthday party, during which their father was taken away. On their return they never asked where their father was.

For the **Third Leg** the child never really knows the person has died, being left in a kind of limbo. By being refused the information and excluded from viewing they have no concrete evidence the person has died.

For the **Fourth Leg** they are not allowed or given the choice to attend the funeral. Naturally, as questions are left unanswered the child's fantasies are left to develop. The child does not know what has happened; they suspect, but the truth eludes them.

These poor quality legs lead to a virtually non-existent seat and there is no way in to a child's grieving process. How can they grieve when they are kept in ignorance of the facts? How can they grieve if they do not know that the person has died? This leads the child to a complex of feelings. There is rage at the exclusion yet this has to be repressed in case this makes the adults angry or upset. The child feels a separation from the deceased yet is unsure. There is fear about the situation, yet a hatred of the deceased because they have died/been ill without informing them. Lastly, the child in their pain/rage/separation anxiety falls into what Lake calls the **Dread Margin**.

The **Dread Margin** is an abyss of pain so great that they are left in a Depressive or Schizoid state. An example of depression is the story of a girl whose father died when she was eight. She asked where he was and was told he had gone away. She kept asking where he was and was eventually told that he would 'be back next year'. Next year she asked and was told 'next year.'

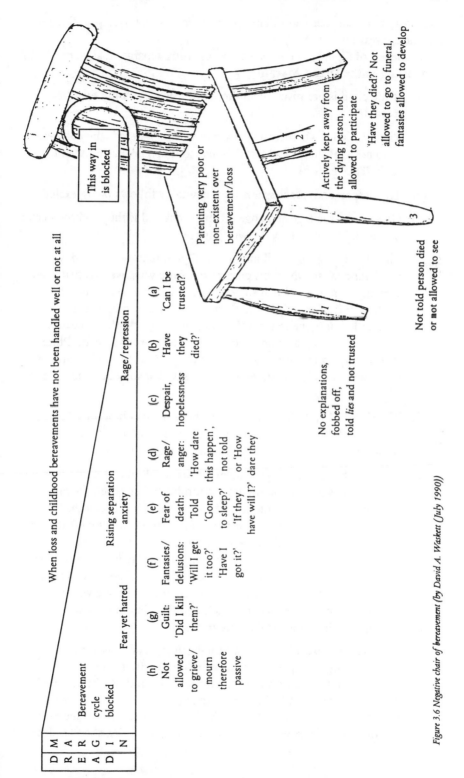

Figure 3.6 Negative chair of bereavement (by David A. Waskett (July 1990))

Over forty years later she was still in a psychiatric hospital having suffered from chronic depression all those years.

To the left of Figure 3.6 comes the area of rising separation anxiety 'a' – 'h' culminating in the **Dread Margin**.

(a) If the child is not given the information they feel 'can I ever be trusted?'

(b) There is doubt whether the person has died. Where is the concrete evidence that they have? Nobody has told me, nor have I seen the body. This leads to:

(c) The despair and hopelessness that inevitably follows being excluded.

(d) Here comes the rage and anger at the event and if they feel the person has died, how dare they die without me.

(e) The use of language is all important. One little boy was told 'we have lost Grandpa', to which his prompt response was, 'we had better go and find him then'! When somebody has died we use wonderful euphemisms, such as 'popped their clogs', 'pushing up daisies', 'eight foot under' or 'gone to meet their maker'. What do these mean to a child? Society has a paradox about the words around death. Phrases such as 'Dying to meet you', 'Deadly dull', 'dead boring' or 'dying trade' abound, yet can we comfortably say that somebody has died? This appears doubtful.

(f) The child is left with fantasies about how the death occurred and, since they know little or nothing, there is a natural fear that whatever the person died of will strike them down too.

(g) Guilt can be caused by ignorance. A doctor told me of a five-year-old boy who was playing on the stairs with his father, when the man fell. He died the following day. The boy was heard to say that 'if only I had made Dad put on his shoes instead of his slippers then he would not have slipped and fell.' Another case was that of a twelve-year-old girl who went out every Thursday with her mother. On this day her mother needed to go out alone, there was a row and as the woman left her daughter screamed at her, 'I hope you die'. The mother had an asthmatic attack and did die. The girl was consumed with guilt, 'I killed my mother.'

(h) If the child is excluded how can they grieve, especially if they are told off for crying? They therefore learn that passivity is the way to act, and this can lead to further problems for the child. Raeburn (1992) mentions the case of Isobel whose mother had died, and how her father never talked about her mother's death or shared his feelings. 'All of this made Isobel frozen too. As she grew older, she found it difficult to form anything other than superficial relationships'. As Johnston (undated) has so succinctly put it, 'To be excluded diminishes one's sense of self – one's sense of membership'.

The three chairs clearly illustrate that children need help in all phases of the grieving process. The positive chair (Figure 3.4) is an ideal model of what should/could happen. I would suggest that it rarely does and the chair of reality (Figure 3.5) is closer to life, when the child receives a variable response to their needs. It is important that the child is recognized as a person of worth and that their mental as opposed to chronological age is taken into account when helping them. However, the negative chair (Figure 3.6) is potentially the most destructive. Here the child receives little or no help and is left to their own devices to try and understand what is happening to them. The chair, however, is not fixed on loss through death and can be adapted to loss by parents separating/divorcing or a child going into care/being in care already.

Some Ideas for Working with Children

Given that the chairs provide a theoretical framework, there remains the need to help children who are in the Negative Chair (Figure 3.6) and to a lesser extent the chair of reality (Figure 3.5).

The ideas following are just some of many that could be used in such cases. The ultimate goal is to enable the child to say a positive goodbye to their parent who has died and to move onto a positive seat of bereavement, when he or she will be able to sit securely without fear of falling off or the chair tipping over.

Use of Faces

On a visit to the social work department of the North London Hospice I saw the sheet of faces (Figure 3.7). Some children find it difficult to express their feelings either because of age or handicap; for instance, there may be insufficient vocabulary. One eleven-year-old boy with whom I worked was furious that his parents had not shared with him that his mother was going to die. At times he was almost incoherent with rage, at others calmer but still distressed. He felt unable to keep a daily diary of his feelings because he felt helpless as to how he could begin to express himself in words. On being given a copy of the faces he felt that here was a medium in which he might begin to record how he felt. This appeared to work for him and each day produced a crop of features (some of which were not on the sheet). Over a period of time, he was able to see that his anger was subsiding and happier faces were starting to appear with greater frequency.

By using the faces the child can start to work through the four legs of the chair, therefore enabling them to be in touch with their feelings on a more positive level. This should enable them to begin to identify each stage that they need to go through to reach a resolution.

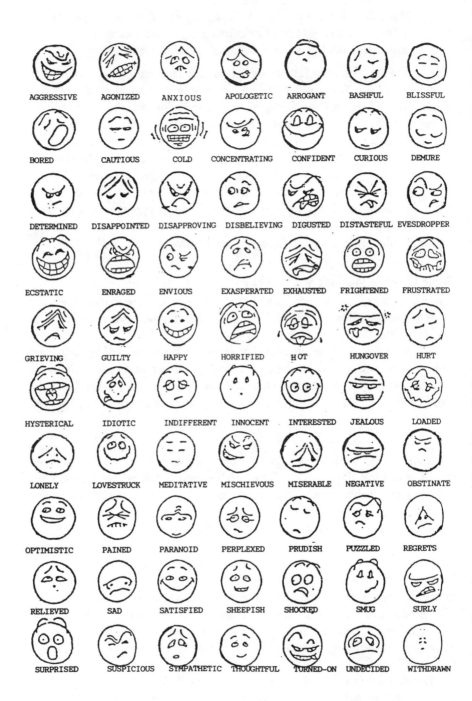

Figure 3.7

Fantasy Journeys

With the negative chair the first and fourth legs are where the child's fantasy world can develop imaginatively concerning what has happened. This is one area where I feel that more work needs to be done in order to help children on a more positive level.

> 'A fantasy journey is an exercise in which people are led by using their imagination, into hypothetical situations that enable them to explore their own fantasy world... A good early childhood nurture will give us a positive inner fantasy world that helps us to relate well with our environment and interpret it with a high degree of accuracy. A bad early childhood nurture will give us a negative one, by which we will often misinterpret the world outside and the behaviour of others towards us.' (Bick undated)

If the child has a negative experience of the first and fourth legs they may in later life find it far more difficult to cope with their fantasies of loss or the ability to say goodbye, whenever they occur. Bick suggests that a guided fantasy might be the answer. In this the child can realize that the parent has died and that there is an unfillable gap in the family. This should enable the child to say goodbye as in the fourth leg or to start the work to enable them to say goodbye. For any worker who wants to use this medium it is best if they experience several fantasy journeys themselves so that they can understand how they work and something of their own fantasy life. This should enable them to deal with any material that a child might wish to disclose. I did my fantasy journey training with the Clinical Theology Association.

Drawing the Family

The use of drawings and paintings by a bereaved child can be therapeutic and my suggestion is to enable the child to draw the family as they see them. Figure 3.8 is a copy of a drawing of a six-year-old boy's family, which comprises himself, his parents – his mother is dying of cancer – his eight-year-old sister and one-year-old brother. His father is a demanding, difficult man to the extent that his wife dies at home, in agony, because he will not let anybody in to care for her.

Most people see the central figure as the mother, his main carer – his brother on the floor, the boy himself on the right, sister back left and father in front of her. In fact, brother is on the floor, the boy himself on the right, the central figure is his sister – his main carer. His mother is on the left front and his father is behind her. This proved to be an accurate portrayal of the family.

For another family where the mother had died (and where the father had described how he and his wife had been so close), I asked the children of eight and nine, separately, to draw their family as it was prior to their mother's death.

Figure 3.8

Both drew the parents on opposite sides of the paper close to the edge. They, however, stood close together in the middle. There was no collusion and their drawings were accurate; the parents turned out to be very much apart.

By this method the worker can begin to understand what the child has experienced and so enable them to move onto the next part, for example the scrap books/diaries.

Scrap Books/Diaries

I have already alluded to this method in the section on the use of faces. However, in fostering and adoption work the use of scrapbooks where the child can record their natural family is well known and this can be used in bereavement. For most people memories fade with time and this also happens to children. How can a child remember what happened when someone close to them died, let alone what life was like with them before the death?

The answer is to help the child to keep a scrapbook. The time of each session will depend on the concentration span of the child, but for a child of five years, fifteen minutes may be the maximum. The scrapbook will enable the child to tell their story of what they remember of the person who has died and what family life was like then. The story can be told in drawings, words and photographs, but always appropriate to each child. Workers need to work on a one-to-one basis if at all possible to give full attention to the child. In some cases it may be important for the surviving parent to take on this task as part of family rebuilding after the event. In this case the worker acts as supporter to the parent.

The importance of the task may not become immediately apparent and it could only become evident in later years when the child reads the scrapbook and realizes what family life had been like. In the cases of the negative chair the work with the child can involve going through the dying process and death of the parent, working through each leg in turn. This will, it is to be hoped, enable an excluded child to begin to understand what has happened and enable him or her to move onto the seat of the chair of reality and react more positively to their loss.

The Ungame

Advertised as a 'Co-operative adventure in communication', 'The Ungame', (by Rhea Zakich 1989) can be used to work with bereaved children as it has questions on cards as a way of eliciting information. 'The Ungame' comes with blank cards which can be used to ask questions about the child's loss.

'The Ungame' has answers that can sometimes be challenged. Examples of questions are: 'What would you want your last words to be?', 'Ages 13 – over: Describe an experience with death as a child. Ages 12 – under: Talk about any experience with death', and 'Complete the sentence: When someone really listens to what I say, I feel _____, because _____'. The board has the game in a circle and players can land on squares with questions such as: 'If you have been LONELY this past week, go to the lonely area.' or 'If you are HAPPY now, go to the happy area.' For the latter if the player does not do so, the COMMENT? square gives another player the right to challenge this.

By using this game at various stages in the child's grieving process, the worker can elucidate how far the child has proceeded in working through the various stages of the chair moving it is to be hoped, from negative to positive. By setting the questions for each game, using the ones provided or writing new ones on the blank cards, the worker can set the pace for each session. Overall the game is a useful diagnostic tool.

Summary

It may need one of these ideas detailed above or a combination of them to enable the child to work through their loss and to be able to say a positive goodbye to the parent who has died. Only then will the child be able to begin to put their past behind them, sit more securely on the chair, remember the journey of grief they have been through and start to look to the future.

Conclusion

Children ARE complex and being an adult or parent gives us the privilege and responsibility to help them on their journey to mature adulthood. How well this happens depends on our efforts. What we as adults need to try to remember is our own childhood – even if that was years ago! We are very good at forgetting what it was like to be our child, especially if painful memories are involved. As a result of this we can miss our children's feelings and underestimate their capacity for grieving.

Children need clear, realistic information and support to come to terms with their feelings. There is no doubt that there is enough evidence that children are damaged by loss. The effects can be ameliorated if they are included in the WHOLE bereavement process. The chairs are an attempt to demonstrate a model of care and what a child's needs are, and what can happen if they are excluded. The basic chair underpinning comes from well rehearsed and accepted theories of grieving.

Ultimately, children themselves are, of course, the best witness to their own feelings. The anger and hurt that can emanate from an excluded child indicates their need to be part of the whole family at a crucial time in their lives. Do we not, as adults, have a duty to give them that inclusion as family members? Therefore our prime role as adults is to aim to build that positive chair for our children to sit on. Sitting on that chair they can and should be able to grow tall, resolve their losses, learn positively from their experience, and, one hopes, cope with any future loss.

References

Bick, D. (Undated) *Fantasy Journey*. Prinknash: Privately Published.

Crain, T.A. (1994) 'Another Taste of Death.' *Contact* 115, 32.

Dyregrov, A. (1991) *Grief in Children. A Handbook for Adults*. London: Jessica Kingsley Publishers.

Jenkins, H. (1986) 'Loss: bereavement, illness and other factors.' In G. Horobin (ed) *The Family: Context and Client?* London: Kogan Page.

Johnston, S.J. (Undated) *Talking Helps*. Cruse Maidstone Branch Pamphlet.

Lake, F. (Undated) *Human Growth and Development*. Nottingham: Clinical Theology Association.

Lendrum, S. and Syme, G. (1992) *Gift of Tears.* London: Tavistock/Routledge.

Raeburn, A. (1992) 'Express yourself.' *Chat,* 12 September, 48–49.

Rando, T. (1984) *Grief, Dying and Death.* Research Press Company.

Worden, W. (1991) *Grief Counselling and Grief Therapy.* London: Tavistock/Routledge.

Wynnejones, P. (1985) *Children Death and Bereavement.* London: Scripture Union.

Zakich, R. (1989) *Ungame.* Anaheim, CA: Talicor, Inc.

CHAPTER 4

Non-Directive Play Therapy
with Bereaved Children

Jo Carroll

Introduction

There has been a growing interest in non-directive play therapy in recent years, largely in response to awareness of the distress and long-term harm suffered by young survivors of abuse. However, this technique was first applied to children experiencing any form of childhood disturbance or unhappiness, including those who were bereaved.

Children bring a range of emotions into play therapy. It is common for bereaved children to deny trauma, feel shock, guilt, anger, fear, confusion and loss following the death of a close relative or friend, and to express these feelings through challenging behaviour or withdrawal (Grollman 1991; Segal 1984; Ward 1993; Webb 1993). Understanding and surviving these feelings can be safely promoted through non-directive play therapy.

The first recorded use of play in therapy is Sigmund Freud's analysis of a phobic five-year-old boy (1909). His work formed the basis of subsequent analytic child psychotherapeutic techniques as practised by Klein (1937 and 1982), Anna Freud (1965) and Winnicott (see Davis and Wallbridge 1983). The ideas of these practitioners have been absorbed into the practice of many who are not qualified child psychotherapists, but who are engaged in therapeutic work with children (Copley and Forryan 1987).

The concept of transference, which underpins psychoanalytic thinking, is particularly valuable. Rosenbluth (1970) describes transference as feelings which are 'transferred from some earlier childhood relationship within the family to the present therapeutic relationship' (p.72). Psychoanalysts see the interpretation of transference as the cornerstone of their work. Non-directive play therapists are unlikely to interpret a transference relationship directly;

however, awareness that feelings expressed in the context of a relationship with a play therapist reflect those between the child and her or his primary carers is invaluable. Bereaved children with a therapist the same gender as the person who has died may introject feelings of anger and grief. A therapist who is the same gender as a surviving parent may find the child clinging and insecure.

As the child psychotherapists were expanding their understanding of such unconscious processes as transference, Axline (1969) and Moustakas (1973) were developing their techniques of non-directive play therapy. Axline (1969) describes non-directive play therapy as an 'opportunity to experience growth under the most favourable conditions. Since play is his natural means of expression, the child is given the opportunity to play out his accumulated feelings of tension, frustration, insecurity, aggression, fear, bewilderment, confusion' (p.16).

Axline's ideas provide the foundation for the current practice of non-directive play therapy. It is distinguished from child psychotherapy in that it views playing itself as the medium for healing; the therapist provides the space in which healing is possible.

> 'It is a way of giving the child an opportunity to 'play out' her feelings and problems and to learn about herself in relation to the therapist, who will behave in such a way that the child is secure.
>
> In this method of therapy, play itself is the therapeutic intervention; play is not used as a stimulation for other forms of therapy. The focus of the theory is on the process of play which heals the child.' (Cattanach 1992, pp.39–40)

There are numerous life events that can trouble children. Moustakas (1973) understood the distress of children struggling to cope with the demands of normal family life, and applied child-centred techniques very successfully. Copley and Forryan (1987), Schaeffer and O'Connor (1983) and Webb (1991) give clear accounts of therapy with children who are unable to come to terms with stressful experiences.

With the current emphasis on the plight of the sexually abused child there is a danger that the distress of other children will go unacknowledged. Attention is paid to the sadness of children separated from families who fail to offer adequate care or protection (Cipolla, McGown and Yanvilis 1992; Jewett 1984). The grief of the child whose parent or sibling has died is as acute as one whose birth family has broken down.

Principles of Non-Directive Play Therapy

Non-directive play therapy is founded on the belief that all children contain within themselves an innate drive towards health; the therapist provides the milieu in which the child can find her or his own road to recovery. Moustakas

(1973) underlines the therapist's 'deep belief that children have within themselves capacity for self-growth and self-realization' (p.4).

Axline's eight principles of non-directive therapy underpin much of my current practice (1969, pp.73–75):

The therapist must develop a warm, friendly relationship with the child, in which a good rapport is established as soon as possible.

In addition to offering a welcome to the playroom, it is important to recognize and accept each child's anxiety. Comments such as 'What a big boy you are!' or 'What a pretty dress!' are inappropriate. The child may feel small, or be made to wear the dress when she would rather be in jeans. We need to be pleased to see the child, however scruffy or miserable she or he may be.

The therapist accepts the child exactly as he (or she) is.

This is the cornerstone of my non-directive play therapy. The therapist never shows impatience, criticism or reproof. Praise must also be avoided. Thus children learn that all feelings and behaviours can be understood. Any anxieties they may have about pleasing me evaporate; they discover the energy to attend to themselves.

The therapist establishes a feeling of permissiveness within the relationship so that the child feels free to express (her or) his feelings completely.

Words alone are not enough. Although children need a verbal introduction to the playroom, and to be told that they may play as they wish, we must also model permissiveness by quiet acceptance of children's play.

The therapist is alert to recognizing the feelings the child is expressing and reflects those feelings back to him (or her) in such a manner that he (or she) gains insight into his (or her) behaviour.

Children in therapy express their feelings in a number of ways. Some use toys to 'play out' events from their lives directly: in such circumstances it is easy for the therapist to identify, name, and empathize with the emotions expressed. Others enact complex scenes involving monsters and demons, which they use to explore fear and powerlessness.

Such children find it difficult if we try to equate feelings with the child's situation, but can tolerate comments about those experienced by the characters in the play. Other children project emotions onto us, and then we may find ourselves overwhelmed with waves of feelings that we may not always understand. Children need their therapists to contain and survive these feelings before they can acknowledge them for themselves.

The therapist maintains a deep respect for the child's ability to solve his (or her) own problems if given the opportunity to do so. The responsibility to institute changes is the child's.

It is difficult for the inexperienced therapist to believe that a child who repeatedly creates havoc in the playroom is finding a solution to her or his difficulties amid the mayhem.

It is also personally stressful, when faced with distressed children, not to try to find solutions. Our natural response as adults is to reassure. Of course, bereaved children need consolation and loving care from those who look after them. However, in non-directive play therapy they reach an understanding of the experience of bereavement, an understanding all the more profound for each child having found it for themselves.

The therapist does not attempt to direct the child's actions or conversation in any manner. The child leads the way; the therapist follows.

When children appear to block all expression of feeling, it is difficult not to challenge them by asking direct questions, or guide them towards play materials related to the child's circumstances. However, many children who suffer in this way cannot face these feelings: questions will be rebuffed or answered untruthfully; materials will be ignored. Given the undivided attention and unequivocal regard of a play therapist, children begin to look at difficult feelings when they are ready.

The therapist does not attempt to hurry the therapy along. It is a gradual process and is recognized as such by the therapist.

The pain of children is hard to bear; it can be almost intolerably painful allowing a child all the time she or he needs to recover. We recognize that bereaved adults may take two years or more to resolve their grief following the loss of a spouse, yet we struggle to permit children the time they need to come to terms with such experiences.

Non-directive therapists must curb this wish to find quick solutions. Their role is to be alongside children while they find solutions for themselves.

The therapist establishes only those limits that are necessary to anchor the therapy in the world of reality and to make the child aware of his or her) responsibility in the relationship.

Non-directive play therapy is not a 'free-for-all'. Children may not hurt themselves, nor the therapist, nor may they deliberately destroy materials. We do not disapprove of the impulses behind these actions, and accept the feelings that are being expressed in the child's wish to behave in this way. Hurting people is not allowed because it hurts, not because it makes us cross!

The setting and maintenance of limits is an important part of play therapy. Without them therapy has no boundary and the child cannot feel truly contained. Within this boundary, the child is free to play and to feel as she or he wishes.

Emotional Content of Therapy

Non-directive play therapy is based on the premise that children can find solutions for themselves. However, during the course of therapy it is important that they also discover and tolerate situations which have no solutions. It is common for children to ask 'why good people die'; it is extremely difficult for them to realize that it is a question with no answer (Segal 1984).

Young children commonly feel a personal responsibility for everything that happens, believing they could have altered events by behaving differently. Col, a small boy in Hill's short story, stomped off up a cliff to sulk, from where he watched helplessly as his father drowned. He believed that his own bad temper had led directly to the death of his father (Hill 1973). The converse of childish feelings of power is the reality of extreme powerlessness. The therapist, while assuring the child of her or his own right to make decisions within sessions, must also enable the child to recognize her or his own helplessness in the face of overwhelming events.

All children entering therapy experience anxiety. Older children may feel embarrassed that they are unable to cope with their feelings themselves. Some may fear that they are going mad. We should identify and accept these feelings: they are natural, understandable and will pass. Many of the feelings children express in the initial stages of therapy are diffuse and generalized (Moustakas 1973). They may experience a sense of emotional overload. Play is likely to be chaotic and the therapist will struggle to contain the muddle of emotions within it. More complex feelings emerge later, but may still be difficult to identify. Children may project these feelings: if we can survive them, then possibly the child will too. In working with bereaved children we should be prepared for waves of projected rage, grief and helplessness. It is common for these feelings to emerge in the course of play; we take the roles offered and play them convincingly: dinosaurs can roar and dolls can weep. We emerge unscathed.

As children settle into therapy, emotions become sharpened and more specific. The child may become able to direct her or his feelings at particular persons or experiences. This is a painful process. Young children find it almost impossible to express negative feelings towards a close relative or friend who has died. The dead person may be idealized; anger at perceived abandonment may be directed at a surviving parent whom the child sees as responsible. It is normal for young children to have jealous fantasies and wish their siblings dead. If this sibling subsequently dies the guilt of the young survivor can be almost intolerable. The long-term consequences for children losing a sibling in this way is only recently understood (Davies 1991). In the safety of non-directive play therapy these feelings can be explored gently, and in the child's own time.

Gradually, positive feelings emerge. At this stage children must tolerate ambivalence, and good memories of the dead person jostle with feeling of loss. Very young children are unable to identify contrasting emotions and tolerance of ambivalence comes with maturity as well as with therapy (Harris 1989). Eventually children begin to put the trauma behind them. Life will never be the same again; but they can talk with love and without tears about the person who has died, and are relaxed enough to have fun. It is time for therapy to end.

Careful preparation must be given to the termination of therapy. It will inevitably mirror many of the feelings of loss that have been raised during the previous weeks or months. Therapists must exercise extreme sensitivity. Gillian, a twelve-year old whose mother had died, was unable to think about her loss until therapy drew to a close: losing her therapist activated feelings about the death of her mother, and were dealt with in the final stages of therapy (Copley and Forryan 1987, p.164).

West (1984) emphasizes the importance of careful preparation when termination is considered, as both therapist and child have feelings to resolve. She brings therapy to a close gradually, seeing termination as a stage during which child and therapist separate gradually and amicably. It is a bridge between the intense relationship of therapy and the child relying solely on the love of family and friends to give her satisfaction and support.

Practical Arrangements for Therapy

We must undertake a full assessment of each child's history, and the circumstances that bring her or him into therapy, before sessions begin. Saravay (1991) regards consideration of the following components essential to a thorough evaluation:

1. The age, developmental stage and cognitive level of the child.

2. The child's previous psychological adjustment.

3. The nature of the child's previous relationship with the deceased.

4. The response of close family members.

5. The presence of available support in the extended family, school and community. (p.178)

Webb (1993) expands on these suggestions, emphasizing the distinction between normal and disabling grief, and considers the possibility that bereaved children may be seriously depressed. She stresses that individual factors in the child should be considered alongside circumstances relating to the death, and the family, social and religious environment (p.19–42).

Other difficulties which exist within the family must also be assessed. For instance, Carol, aged thirteen, was referred to a Child and Family Guidance Clinic presenting with challenging behaviour when her mother prepared to remarry following the death of Carol's father. The therapist had to attend to the mother–daughter relationship, and family secrets surrounding the death of her father as well as Carol's unresolved grief (Lask and Lask 1981, p.121).

Consideration must be given to the question of confidentiality. It is reasonable for those who care for children to seek involvement in their therapy. Many children's behaviour appears to deteriorate during the early stages of therapy, and the support and understanding of carers is essential if therapy is to be successful. However, it is not appropriate to share the minutiae of play. I tell children that I shall not discuss the details of our sessions, but shall be talking with her or his carers to outline the progress of therapy, and shall make a point of telling them if she or he is upset.

When sharing information with surviving parents sensitivity to their feelings is essential. Unresolved mourning may inhibit this parent's ability to meet the needs of the child. A therapist working with Max, a small boy who had witnessed the accidental death of his father, recognized that his mother could not express her own anger, and (unusually) permitted Max's mother to watch the sessions through a one-way screen. She could empathize with the feelings Max was expressing, and this led to an appropriate release of her own feelings (McMahon 1992, pp.140–141).

Attention must be paid to accurate recording. I try to record each session in as much detail as possible (although not in complete sentences). I spread my notes over two-thirds of the page only, and, alongside these records, I comment on the child's play and my feelings about it. It is then easy to monitor the process of therapy, and to attend to the projections of the child.

Non-directive play therapy with bereaved children is stressful and demanding work for the therapist. Good supervision and support is essential, as are opportunities to work in other fields from time to time. Feelings projected by grieving children are intense and distressing; therapists who cannot look after themselves and relieve their own emotions cannot contain and tolerate the feelings of the children.

Children need predictability in therapy. Many feel that their lives have turned 'upside down'; security offered by regular sessions, at the same time and in the same place each week, offer a certainty that the rest of their lives may lack. When all else is failing the certainty of play therapy is there to hold on to.

Whilst a well-designed playroom may be ideal, few of us have this luxury. Yet, with imagination and foresight children can be seen almost anywhere. If I can ensure that we will not be disturbed, the child can be offered therapy. We can look for a room with the minimum of distractions and few opportunities for the child to damage property. Ideally, running water affords the opportunity for paint and messy play. Too large a room, and children may keep so far from us that they never experience the relief of having feelings contained and understood. Too small a room, and anxious children cannot find enough space between themselves and us to consider their feelings in peace, and may panic.

It is essential to attend to the child's physical needs. It is reasonable to offer a drink or snack if the child has travelled a long way, or it was a long time since breakfast. In addition, children need the toilet more frequently than adults, and anxious children need the toilet all the time!

The selection of material should be made with care. Many writers have offered suggestions of materials suitable for use in play therapy (Ginott 1982; Reismann 1973; McMahon 1992). Few agree as to which toys are most effective in enabling children to play imaginatively and prompting the expression of feelings. Axline (1969) found the following toys the most successful:

> 'nursing bottles; a doll family; a doll house with furniture; toy soldiers and army equipment; toy animals; playhouse materials, including table, chairs, cot, doll bed, stove, tin dishes, pans, spoons; doll clothes, clothesline, clothespins, and clothes basket; a didee doll; a large rag doll; puppets; a puppet screen; crayons; clay; finger paints; sand; water; toy guns; peg-pounding sets; wooden mallet; paper dolls; little cars; airplanes; a table; an easel; an enamel worktop for finger painting and clay work; toy telephone; shelves; basin; small broom; rags; drawing paper; finger-painting paper; old newspapers; inexpensive cutting paper, pictures of people, houses, animals and other objects; and empty berry baskets to smash.' (p.54)

It is essential that small figures and dolls reflect the racial mix of our society, without prejudice or stereotyping. Children should never feel that they cannot find dolls to represent themselves.

I lack the luxury of my own playroom, and must use toys that I carry with me. Since I cannot carry everything, I have to make a careful selection which I feel meets each child's needs. During my initial assessment I talk with the child's carer, to discuss how she or he spends free time, and ensure I have materials with me which are likely to be popular. My next priority is to find toys which stimulate imaginative play: small figures, domestic and wild animals, fantasy figures and dinosaurs. I include puppets, a doctor's set and woollen dolls, to encourage both nurturing and revengeful play (it is extraordinary how much aggression can be expressed giving an injection). A doll and baby bottle can enable children to retreat to the relative safety of infancy. If possible I include a tea-set, which can lead to exploration of the personal meaning of feeding experiences; and a telephone, which may enable a child to say something which she could not reveal directly. If there is anywhere we can wash our hands, I always include playdough: it is easy to knead and manipulate, can help anxious children to relax and withdrawn children to express anger. If water is available I include paints; if not felt tip pens have to suffice.

I make a point of providing toys which encourage aggression: my dinosaurs are carnivorous, with open mouths and huge teeth, and my lions and tiger look far from docile (although I include fences to keep them in). Children also need opportunities for gentle, nourishing play: this is seldom easy for boys, who spurn more traditional 'girl's toys'. However, many find a toy car in need of constant mending, or a puppet requiring frequent feeding, fulfils this need for reparative play. Highly anxious children value opportunities for regressive play, and respond to tactile material such as playdough.

Many respected therapists, including West (1992) and Wilson, Kendrick and Ryan (1992) are comfortable using guns. I am not. Modern toy guns are almost exact replicas of real ones; I want to explore children's fantasies, not to engage in play which reflects films or television programmes they may have seen. Children can find enough 'props' to pretend to kill me without the provision of guns. However, the survivors of violence are my one exception. As children who have lost a loved one in a road traffic accident play car crashes endlessly, so children whose relative has been murdered need material for comparable play. Children who have witnessed violent assault against their parents can be particularly disturbed by the experience (Hendricks, Black and Kaplan 1993; Pynoos and Eth 1984). These children have experienced such profound trauma that they need highly skilled and prolonged intervention.

If the death followed months in hospital, plenty of hospital and nursing equipment should be included. However, we must concentrate on the child's experience: it is easy to be diverted by the patient and lose sight of the child who visits each day and must leave. Some children are sent to stay with relatives when it is known that a parent or sibling is dying, or not permitted to visit a much-loved grandparent: these children may find it impossible to believe that the death has occurred and their play will be full of fantasies of resurrection.

Children need toys which help re-enact a funeral. We should try to be familiar with the funereal arrangements of different cultures, and make sure that the material they provide is appropriate for each child (Ward 1993). Some families do not permit children to attend the funeral. These children may need to create their own rituals to say 'goodbye'; the therapist can enable the child to choose her or his own ceremony (Crompton 1990).

Application of this Technique with Bereaved Children

Many children recover from the shock and grief of bereavement without professional intervention. If the support, understanding and opportunity to express their feelings openly are available in the child's environment, and she or he has had a relatively trouble-free childhood prior to the death, it is possible for time ultimately to heal the wounds and the child to make a healthy adjustment.

However, research shows that adults who were bereaved as children suffer a higher incidence of depression (Hurley 1991); therefore a thorough assessment and appropriate help is essential if children are to mourn successfully. Regrettably, many families cannot tolerate the distress of their children, denying them space for open expression of grief. It is also common for children to be unable to communicate feelings about the loss of a loved one (Segal 1984), and parents or carers may not be skilled at recognizing the child's non-verbal communications.

Children should be given opportunities to share their grief and sorrow with others who are mourning, and questions should be answered openly and honestly (Excell 1991). Children without the loving support and understanding of their families may suppress feelings, or act them out. They may withdraw, become aggressive or attention-seeking. In time, the children themselves lose sight of the origins of their distress; management of challenging behaviour becomes the focus of professional intervention. Some of these children are unable to respond to directive techniques, which take for granted the child's ability to associate feelings with their external causes. Occasionally they are aware of overwhelming unhappiness; more often they present as angry, confused or withdrawn.

For some families, bereavement exposes severe distortions in relationships, and emotional difficulties which were not evident before. All families need to adjust their relationships following a bereavement; this is made all the more difficult by enmeshed or anxious attachments amongst surviving family members. Families which lose a member through suicide commonly have distorted relations prior to the death, which impinge on individual and familial grieving (Hurley 1991; Webb 1993). Such families need skilled intervention and children may need individual help to separate their feelings of grief from other family problems.

Children who struggle to recover from bereavement need careful assessment to consider appropriate interventions. Guerney (1983) considers non-directive play therapy to be applicable to all distressed children, because of its commitment to the unique quality of each child. Other practitioners take a more eclectic approach. Contributors to Webb (1993) each assessed the difficulties of the children referred to them, and selected an appropriate response. In non-directive play therapy grief can emerge gradually. It is contained by an adult who does not judge the child and empathizes with the sorrow behind challenging behaviour. The child can mourn in safety, emerging able to enjoy her or his surviving relationships. Thus non-directive play therapy is highly effective for those children who, for whatever reason, have not mourned the loss of a loved one appropriately, or for whom the repressions of feelings has led to long-term behavioural or emotional difficulties. These children need space, time and unconditional acceptance of themselves and their distress, and then they can begin to resolve long-standing difficulties.

Non-Directive Play Therapy in Practice

Celeste

Celeste's father died in hospital after a long and painful illness. Her mother brought her for therapy following outbursts of aggressive behaviour which did not decrease in the months following the death. Celeste had known that her father was ill and would not recover, and visited him in hospital; however, she was unable to visit as often as her mother or younger siblings as she was at school. Le Vieux (1993) selected non-directive play therapy techniques to help Celeste, as they offer opportunity for symbolic expression of feeling and emphasize the importance of the child's need to be heard.

From the outset, Celeste was able to describe her sadness at the death of her father, and to illustrate this by deliberately placing a male figure in the corner of a sandbox whilst Disney characters enjoyed themselves elsewhere. Her feelings were evident in the tone of her voice, and were reflected by her therapist. During the ensuing months, Celeste was able to explore happy memories of her father alongside the sorrow she so clearly felt; she recalled small details such as his hazel eyes and the way her hand felt so small when holding his. She projected great sadness on to her therapist as she described such incidents; and she used drawings to illustrate many of her feelings. Gradually, she was able to recall happy memories of her father, and was less disabled by her grief. There were times when her play seemed less purposeful, but her therapist concluded that this mirrored many occasions when she would play alongside her father. Celeste's therapy continued weekly until after the anniversary of her father's death, when termination was approached gradually.

Her therapist also made a point of spending ten minutes with Celeste's mother before each session; this was extremely supportive for her mother, who was struggling to cope with her own grief as well and the demands of young children, and ensured good communication between all those caring for the child.

Gerald

Hellendoorn (1988) describes a case reported by Donker-Raymaker (1982). Gerald, aged ten, lived with his father and three older siblings following the death of their mother. Gerald showed no emotion at the funeral, appearing to be the least affected member of the family at the time. However, eighteen months later he was friendless, underachieving and withdrawn.

In his play he repeatedly buried his favourite toy, saving it only at the last minute. In his third session he turned to the doll house, and enacted a scene of mother leaving and returning to the family, with the children's anxiety relieved by her return. Thus Gerald disclosed his denial of this mother's death. His therapist attempted to confront him by creating a small cemetery in the sandbox; Gerald was clearly threatened, responding by making the dolls in the house even safer by adding blocks to the walls. The therapist, wisely, acknowledged this anxiety and helped to build the walls. An attempt to hurry Gerald's recovery through directive techniques was rejected by the child, who felt safer in the context of non-directive play therapy.

As Gerald's trust in his therapist grew stronger, his play changed. The father figure took an increasing prominent role, and the mother figure gradually disappeared. However, the world was still a dangerous place, and figures were introduced who promptly died in the sand. Gerald and his therapist made a solemn burial ground for them, decorated with trees and flowers.

During the closing sessions the father figure became increasingly central and protective. Only then could Gerald begin to talk openly about his mother.

Gerald's therapy lasted over six months. The therapist's attempt to hasten his treatment met with heightened anxiety and an emotional retreat: only by adopting a non-directive approach could the therapist enable Gerald to accept his mother's death and mourn for her (Hellendoorn 1988, pp.57–59).

Chris

Masur (1991) employed non-directive play therapy when she worked with Chris, a six-year-old whose mother had died of leukaemia when he was eighteen months old. Behavioural difficulties in a subsequent foster placement exposed unresolved feelings about the loss of his mother.

Chris selected a soft panda to illustrate his pain. He needed to master the experience of the death of his mother by becoming an active participant in the event; this he achieved by deliberately losing and finding the panda during sessions. His wish to take the toy home with him reflected a wish that his mother were still with him; tolerating weekly separations from panda helped him to accept the finality of his mother's death.

It then became clear that Chris had failed to mature following his mother's death; many of his symptoms were normal behaviour for toddlers. In addition, he believed that his mother had left him as a punishment for this behaviour. After a year, Chris' play became more aggressive, as he felt safe enough to express anger; once punished, panda lost the persona of his mother and became the small boy the Chris would like to be. Non-directive therapy allowed Chris to explore the wide range of his feelings following the death of his mother, and to consider the future with hope.

Terry

I recall working with Terry, a nine-year-old boy whose father had died when he was three. Like Chris, his distress was unrecognized, although his behaviour had deteriorated. Eventually his mother had been unable to cope with him, and he had moved to a foster placement. He was offered play therapy to help him express feelings about the loss of his natural mother; in his sessions it became clear that this recent loss had awakened feelings which he could not express when his father had died.

I found a room in a Children's Resource Centre in which to see Terry; it was small, with several inviting cupboards which he was not allowed to explore, but our privacy was assured. His school agreed that he could arrive late once a week. A conversation with his foster mother revealed that he liked army toys (he lived in an area where army manoeuvres are a common sight), fantasy toys such as 'Star Wars' figures, cars and playdough. My repertoire of 'Star Wars' figures was limited, but I was able to provide the rest. I added small figures, dinosaurs, farm and wild animals, puppets and woollen dolls, paper and felt pens, a telephone and doctor's set.

Terry was enthusiastic at the prospect of playing with me; he was told that this would help him feel less muddled about all the changes in his life. Early themes in his play included a need to experience omnipotence and power: this was displayed in prolonged battles between armies or groups of animals in which he destroyed his enemies totally and emerged unscathed. Some of these fantasies were extremely violent. There were occasional glimpses of more vulnerable feelings, and infantile games such as 'peek-a-boo', but he was unable to sustain these for long and returned to more aggressive play. However, these brief returns to the comforts of infancy were the first indication I had that feelings about the early loss of his father remained unresolved.

After three months of therapy, Terry began one session by announcing that one dinosaur was the father: this figure began by stomping around aggressively and eating other animals. He introduced a baby dinosaur, which the father initially ate. Revived, the baby was nurtured by the father, given food and shelter and protected from intruders. Terry took the dinosaurs to the playdough, and repeatedly hid the baby in it, making the father look for it, At the end of the session, he left both father and baby dinosaur safely together. Thus Terry was displaying some of the fantasies he had about a father of whom he had no concrete memories. Initially he perceived his father as fierce and aggressive, following this with a wish that his father would find and nurture him. He retained a fantasy that his father was still alive and would one day return to care for him, and he clung to this belief in the context of subsequent loss.

This play gave Terry great relief. Before he left he turned to me for a hug: the first I had had from him. He looked directly at me, and mumbled 'thanks'. Having been able to face the feelings associated with this initial bereavement, and have those feelings validated, enabled him to move on in subsequent sessions to think about more recent disruptions to his life.

Summary

Non-directive play therapy is not a panacea. Originally children with many varied difficulties were offered play therapy; in recent years young survivors of abuse are more likely recipients. Regrettably, there have been occasions when children and young people who have suffered other traumas, such as bereavement, have not had their distress acknowledged nor their emotional needs met. Non-directive play therapy offers these children a space where they can be themselves, and where they can begin to express feelings in safety and comfort. The total acceptance of each child underpins the practice of non-directive play therapy, providing the context in which children explore feelings in their own time and in their own way.

Sound practical preparations are important if therapy is to be effective. This includes comprehensive assessments of children and their difficulties, as well as finding appropriate space and materials. Sound supervision and support for the therapist is essential.

Some children receive the love and care they need within their families to enable them to express themselves freely and recover from the trauma of bereavement. However, those children who, for whatever reason, are unable to grieve openly, are likely to display behavioural symptoms of distress which may ultimately over-shadow their origins. These children respond well to non-directive play therapy, where their behaviour is not judged. Given time, and the unconditional support of a skilled therapist, each child can find her or his personal route to recovery, and emerge able to enjoy themselves again.

References

Axline, V. (1969) *Play Therapy*. New York: Ballantine Books.

Cattanach, A. (1992) *Play Therapy with Abused Children*. London: Jessica Kingsley Publishers.

Cipolla, J., McGown, D.B. and Yanulis M.A. (1991) *Communicating Through Play Techniques for Assessing and Preparing Children for Adoption*. London: BAAF.

Copley, B. and Forryan, B. (1987) *Therapeutic Work with Children and Young People*. London: Robert Royce.

Crompton, M. (1990) *Attending to Children – Direct Work in Social and Health Care*. London: Edward Arnold.

Davies, B. (1991) 'Responses of children to the death of a sibling.' In D. Papadatou and C. Papadatou (eds) *Children and Death*. London and New York: Hemisphere Publishing Corporation.

Davis, M. and Wallbridge, D. (1983) *Boundary and Space: an Introduction to the Work of D.W. Winnicott*. London: Karnac Books.

Donker-Raymaker, Th. (1982) 'Beeldcommunicatatie bij een rouwproces', quoted in J. Hellendoorn 'Imaginative play techniques in psychotherapy with children.' In C.E. Schaeffer (ed) *Innovative Interventions in Child and Adolescent Therapy*. New York: John Wiley.

Excell, J.A. (1991) 'A child's perception of death.' In D. Papadatou and C. Papadatou (eds) *Children and Death*. London and New York: Hemisphere Publishing Corporation.

Freud, A. (1965) *Normality and Pathology in Childhood.* Harmondsworth: Penguin.

Freud, S. (1909) 'Analysis of a phobia in a five-year-old boy.' In J. Strachey (ed)
The Standard Edition of the Complete Psychological Works of Sigmund Freud, Vol.10.
London: Hogarth Press. Also published in S. Freud (1959) *The Psychoanalytic
Treatment of Children.* London: Hogarth Press.

Ginott, H.G. (1982) 'A rationale for selecting toys in play therapy.' In G.L.
Landreth (ed.) *Play Therapy: Dynamics of the Process of Counselling Children.* Illinois:
Charles C. Thomas.

Grollman, E.A. (1991) 'Explaining death to children and to ourselves.' In D.
Papadatou and C. Papadatou (eds) *Children and Death.* London and New York:
Hemisphere Publishing Corporation.

Guerney, L.F. (1983) 'Client-centred (non-directive) play therapy.' In C.E
Schaeffer and K.J. O'Connor (eds.) *Handbook of Play Therapy.* New York: John
Wiley.

Harris, P. (1989) *Children and Emotion.* Oxford and Cambridge: Blackwell.

Hellendoorn, J. (1988) 'Imaginative play technique in psychotherapy with
children.' In C.E. Schaeffer (ed) *Innovative Interventions in Child and Adolescent
Therapy.* New York: John Wiley.

Hendricks, J., Black., D. and Kaplan, T. (1993) *When Father Kills Mother: Guiding
Children Through Trauma and Grief.* London: Routledge.

Hill, S. (1973) *The Badness Within Him.* Bristol: Hamish Hamilton.

Hurley, D.J. (1991) 'Crisis of paternal suicide: case of Cathy, age 4½'. In N.
Webb (ed) *Play Therapy with Children in Crisis: a Casebook for Practitioners.* New
York: Guilford Press.

Jewett, C. (1984) *Helping Children Cope with Separation and Loss.* London: Batsford
Academic.

Klein, M. (1937) *The Psychoanalysis of Children.* London: Hogarth.

Klein, M. (1982) 'The psychoanalytic play technique.' In G.L. Landreth (ed) *Play
Therapy: Dynamics of the Process of Counselling Children.* Illinois: Charles C. Thomas

Lask, B. and Lask, J. (1981) *Child Psychiatry and Social Work.* Suffolk: Tavistock
Publications Ltd.

Le Vieux, J. (1993) 'Terminal illness and death of father: case of Celeste, aged
5½'. In N. Webb (ed) *Helping Bereaved Children.* New York: Guilford Press.

Masur, C. (1991) 'The crisis of early maternal loss: unresolved grief of six-year-old
Chris in foster care'. In N. Webb (ed) *Play Therapy with Children in Crisis: a
Casebook for Practitioners.* New York: Guilford Press.

McMahon, L. (1992) *A Handbook of Play Therapy.* London: Routledge.

Moustakas, C. (1973) *Children in Play Therapy.* New York: Aronson.

Pynoos, R.S. and Eth, S. (1984) 'The child as witness to homicide.' *Journal of Social
Issues 2,* 4, 72–78.

Reismann, J.M. (1973) *Principles of Psychotherapy with Children.* New York: John Wiley.

Rosenbluth, D. (1970) 'Transference in child psychotherapy.' *Journal of Child Psychotherapy 2,* 4, 72–78.

Saravay, B. (1991) 'Short-term play therapy with two pre-school brothers following sudden paternal death.' In N. Webb (ed) *Play Therapy with Children in Crisis: a Casebook for Practitioners.* New York: Guilford Press.

Schaeffer, C.E. and O'Connor, K.J. (1983) *Handbook of Play Therapy.* New York: John Wiley.

Segal, R.M. (1984) 'Helping children express grief through symbolic communication', *Social Casework 25,* 10, 590–599.

Ward, B. (1993) *Good Grief: Exploring Feelings, Loss and Death with Under 11s, A Holistic Approach.* London: Jessica Kingsley Publishers.

Webb, N. (1991) *Play Therapy with Children in Crisis: a Casebook for Practitioners.* New York: Guilford Press.

Webb, N. (1993) *Helping Bereaved Children.* New York: Guilford Press.

West, J. (1984) 'Ending or beginning: discussion of the theory and practice of termination procedures in play therapy', *Journal of Social Work Practice 1,* 2, 9–65.

West, J. (1992) *Child-Centred Play Therapy.* London: Edward Arnold.

Wilson K., Kendrick, P. and Ryan, V. (1992) *Play Therapy: A Non-Directive Approach for Children and Adolescents.* London: Balliere Tindall.

Part Two

Family Work

CHAPTER 5

It is Impossible Not to Communicate –
Helping the Grieving Family

Barbara Monroe

Introduction

It is impossible not to communicate with children. All adults will have experienced their unerring ability to pick up the very pieces of information we would rather keep private, the acuity of their questions about issues we would rather not talk about. In general terms adults see it as their role to help children gradually gain more understanding of the world around them, yet when children are facing bereavement adults often fall strangely silent. Parents and professionals alike want to protect children, but in doing so often succeed in excluding and isolating them, leaving children confused, unsupported with their feelings and unprotected from their fantasies. The way in which children are helped to deal with loss will have a profound impact on their future emotional development.

Research indicates that the death of a parent, sibling or close family member can put children at risk of developing serious emotional problems (Black 1978) and that since children's grief unfolds and is experienced differently over time and with new levels of developmental understanding, it may be many years before the full impact of a death is seen. However, grief is not an illness and separation is a normal human experience that we must all learn to live with. Children need support as they attempt to manage this transition and the inevitable adjustment in their life style, but professional attention centred on the individual child can stigmatize and isolate the child. The child can become defined as 'the problem', a focus of negative family attention, a distraction from the needs and hurts of other family members. Evidence increasingly suggests that a child's adjustment after a death is influenced by the openness of family communication patterns, the amount of emotional support in the family, the child's ability to understand the dying process, their relationship with the dying person and their involvement in the dying person's care. All of these factors indicate that wherever possible help should start before the death and should focus on the child within the family rather than the individual child alone. The objective should be to support parents in their role, to help the family to develop better methods of communication.

It is not an adequate substitute for professionals to take over from parents in efforts to support their children. Children need the help of their families who will be around long after the professionals have disappeared. Professionals who do too much will simply reinforce family feelings of helplessness. Parents want to do the best for their children. They are the experts on their children but may also need encouragement and support to understand how best to communicate with them and involve them. This chapter will examine the task of helping parents to help their children.

It is Impossible Not to Communicate

A terminal illness or death in a family causes enormous changes and children quickly sense when something so serious is happening. They pick up the emotions around them, notice changes in routine, read body language and overhear conversations. However, a child's silence, lack of questions or apparent indifference may be interpreted by adults as a lack of awareness or a state of coping which should not be disturbed. Children want to protect their parents and often attempt to obey family rules even if they are unwritten. If the whole emotional atmosphere of the family is saying 'don't ask, we don't talk about it' children may try to join in the pretence that nothing is happening. When seven-year-old Mark's father was admitted to the hospice with a terminal brain tumour his mother told staff that he did not know what was actually wrong with his father, just that he was ill. When Mark was given the opportunity to write down his questions for the doctor, he did so: 'Can you stop the bad thing in daddy's brain? Can daddy come home? What will happen to daddy's heart? Will the bad thing grow in the rest of his body?' It was important that Mark received honest answers to these questions rather than being left to imagine his own. Fantasies are often worse than the reality and can be very frightening. One nine-year-old child thought that death inevitably involved copious bleeding from the mouth and ears and was relieved to hear a description of a gradually deepening loss of consciousness. The only certain way to find out what children understand about the circumstances in which they find themselves is to ask them.

Parents have good reasons for their reluctance to share information about illness and death with their children. They are often struggling to maintain some control in an uncertain situation and they can feel overwhelmed by their own raw and confused emotions. They may wonder if they can cope with the child's grief, they themselves may be avoiding the truth, they may be anxious about, or underestimate, what their child understands and they will worry that saying the wrong thing may make an already difficult situation worse. In short they do not know how to begin or what to say.

Be Proactive – Treat Parents as Colleagues

All too often professionals join the conspiracy of silence. It is important to make a direct offer of help, 'Hello, I'm the social worker on the team. A lot of parents worry about their children at times like this and I wonder if it would help to talk' and to recognize that this does not abrogate or interfere with the parental role. Professionals must stop seeing parents as a potential hindrance to work with children. Parents quickly sense judgement but most welcome a separate opportunity to talk about their own anxieties and their own reactions to the death. It is often necessary to work with parents alone before children's needs can be addressed. For example, a couple who cannot openly acknowledge impending death between themselves are not well placed to help their children. They may also need more information. No one can be expected to explain things to children if they are not yet clear about it themselves. We should remember that many parents need time to assimilate information about children's needs and the opportunity to change their opinions about involving them.

Where to Start – Parents Need to Have their Feelings Recognized

Bereavement begins before the physical event of death and wherever possible emotional help for the family should start before the death. Professionals need to reassure parents that they understand their concerns about their children and to acknowledge that it is not easy to talk to children when what you say is going to hurt them: 'This is one of the most difficult things a parent has to do.' We can then begin to offer parents suggestions from our own and other families' experiences, not blueprints, not the right things to say, but practical hints on management and some possible paths through the wilderness, 'some parents seem to find it helps if...' Parents will also need to discuss strategies for managing other family members who may be resistant to the idea of involving the children. Bereaved children need help in four main areas: information, reassurance, the expression of feelings and an opportunity to be involved in what is happening. Bereaved parents need much the same things from the professionals they encounter.

Information
Make it Manageable
Parents may need prompting to see that since communication of some sort will occur anyway with children it is better for it to be consistent and regularly updated information provided by the parents who love them, than confused,

incomplete and often contradictory snippets of gossip from a variety of sources. It is important to reassure parents that the words said are not as important as how they are said; they need to be conveyed with warmth and love, often best transmitted through physical touch and hugs. Information needs to proceed at the child's pace and should be clear, simple, truthful and repeated. Parents may appreciate advice about vocabulary and explanations of death appropriate to their child's age and understanding. They will want to know that the task of talking to children does not have to be accomplished all at once. The objective is to create an atmosphere where questions are acceptable. Children should not be pushed to talk or frightened with excessive medical detail. Parents can be told that children often wander off physically or change the subject when they have had enough and that children's questions often come in the middle of a mundane activity rather than during a specific conversation about death and loss.

Children need to know what has happened and why and what will happen next. Obvious changes in routine need an explanation but things should ideally proceed gradually. 'Daddy's very ill. Daddy is so ill the doctors aren't sure they can make him better. Daddy is so ill we don't think he will live more than a few days now. Daddy is dying.' Parents may need help to understand that any information will need to be repeated over and over again as children check that what is happening is still true. Vocabulary should be factual, direct and accurate and it is important to check that the child understands the meaning of any words used. 'When someone dies their body stops working, it is not the same as being asleep, the body will never wake up again. It will never eat, drink, feel sad or happy again. It cannot feel pain.' Confusing explanations of death should be avoided. 'Daddy has gone to sleep, granddad has gone on a long journey' can lead to the responses 'I'll stay awake all night' and 'please don't get on the bus mummy'.

Anticipate Difficulties

We can help parents to anticipate difficulties in advance and to think about how they would like to cover the problem. Examples would be deciding whether the children should attend the funeral and thinking about how to describe it, or pointing out that the child who shares a room with a dying sibling may want to talk about his fears of waking up to find the child dead and may appreciate the offer of changing rooms or at least talking about it. For some parents such discussion will be sufficient. They will want to speak to their children alone, having rehearsed what they are going to say and having been offered the opportunity to come back and share how the conversation with the child went. Other families may welcome the professional joining them with the children to help answer questions and to open up areas for discussion. Many parents respond to the suggestion that they help children make a list of questions in preparation for such a meeting. Six-year-old Pat, whose mother had cancer of the breast with secondaries in the bone and brain, wanted to know 'Why can't mummy walk, why is she so fat, why does her breathing sound funny?' Simple, honest answers to these questions by the doctor and social worker created an atmosphere in which Pat was able to look directly at her father and ask, 'Is my mummy going to die?' Her father nodded and they cried and hugged one another. Parents learn fast and being part of just one direct conversation with a child and a professional can give them the confidence to continue for themselves. The suggestion should be made that wherever possible children be included in family discussions.

Of course death is sometimes sudden and unexpected. Parents and professionals may have to act quickly and in such circumstances professional clarity is vital. Parental shock may initially demand that the professional does much of the work of talking to the child but he or she should be constantly alert to opportunities to involve the parent and affirm their role and capabilities. For example, a young woman whose husband died suddenly fetched her children from school to see him. She asked the professional to tell the children that he had died but remained present while this happened and when the professional gently suggested that the mother take the children to see their father, she was able to do so. In such circumstances children may be angry that their parents have not told them about the gravity of the situation earlier. Part of the professional's role is to help children understand why their parents have behaved the way they have. 'Everyone was hoping daddy would get better. Things have happened very suddenly.'

Offer Resources

Parents may welcome the provision of booklets about childhood grief (e.g. Couldrick 1988) to read for themselves in order to gain some intellectual mastery over an emotionally unfamiliar subject. It is also helpful to give parents suggestions of books suitable to read with children or for older children to read for themselves. Books often help a child to feel that others have similar experiences and feelings. Some years ago the social work department at St Christopher's Hospice resolved to take action on the dearth of simple materials aimed directly at bereaved children themselves. This was partly prompted by the warm response to written materials for adults, for example a simple bereavement leaflet describing some of the thoughts, feelings and experiences that commonly follow a loss. Brainstorming sessions in the team produced the texts and they were illustrated either by team members or local artists. The development and printing costs of the booklets were initially funded by the B.B.C. Children in Need Appeal. We recognized that the pictures were as important as the text and conveyed powerful messages, for example 'men cry' (see Figure 5.1)

How do we feel ...

The death of someone important to us makes us very sad. You will find that crying makes you feel better. Everyone needs to cry – men, women and children. Sometimes we feel we shall never stop crying. Both these feelings are normal and we must be patient with ourselves.

Figure 5.1. Someone Special Has Died (Department of Social Work, St. Christopher's Hospice 1989b)

This is _ _ _ _ _ _ _ _ _ _ (name)
Draw the bit of their
body which is ill.

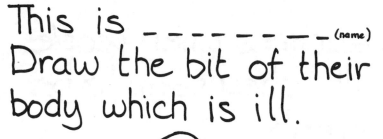

The Hospice helps them
to feel comfortable
even when they are very
ill.

Figure 5.2. My Book About (Department of Social Work, St. Christopher's Hospice 1989a)

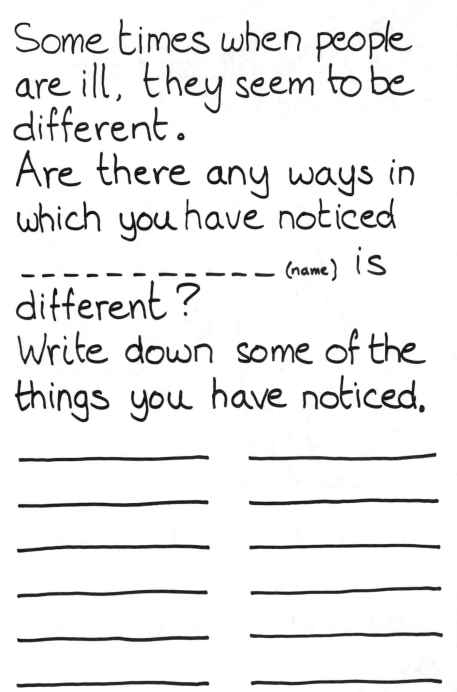

Some times when people are ill, they seem to be different.
Are there any ways in which you have noticed

_____ (name) is different?

Write down some of the things you have noticed.

_____   _____

_____   _____

_____   _____

_____   _____

_____   _____

Figure 5.3. My Book About (Department of Social Work, St. Christopher's Hospice 1989a)

The things I can do to help
— — — — — — — — — — — are:—

Here are some spaces for you
to draw what you can do.

* visiting them

*talking together

*making things for
them

*what else can you
think of ?

*Figure 5.4. My Book About (Department of Social Work, St. Christopher's
Hospice 1989a)*

We were also careful to include a variety of racial models. 'Someone Special Has Died' is a bereavement leaflet for children up to the age of about eleven and is complemented by 'Your Parent Has Died' which is suitable for adolescents. Both are available from St Christopher's Hospice (price £1). We have also developed a workbook 'My Book About...' for using with children during the illness of any relative. We produce this in two sizes; A3 for younger children who need space to express themselves clearly and A4 to offer a more sophisticated looking text for older children. It, too, is available (price £1.50). The workbooks are designed to be used by children with parental involvement. For many parents workbooks represent a less direct and therefore less threatening way to begin difficult conversations with their children. Many have commented, for example, on how helpful they have found the simple body outline with the instruction 'Draw the bit of their body which is ill' (Figure 5.2) in starting to talk about cancer and its effects.

Such books can assist parents to find out what the child already knows and help them to link explanations to things the child has already noticed. 'Sometimes when people are ill they seem to be different. What have you noticed that is different about mummy?' (Figure 5.3) 'She sleeps a lot. Her hair has fallen out.' 'Why do you think this has happened?'

Such work allows the opportunity to validate the child's experience, to assess their level of understanding and to correct any misapprehensions. It also helps children to experience a sense of control and involvement. Children seem to value their completed books and like to keep them as a memorial (Figure 5.4).

Children will pick up a great deal through observation but may lack the knowledge to interpret their insights correctly. Parents may need assistance to answer the question that is actually being asked. 'What happens to you when you are dead?' may be a request for information about coffins and funerals rather than the existence or not of heaven. Parents also need reassurance that they do not have to have an answer to every question. Children will accept 'I don't know' or 'I'm not sure about that' or 'I'll try to find out.' Professionals must be aware of the family's culture and belief system. Any help offered should not conflict with it. If the professional is uncertain about this, it should be discussed with the adults in the family in advance of any conversation with the children.

Reassurance

Professionals can help parents by reminding them of bereaved children's needs for extra security and consistent routine along with as much physical affection as possible. A teenage girl ran away from home after her father's death because her mother stopped telling her off when she got in late at night. The girl felt that no-one cared about her now that her father was dead. Her mother had been trying to be gentle with her. It needs to be emphasized that children of all ages require quite explicit reassurance that nothing they did or said could have caused the death and that death itself is not contagious. For example, many children worry that cancer is catching or that they themselves or a parent or other family member will also become ill and die. Parents often look for advice about the appropriate level of reassurance. Security is important in a world that has become suddenly unreliable and unsafe, but it should be consistent with the truth. 'It is very unusual for someone as young as mummy to be so ill that the doctors can't make her better.' Bereavement leaflets written specifically for young children (Department of Social Work, St Christopher's Hospice 1989b, see Figures 5.1 and 5.5) and adolescents (Department of Social Work, St Christopher's Hospice 1991, see Figures 5.8 and 5.9) can help to reinforce these messages and many parents comment on how they themselves have been more helped by the explicit reassurance of such child-oriented literature than those aimed at adults.

Be Gentle with Yourself

Parents coping with children facing bereavement should be encouraged not to be too hard on themselves. Most parents under stress sometimes find themselves shouting at their children. Bereaved parents may need professional reassurance that the death of someone close has not turned them into a selfish monster. However, it will help children if parents can explain their behaviour later. 'I'm sorry I got so angry. I'm not really cross with you, I'm just feeling very sad because daddy is dead.' Parents may need help to anticipate, understand and accept altered or difficult behaviour in children, especially when they are grieving themselves. For example, a man whose wife has died may interpret his children's unruly and erratic behaviour as evidence of his own failure as a parent rather than an expression of their grief.

You Don't Have to Go It Alone

Parents need to know that they do not have to do it all themselves. Parents overwhelmed by their own grief and the practical difficulties of coping alone may find their children's needs threatening. Professionals can encourage them to widen their child's support network by involving other adults close to them, a relative, a member of the clergy, a youth club leader and, very important, the school. Parents do not always understand the importance of the part the school can play in helping the grieving child. School often represents a welcome haven of routine and safety away from the confusing emotions of the grieving family. The professional may simply encourage a parent to contact the child's teacher and discuss their needs. Sometimes, with permission, the professional will contact the teacher on the parent's behalf. The teacher may well appreciate a formal discussion of a situation with which he or she is unfamiliar. We can also help a parent to think ahead about possible areas for discussion and negotiation with the teacher. For example, what is to be said to the class before the child

Often people find it hard to concentrate at school, or they may feel too upset to be helpful at home. Grown-ups feel this way too, so that it sometimes seems that they haven't as much time for you as they used to have. But gradually everyone begins to feel better.

Figure 5.5. Someone Special Has Died (Department of Social Work, St. Christopher's Hospice 1989b)

returns to it and how will the child be informed about this, the need to ensure that all staff are told about the bereavement, the possibility of the teacher helping a few friends to overcome their embarrassment by exploring ways of being supportive, the need for the bereaved child to have a quiet corner to escape to if he or she feels overwhelmed.

Is There a Future?

Children need reassurance about their practical anxieties and the professional can help the family with questions to elicit the impact of changes in family life and the child's feeling about them. 'What has changed at home? What are you worried about?' 'Who will take me to school? Who will come to me if I cry in the night? Will I still be able to go away to college?' Parents and children are often relieved when such painful issues are openly addressed. Realistic discussions to involve the child in issues about their future care are even more important when a single parent is dying. Saying the worst out loud can rob it of some of its secret power. 'I think what everyone in this family is worrying about is how you are going to manage when mum isn't here to look after you.' Parents should tell children about what will not change as well as what will; they can be prompted to offer the child some small fixed point in a world which has become chaotic. 'I will still take you swimming on Sundays.' Children need to know that life will go on and how it will do so. They need reassurance that anger is normal, that sadness does not last for ever and that it is still acceptable to have fun sometimes.

The Expression of Feelings

Grief is neither expressed or answered simply through words. It goes much deeper than that. Children can sometimes upset adults by seeming to be casual or callous, like the little boy who greeted his brother's death with the announcement 'I always wanted my own room anyway'. Such behaviour does not mean that they are not also very sad. Parents will appreciate some discussion about their children's feelings and help to understand their sometimes altered behaviour, since children's grief, much to their parent's consternation, is often acted out in behaviour rather than through words. Grief is an unhappy feeling and parents need to know that children's reactions of fear, guilt, anger, sadness, denial and exhaustion are normal. Parental feelings of competence can be increased by anticipation of the toddler's clinginess, the confident eight-year-old's return to fear of the dark, or the teenager's lack of concentration at school and discussion of possible coping strategies such as regular quiet cuddle times, night-lights and help with lists and planning. Parents need to encourage their children to express their feelings which does not mean telling them how to feel. 'You have got to be brave now, don't upset your mother' denies a child's right to grieve.

Play is Communication

Many children express their feelings more easily through games and drawing than in the unaccustomed medium of a long conversation. Modelling clay, dolls houses, medical kits, puppets, telephones, a doll in a bed, can all help younger children to act out their concerns and articulate their questions. One little girl drew 'her world', a circle with her mother in the middle of it, in bed near a large bottle of medicine. On the top of the world were a series of circles in squares. The seven-year-old confided that these were bodies in coffins. Discussion revealed that she lived near a car scrapyard. Although she knew that dead people were put in coffins she had not been informed about funerals, burial or cremation. She feared that somewhere there was a huge coffin scrap yard and that her dead mother would be left there. This child was greatly relieved to receive some simple information about the funeral service and what happens to

Figure 5.6. Modelled on Heegaard, M. (1988) **When Someone Very Special Dies**

dead bodies. She later chose a hymn for the service and said with great satisfaction that the funeral had been 'a proper goodbye'. Following a death many children enjoy completing a home made workbook which might be based on that published by the American social worker Marge Heegaard [1988]. Each page carries a simple instruction: 'draw something sad, sometimes I get angry because... I worry a lot about...'

Wherever possible the parent should be there with the professional whilst the child completes the material so that the child is aware of the parent's attention and concern. The parent also then knows what the child has said and can follow up on it in a natural way. Such work also often helps parents to access their own grief. At the end of such grief work sessions the child will need time to re-orientate to everyday demands. The professional should check that the child feels comfortable to continue with the next activity of their day and offer some bridging conversation about less emotive topics such as a hobby or school.

Children Learn How to Grieve

Children learn to mourn by observing others. One of the most powerful messages for parents is the importance of sharing their feelings. Children are often uncertain about what is allowed and need to see others crying, especially their parents, and to know that others, too, feel confused and hurt. The taboo against sharing adult grief with children needs to be broken. Children are helped most when they are allowed to comfort as well as to be comforted. A seven-year-old boy whose father was dying commented that he had a special medicine for his mother, 'hugs and kisses'. Exclusion hurts more than painful but shared feelings, provided that children also understand that the adults around them are strong enough to carry on caring for them.

Adolescents Need Space

For adolescents grief comes on top of all kinds of developmental issues as they struggle to find a new identity and a new balance between dependence and independence. Death presents a profound challenge and threat to the teenager at a time of great natural self-absorption and great uncertainty. Young people may feel very resentful that their life has been disturbed. 'Why did dad die just when I'm doing my 'A' Levels?' However, their awareness that such thoughts would be judged 'selfish' may induce guilt and they are in any case difficult to express to other members of the family.

Adolescents may also struggle with the inexpressible thought that the 'wrong' parent has died. 'Why didn't dad die instead of mum?' They may sometimes welcome a private meeting with a professional to be reassured that others feel like this. The adolescent needs information to try to gain some control over his or her life. 'What is grief, why do I feel so muddled?' They are often responsive to this in a written form that they can manage for themselves (eg Department of Social Work, St Christopher's Hospice 1991. See Figures 5.7 and 5.8) even when they appear to be uninterested during conversations. When a family member is ill it may help to suggest to parents that the adolescent has a separate opportunity to talk to the doctor or nurse about the illness. Young people may also want to talk about difficulties in relationships with their friends,

Figure 5.7. Your Parent Has Died (Department of Social Work, St. Christopher's Hospice 1991)

Figure 5.8. Your Parent Has Died (Department of Social Work, St. Christopher's Hospice 1991)

sensing that death is both frightening and embarrassing for their peer group and worrying that it is something that makes them different just when they most want to be the same. Some teenagers seem more able to discuss their feelings by talking about their dreams or nightmares, as if this in some way legitimizes powerful emotions. In any separate work with adolescents it is important to come to clear agreements about confidentiality with both them and their parents.

Individual meetings with adolescents are often helpfully interspersed with meetings with the family. Adolescents should not be expected to take on the responsibilities of the dead parent, but may realistically have to do more around the home. A family meeting with a professional may aid their involvement in decisions about the allocation of household tasks or a discussion about loss of finances and their own expectations for the future. Parents and professionals should try to remember that when helping teenagers talking is not everything. Keeping a diary, watching films and reading books, using sport as a release or practising relaxation techniques can all help adolescents to express their feelings.

Involvement

Parents and adult carers benefit enormously from being involved with the support offered to their children. In addition they tell us how much they appreciate being involved in helping the person who is dying or in sharing in the rituals that follow a death. Most children also like to feel useful and memories of helping can be important later on. Practical tasks can ease the strain and artificiality of being a 'visitor' to the patient. At home children might like to read the newspaper aloud or provide drinks. In hospital they might arrange the flowers or take in a drawing or a tape recording of their music practice. However the nature and degree of children's involvement should, as far as possible, be the result of their own informed choice.

Parents may need to be reminded that although grief is common to all, it is expressed and managed differently by everyone. One child may wish to spend as much time as possible with a dying parent, another may only be able to visit if he/she knows it is permissible to stay for just five minutes. Some children find visiting easier if they take their homework along, others may not want to visit at all. They may prefer to write a letter or make a telephone call, or may distance themselves by increased leisure activities or by spending more time with friends. Adults' feelings can be hurt if they are not helped to understand that these reactions are often just another way of coping for the child. Professionals may also need to help parents to negotiate compromises between seemingly impossible conflicting demands, such as staying with a dying person and being at home for a child returning from school. A parent who is struggling with the impending death of a partner may lose sight of their child's fear that they are losing not one parent but two.

The Environment

The physical environment of hospitals, hospices or the patient's room at home can have an enormous impact on children's comfort and the parent's feeling about involving them. Some institutions seem to work hard at deterring the presence of children. Children's murals or displays of their art, a designated area with small chairs, a toy box, can all display messages of a positive welcome for children. Staff should always make a particular effort to introduce themselves to children and to explain medical equipment and treatment to them in a straightforward way. For example, 'what is a syringe driver?' Most children are fascinated by simple mechanics and explanations help them to get a strange world under some control. Children will respond to explicit permission about where they can display their pictures or written work by the bed and will be reassured to be shown the trolley telephone for goodnight calls.

A Chance to Say Goodbye

Children need clear acknowledgement of their loss and a chance to say goodbye. They also need experiences that help them to confront the reality of what they have lost. For example, one little girl who came to visit her dying father left a toy rabbit with him to look after him. She later asked for it to be placed in his coffin. In her bereavement she spoke frequently of her satisfaction at her special goodbye to her father. Children will appreciate the chance to see the death certificate and, if offered, many will accept the opportunity to view the body. Children will need a description of the viewing room, of whether the body will be in a bed or a coffin and a warning that it will be cold. They will want to know who will be with them and often respond to suggestions that there might be things they want to say to the dead person and to the prompt to touch them. Parents will often feel more confident about these matters if they are discussed in advance.

Parents are often anxious about funerals and whether or not their children should attend. Funerals allow children to recognize that a change has taken place and to see that other people loved the dead person and are sad just as they are. Professionals can help parents give their children information in advance about what to expect so that the child and family can decide together what they feel comfortable with. For example, children need to know what a coffin is, where the funeral will take place, what the church or crematorium looks like, who will look after them, what emotions the adults will display, what will happen to the coffin and the body inside it. It will usually help parents to suggest that a friend or relative be particularly responsible for children at a funeral where the death closely involves the parent. It also helps to find out whether other children will be attending. However, if parents feel they cannot cope with their child at the funeral it will not help to suggest that they will have done irreparable damage to the child by denying him this experience. We must always work within what parents can manage at the time. It is then important to help them explore alternatives, for example to remind them that the child should be told as soon as possible after the funeral what happened and perhaps offered a later visit to the church, crematorium or grave.

Remembering

Parents will sometimes need reminding of the importance of giving the child a memento of the person who has died as a tangible reminder of their existence and importance. It could be a watch, a photograph, some tools, a book or a piece of jewellery. Some dying parents or siblings will want to create a special memory book for their family. These often helpfully include descriptions of shared experiences, photographs of holidays spent together and concrete facts such as a record of favourite music, food, colours and clothes. Such books can be of enormous help to children and are particularly valuable for very young children as a way of preserving memories for the future that the child may have been too young to be able to recapture without help. In such circumstances it may assist to suggest taking a photograph of the dying person with the baby or toddler for use later on.

Children need to talk about the person who has died and families can be encouraged to do so together by reminiscing, looking at photographs or visiting favourite places. We must remember that a child does not stop being her father's daughter because he is dead. She is still connected to him but needs to find a new place for her relationship with him. This is achieved by talking and remembering, not by forgetting or being encouraged to do so. Research (Silverman and Worden 1993) now indicates that children making healthy adjustments to a parental death often dream about their dead parent, talk out loud to them and do things to please them. Our experience at St Christopher's Hospice is that help offered to the whole family before a death occurs can often reduce the need for professional help for children (and their parents) following the death. However, in such circumstances many children will also benefit from brief group involvement to experience peer support, to know that they are not alone and that their experience is not unique. Such groups for bereaved children are described in Chapter 9 of this book by my colleagues.

What About Us?

Working with children experiencing loss involves adults in considerable pain. All professionals, like all parents, need to remember to be realistic. Children cannot ultimately be protected from the truth. When someone important to them has died we cannot make things better, we cannot take their pain away. They will be sad. However, if they are given the opportunity to be aware of the death and to join in family grief, the adults around them can offer them support with their sadness. Just as it is important to help children to share their feelings, so it is important that we acknowledge our own. The bereaved child arouses strong feelings in all of us. We are reminded of ourselves as children, of our own children, or the children we hope for. We should also remember that children are survivors. Offered the truth with love they can and do respond to the challenges of bereavement.

References

Black, D. (1978) 'The bereaved child.' *Journal of Child Psychology and Psychiatry 19*, 287–292.

Couldrick, A. (1988) *Grief and Bereavement: Understanding Children.* Oxford: Sobell Publications.

Department of Social Work, St Christopher's Hospice (1989a) *My Book About...* London: St Christopher's Hospice.

Department of Social Work, St Christopher's Hospice (1989b) *Someone Special Has Died.* London: St Christopher's Hospice.

Department of Social Work, St Christopher's Hospice (1991) *Your Parent Has Died.* London: St Christopher's Hospice.

Heegaard, M. (1988) *When Someone Very Special Dies.* Minneapolis, MN: Woodland Press.

Silverman, P.R. and Worden, W.J. (1993) 'Children's Reactions to the Death of a Parent.' In M. Stroebe, W. Stroebe and R. Hansson (eds) *Handbook of Bereavement.* Cambridge: Cambridge University Press.

CHAPTER 6

A Cradling of a Different Sort

Ann Couldrick

Introduction

Brian Keenan (1992) used the title *An Evil Cradling,* for the account of his ordeal of being a captive in the hands of fundamental Shiite militiamen for four and a half years.

Bereaved children are captive too, captive of their circumstances. A parent immersed in their grief journey is frequently anxious about finance, full of dread for the future and often unable to take pleasure in the child's development or behaviour. Children have to survive, to make sense of their changed world and to take upon themselves the biggest burden of all, that of keeping a watchful eye upon and consoling the very person who they might expect to console them. Other chapters in this book illuminate direct work with bereaved children, but most of the caring professions that are likely to be involved – general practitioners, health visitors, community nurses and teachers, frequently feel ill equipped to work with the sense of loss that the children are experiencing. But they meet these families and witness the distress. If they allow this to render them helpless, they abandon bereaved children to their captivity, just as the world abandoned Keenan, McCarthy and many others to their evil cradling.

The professional's cradling of the bereaved family through the first bewildering months after the death of a parent can offer the child or children hope that their circumstances will slowly become more secure.

By opening themselves to the pain and grief of the bereaved parent, by giving regular committed attention to their needs, their confusion and uncertainty, they can fulfil two important functions. First, they can provide a safe place for the expression of feelings that might otherwise engulf the child, and second, they can give an opportunity for the parent to explore the child's

---

In this chapter, he or she can be applied, unless the gender is obvious from the context.

behaviour and reactions with someone who has knowledge and experience of other bereaved children. Perhaps most important, they hold onto hope, mark the progress and growth of each member of the family, and help them celebrate what they achieve through this uncertain time.

Does this Cradling Affect Longterm Outcome?

This is difficult to research because most of our knowledge and understanding comes from studies done with the bereaved child who is in trouble. Behaviour problems such as aggression and truanting, or involvement with and misuse of drugs and alcohol, are common so that social services, child guidance centres and the police may have become involved. The studies do not tell us much about the prospects for children who are well taken care of following the death of a parent. Research undertaken by Black and Urbanowicz (1987) followed up an unselected group of children aged sixteen years or under for two years after the parent's death. This study indicated that the group offered treatment found the intervention helpful and that the period of distress was shortened compared with the control group. The findings of Harris and her colleagues (Harris, Brown and Bifulco 1986) support the suggestion that whether a woman who had been bereaved in childhood developed an adult psychiatric disorder, was dependent on whether her care subsequent to the loss was adequate.

I want to explore in this chapter how the professional (the teacher, the health visitor or family doctor, for example) can cradle the bereaved parent so that their care of the child *is* adequate. Perhaps the most important help that parents can give their bereaved child is to care adequately for themselves and to know to whom they can turn in order that their own feelings of abandonment and pain do not impede the child's grief work.

Preparation

If there is time to prepare, anticipatory grief work, supported by staff that have some knowledge of the situation that the family will face as death approaches, can bring the family closer and set a pattern of communication for the troubled time after the death. Two of the issues that cause concern are how and when to tell the children. Communication of some sort will be taking place, for children sense fear and anxiety. The professional cannot take the place of the parents in communicating with their children, but parents value opportunities to discuss and rehearse what to say at different stages in the illness.

Faced with decisions that they had never expected to have to make, Mary and Robert turned to their family doctor for help with preparing their sons for the death of their father. He advised that they should be as open as possible.

> Mary and Robert told their sons Richard, who was twelve, and Martin, who was nine, that Robert had cancer of the lung and that it was difficult for him to get better. Martin wept a good deal and Richard

asked many questions about the illness and the treatment. Together, the parents tried to comfort, answering their questions to the best of their limited knowledge. Two weeks after this Robert went into hospital for a course of chemotherapy. Again they explained what chemotherapy was intended to do and warned the boys that for a time Robert would lose his hair. Four days after admission Mary visited her husband and found him desperately ill. The oncologist confirmed that Robert was dying, and Mary decided that she had to tell the boys the truth.

On the way home from visiting their father she started by asking them what they had thought when they saw their father. 'Well he's worse isn't he?' said Richard, so she said 'I don't think he's going to come home again'. Martin cried all the way home and allowed her to cuddle him. When they reached home Richard went upstairs and locked his bedroom door. The same night she was called to the hospital, so she called a neighbour to sit in the house and drove to Robert's side to be with him.

He died, and she came straight home. When her sons came down for breakfast, Richard looked at her and said 'he's died hasn't he?' Then he ate his breakfast and went to school refusing to talk to her. Mary, feeling numb, rang the school and told them what had happened. Martin stayed with her. Because she had found her doctor so empathetic, she sought help again from him who then invited her to meet the practice counsellor. She described the peacefulness of Robert's death, how unfrightening it had been, how important it had been to say goodbye. The counsellor said 'Do you think Richard and Martin would like to say goodbye? After all they are struggling to make sense of being told that their father is not getting better and now he is dead.' 'Do you mean – see his body?' Mary was horrified. She had a strong sense that children should be protected.

The counsellor pointed out that many children who had been denied the opportunity had said that they wished they had been able to say goodbye but that it would be important for her to be reassured first by the undertaker that it was acceptable to bring the boys before she gave them the chance. 'But I don't want to say goodbye either!' she cried.

She came to surgery the day after the funeral to tell the doctor what she had decided. Bravely she had gone on her own to the chapel and finding Robert looking so free from pain and illness, she had no doubts that it would be the right thing to take the children. Together, as a family they had closed the circle left jaggedly open by the sudden deterioration and death. This simple decision had allowed the children to support her and each other, to ask questions – why had the prognosis changed, why had the treatment failed, was this cancer something they might catch? Martin had said sadly 'I always thought my dad was the strong one in the family'.

So they faced together the future without him.

Mary continued to check out her understanding of her sons for many weeks and began to see that like Richard, she could only deal with Robert's unexpected death at a cognitive level. She felt that her feelings were frozen. She envied Martin because he could cry and say how much he missed his father. She could comfort him, but felt that the only person who could comfort her was dead. The counsellor, who she came to see regularly for a few weeks, pointed out that Richard too might be feeling this and so was holding himself together until it felt safe enough to let go.

Gradually she started to look at her relationship with Robert, what needs they had met in one another. This led her to look at her own previous experience of loss. She had been fourteen years old when her own mother had died. Her father, who was Italian, had 'given himself up to grieving' for many months, and been quite unable to see the effect his wife's death had had upon Mary. She had come through the experience by working hard at school and had gladly left home when her father remarried a year after his wife's death. As Mary allowed herself to be comforted and listened to, she began to mourn for her mother, using photographs and letters to get in touch with that vital relationship. Only then could the feelings of loss for Robert surface. Feeling cradled was new for her. It allowed her to experience the confusion and anger that. once again, she had been left to manage on her own, without feeling guilty because she did not always manage to cope the way she thought she should. When the time came to carry out her husband's wishes to scatter his ashes in Wales, she listened to Richard and Martin, who stated very firmly that they wanted a place and a stone to visit. Together they chose a place in a nearby churchyard.

Thomas Mann (1969) said 'a man's dying is more the survivor's affair than his own' and this has to be remembered when the survivors' wishes clash with those of the dead. The boys, given a part in the decision knew best what was right for them.

Sudden Death

There is not always time to prepare the children. A road traffic accident, a sudden collapse of a partner will mean that the parent who is left has had to do the best they can, given that they were in acute shock. It is essential that they are allowed to explore the experience of how *they* were told, by whom, where they were at the time; whether they were able to view the body; how and who told the children. For in the re-telling, they often are able to understand the children's reactions.

> Sonia woke to hear a police car pulling up at her front door. The milkman had found her husband dead in his fume filled car. She was so stunned that she allowed the police to wake Edward who was three years old at the time. She does not know what they said, she only remembers Edward wailing loudly for her. She woke Moira who was nine years old and holding Edward tightly to her, she told her daughter that their father was dead and had probably killed himself. For several days the house was full of people. Sonia's mother took Edward home with her until the inquest was over. Moira refused to go and assumed an adult responsibility for her mother, making sure she ate, making her rest when she looked tired. Sonia talked, raged and wept and about three months later she began to accept that these feelings were normal, acceptable and would continue. Once she could tolerate them in herself she began to want to understand how this tragedy was affecting her children and to appreciate how frightened they were of losing *her*.
>
> Edward's terror of her going out of his sight, of being left alone in his bed somehow became tolerable. She started putting him to bed in her room, leaving the door open so that he could hear her downstairs. And she understood that Moira could not stop worrying about her mother until she felt that Sonia was looking after herself. As Sonia began to get some order and pattern into her life, knowing that she had a regular outlet for her feelings, Moira became sadder and more able to talk about her father and understand that his mind had got so sick, that like a body that is dying from disease, his mind had died too.

Attitudes to Death and Grief

1. *Avoidance*

Erma Furman (1974) says,

> 'the child's grasp of death does not solely depend on the maturation of his thought process. It is affected by many factors from within his personality and without, by the nature of his experience with death, his adaptation to or identification with adult attitudes to death, and the amount of correct or incorrect information he receives.' (p.271)

Everyone dies eventually but in some families it would seem that no-one ever dies. Death is never, ever talked about. So adults who deny that it will ever happen to them find the task of talking to their children intolerable. Preparation time is lost, and the children find themselves in a dark, confused world in which nothing and yet everything is changed. Euphemisms are used like, 'grandad has gone to sleep' or 'Jesus wanted him to live with him because he was so good'. How then does the child accept that the person they loved died because they were too ill to get better or because some accident caused them to stop living? Before the child can receive any help, the parent has to risk testing this denial for him or herself.

> Geoff came to talk about his five-year-old son David. He was deeply troubled because David claimed to 'see' his mother who had been dead for a year. He would talk to her and get very cross with his grandmother when she told him not to be so silly. The story was that Anna had been ill for many months before she died. Because David was pre-school, he often went away to stay with his grandmother. After one visit he returned to find Anna had gone. *He didn't ask where she was, much to his father's relief.* So Geoff got on with the business of being a single parent. Anna was not talked about, there were no photographs about because granny had advised that they be hidden in case they reminded David of his mother. My task was not to disapprove of those decisions. Geoff had entered a new world, a world that had no landmarks. He was learning to mother a small boy, keep his job and a roof over their head, and master a myriad different skills that hitherto had been his wife's province. His only support had been his mother who held firmly to the belief that 'what children don't know can't hurt them.'

> But it was not working. Geoff was depressed and lonely and now David's behaviour was worrying him. It was hard for this man to learn that difficult feelings, such as sadness and anger, are normal. He felt abandoned too, and longed to 'see' his wife again. As Geoff gradually grew to trust me, he began to see that David shared these feelings, but had no information. How could he let his mother go, when he had not even been told that she had gone? Slowly and painfully Geoff practised different responses to David's behaviour. We found books for Geoff to read to him (see suggested reading). Together, father and son began to talk about Anna, about how sick her body had got and how eventually it broke like a toy that could never be mended. The photographs were reinstated and eventually David started to talk. He asked the same questions over and over again about his mother's disappearance. His father was helped to understand that his little son was checking out the story, expressing his disbelief, which is readily understood in adults when they say things like, 'I keep thinking it's a bad dream.' It got harder for Geoff, because David began to act out his feelings, breaking toy after toy and bringing them to his father to be mended. Because he could talk about this behaviour, Geoff began to understand that the little boy was trying to come to terms with the fact that his mother

could not be mended. At the same time he was preventing his father from avoiding his own feelings.

How respectful small children are of the adults in their world. David knew not to ask questions until his need to be whole asserted itself. His 'contentment with being captive' (Keenan 1992) disintegrated so he forced his father to take action. He reminds us of what we have learned from mothers who were denied the right to see and hold their stillborn child; that human beings must mourn a lost loved object lest their inner world be coloured with sadness. The price of attachment is the pain of separation. The cradling that Geoff needed allowed him to 'hold' his little son through the difficult time of adjustment to his mother's death.

2. Ambivalence

All relationships are ambivalent to some extent. The death of a loved person can heighten the component of hatred and the task of dealing with this is always part of the mourning process (Freud 1931). At the earliest developmental phases the mixture of aggression in relationships is particularly strong and inadequately tempered by love. The toddler's difficulties in dealing with his aggression may well jeopardize his mourning process. Older children, too, may find their mourning tempered by mixed feelings because of the nature of their relationship with the dead parent. When we are working with bereaved adults it is often a turning point when they stop sanctifying the dead and can acknowledge other more difficult facets in the relationship. A child may simply find it is too difficult to work through and turn to gross avoidance techniques like refusing to visit the parent when he or she is near to death or refusing to talk about them, even to simply walking out of the room when the dead person is mentioned. Ambivalent feelings towards the parent who is left may be expressed clearly – 'I wish you had died' may be hurled angrily at the mother or father who is not dead. More often these feelings are acted out unconsciously.

> Alan, aged ten when his mother died, retreated into forgetfulness and a degree of slovenliness, unconsciously designed to provoke his orderly father into a rage. Only when his father had lost his temper and punished him, could Alan weep and write angry letters to his mother, cursing her for dying.

Alan's father needed help to understand his son's behaviour, to bear the anger that Alan expressed for both of them.

The upset toddler unable to understand the permanence of the separation caused by death has to find ways to express these feelings that are beyond their developmental capacity to express in words.

After her father died, Gemma aged three started wetting and soiling. She became aggressive to her baby brother to the point where it was not safe to ever leave them together unattended. She constantly searched for her father in the parts of the house that she had always been at his side – the garden shed, the garden, the bedroom. Every decision her mother made met with a fight – even getting ready to go out for a walk, which she loved. At her wits end, Pippa, her mother turned to alcohol to get through the day until the neighbours alerted the family's health visitor.

A package of respite care was arranged that included play therapy for Gemma to help her work through her mixed up feelings and nursery care for the baby. Once the drinking was under control, her mother was referred for counselling. The health visitor had never experienced someone so 'rent asunder' by grief. At first, Pippa was pre-occupied by the loss of a 'wonderful husband.' He was her second husband. Pippa had left a poor and violent relationship and had lost custody of her first child, who was now thirteen years old. She had lost contact with her beyond sending birthday and Christmas cards. She was so ashamed of this that she had never told her second husband, nor had she told him that between the marriages she had resorted to quite heavy use of alcohol. I asked who she had received support from during these years. She had turned to her father who had told her that she was 'no daughter of his'. The rift had never healed and he had died without reconciliation around the time of her re-marriage.

She tried so hard to make me condemn her and when I pointed out that she had punished herself for long enough, she began to talk about John in a much less idealized way. John had wanted the two children. Against her deepest wishes she had borne Gemma and the baby boy. But she could not let herself love Gemma, for she felt so guilty about abandoning the first daughter.

John had taken over more and more of the care of his small daughter. Pippa tentatively began to express her anger with John for dying, leaving her in charge. 'He must have known I'm not fit to be a mother!' she exploded. So we explored the options; facing up to abandoning a second daughter, or with the help of social services – a family aide, and child minding support, picking up the mantle of motherhood. She chose the latter. As she came to understand herself and to feel held and accepted, she began to feel the first flickerings of love for her little daughter who was fighting so hard to be heard and valued.

As the relationship strengthened, Gemma fell prey (as many sad children do) to infections which, although they tested poor Pippa to the limit, in terms of physical stamina, evoked a capacity for tenderness in her that she thought had long since atrophied. It is important to recognize that this sort of damage is threaded permanently into the rope between Pippa and Gemma. Both will re-visit these feelings of hostility and rejection. But it is to be hoped that Pippa will have used the experience of being cradled, to seek it out again.

3. Delayed Grief

'How we mourn and how our mourning is resolved will depend on

- how we perceive the loss
- our age
- the age of the person dying
- how prepared we are
- our inner strengths and resources
- our relationship with the person who died.'

(Couldrick 1992)

In the light of the above, an adult child whose parent dies in her sixties after a lengthy illness in which she was nursed at home by her daughters and close extended family, might be expected to have come through the experience sad, but satisfied that she had fulfilled her obligations.

Nimocks, Webb and Connell (1987), suggest that when we think of a good death experience, we mean that goodness can be defined in terms of the extent to which the interactants accept the impending death, receive mutual emotional care and spiritual support, mitigate the dying person's discomfort and isolation and complete unfinished business.

The death of Janna's mother met the above criteria. She died well symptom controlled, and supported by her large muslim family, who live close to one another in Britain. They believe firmly in the will of God and the abiding support of the family. Janna's father died when the youngest child in the family was four years old.

After their mother's death, the three daughters, Janna aged 19, Kairi aged 16 and Shushila aged 14, lived in the home of an uncle, his wife and baby girl born two weeks after Mrs K's death. Kairi and Shushila continued to attend the same senior school as before. Janna, who had abandoned her A level course in order to nurse her mother, kept house and looked for a job that would enable her to study part-time.

For eighteen months, the family supported one another and only sought help for Shushila who started having 'fits' the day after the funeral.

Having eliminated all organic causes, the family doctor asked if I thought bereavement counselling might help. By then the sisters had decided that Shushila sometimes could not bear her feelings and so would faint. Shushila welcomed an opportunity to talk about herself and her mother.

She was quickly able to associate 'the fits' with confrontation with the reality of the loss of her mother. For example she was sent home from school one day with dysmenorrhoea,(stomach pain which can accompany the onset of menstruation) and had a 'fit' on arrival at home. She herself decided that it was awful to come home to be faced with no mother to put her to bed with warm bottles, no mother to tempt her with little delicacies, no mother to sing to her and 'baby' her. The older girls and Shushila made a special effort to mother one another when they felt low or ill. Eventually the 'fits' ceased.

Kairi did well in her GCSEs, and went on to prepare herself to study medicine. They were able to talk openly about their mother, to look at photographs and express how sad it is to be without both parents.

Two years after the mother's death, the employer of the eldest daughter, Janna, rang to say that she was about to lose her job. She was frequently late for work, consistently careless and had become intolerably slovenly in her personal hygiene.

We met and I was shocked by her appearance. She had lost weight, her long dark hair was unwashed, and her eyes were hollow and empty of expression. Gone was the intrepid older sister who had picked up the mantle of mothering. She found it hard to acknowledge that she had changed, but her voice was flat, discouraging intrusion into her world. Only when she talked of the younger girls and the toddler in the house did any warmth come back. Work was 'all right' but she had not taken up any opportunities for further training. 'Why was that?' I asked. She shrugged and said, 'What's the point?' I said 'It seems you feel there's no future worth looking forward to, is that right?' She seemed totally apathetic.

I felt very concerned about her and eventually she was given a course of anti-depressants. As the depression began to lift, Janna began to talk angrily about her life, caring for the others, the loss of the dream of studying to become a pharmacist and returning to India, and as she began to name the hurts, she started to dream at night about her mother. In these dreams her mother appeared, looking terrifying, as if she would hurt her daughter. 'She's angry with me' said Janna, 'because

I'm not content to do God's will'. 'Which is what?' I asked. 'To accept that I won't marry until my sisters have finished their education.'

I suggested that Janna might be very angry with her mother for dying and stopping so many hopes, however unfair that sort of anger is. Janna became very agitated and upset at the thought of expressing anger with a beloved, much longed for parent. It was many weeks before she could acknowledge these strong feelings, and in doing so, she began to be very sad, acknowledging how much she missed her mother, how tired she was of being the eldest child. Janna lost her job, but talked with her uncles about arranging her marriage, a system which she believed in.

She has learned that she is considered worth attention outside the family, but she still has the difficult task of accepting that the road ahead is not necessarily a hopeless substitute for her earlier dreams.

Looking After Ourselves

We are the tool in this process of cradling. Unless we look after ourselves, we will be unable to sustain care for others.

Some important points in self-care are:

- to learn about our own reactions. It is helpful to have reflected on our own losses so that we do not load unfinished grief onto the family.

- to anticipate that we will experience emotional reactions if we are supporting children. We react more strongly to them for it touches our own vulnerability.

- to have someone we can share responsibility with, or someone we can seek advice from.

- to remember that we cannot carry away the family's grief, but we can help and support them.

- to have good colleagues to share with and to seek supervision for the work.

- to remember that to be any use, we need to take good care of ourselves.

What Skills are Needed?

- awareness of normal grief processes
- knowledge of children's understanding of death according to their age and development
- core counselling skills of respect, empathy and genuineness

- respect and concern for the bereaved child and his parent (see suggested reading).

If we take for granted that the concern for the family is inherent, these skills are accessible to:

- family doctors who are the best placed professional to identify the vulnerable family.

- health visitors who have wide experience of both the normal and the dysfunctioning family.

- community nurses who have a very special role in helping the family prepare for death and who are often trusted by the family.

- social workers who are involved through the hospital.

- teachers who have care of the child for a third of the day.

In Summary

- Parents need information about grieving children and what they understand, depending on their age and development.

- Parents need support and attention so that some of their own emotional needs are met. The experience of losing a partner, leads to loss of self esteem and loss of confidence in themselves. They no longer have someone with whom to share uncertainty.

- Parents need guidance to reading matter for themselves and the children. The two small booklets, 'Grief and Bereavement, Understanding Children' and 'When your Mum or Dad has Cancer', were written in response to requests from parents for something straightforward and easy to read. (see suggested reading)

If we remember the old nursery rhyme

> Rock a bye baby on the tree top
> When the wind blows the cradle will rock
> When the bough breaks, the cradle will fall
> Down will come baby, cradle and all

The bough does break, the cradle does fall, so any effort to prevent this is worth trying.

Keenan (1992) reminds us

> 'There is a capacity in each of us and sometimes I think even a need to reach out to others in pain.' (p.46)

> 'We cannot abandon the injured or the maimed, thinking to ensure our own safety and sanity. We must reclaim them, as they are part of ourselves.' (p.288)

He had to learn the hard way, because the situation was beyond his control.

Cradling is both holding on and holding up, conveying that someone believes that the parent can get through the experience, to a quality of life that will be worth living for. Unless the parent feels supported and valued, the bereaved children will struggle through the experience of loss. Their lives will be coloured by the absence of the parent who has died, however well the parent survives, but their suffering can be mitigated.

Let us not abandon the bereaved child and his parent.

References

Black, D. and Urbanovitch, M.A. (1987) 'Family intervention with bereaved children.' *Journal of Child Psychology and Psychiatry 28*, 467–476.

Couldrick, A. (1992) 'Optimizing bereavement outcome: reading the road ahead.' *Soc. Science Medical 35*, 12, 1521–1523.

Freud, S. (1931) 'Totem and taboo.' *Standard Edition* Vol.13, 1–161. London: Hogarth (1955).

Furman, E. (1974) *A Child's Parent Dies.* London: Yale University Press.

Harris, T., Brown, G.W. and Bifulco, A. (1986) 'Loss of parent in childhood and adult psychiatric disorder.' *Psychological Medicine 16*, 641–659.

Keenan, B. (1992) *An Evil Cradling.* London: Hutchinson.

Lansdowne, R. and Benjamin, G. (1985) 'The development of the concept of death in children aged 5–9 years.' *Child Care, Health and Development 11*, 13–20.

Mann, T. (1969) *The Magic Mountain* (originally published in German (1924) and in English (1927)). New York: Random House. (Vintage Books paperbacks.)

Nimocks, M.J.A., Webb, L. and Connell, J.R. (1987) 'Communications and the terminally ill, a theoretical model.' *Death studies 2*, 323–344.

Suggested reading

Couldrick, A. (1988) *Grief and Bereavement, Understanding Children.* Oxford: Sobell Publications.

Couldrick, A. (1991) *When Your Mum or Dad has Cancer.* Oxford: Sobell Publications.

Dyregrov, A. (1990) *Grief in Children: A Handbook for Adults.* London: Jessica Kingsley Publishers.

Furman, E. (1974) *A Child's Parent Dies.* London: Yale University Press.

Mellonie, B. and Ingpen, R. (1987) *Beginnings and Endings with Lifetimes in Between.* Limpsfield: Dragon's World.

Parkes, C.M. (1972) *Bereavement Studies of Grief in Adult Life.* London: Tavistock Publications.

Papadatou, D. and Papadatou, C. (eds) (1991) *Children and Death.* New York: Hemisphere Publishing Corporation.

Rogers, C.R. (1951) *Client Centered Therapy.* London: Constable.

Stickney, D. (1984) *Waterbugs and Dragonflies.* Oxford: Mowbray.

Varley, S. (1985) *Badger's Parting Gifts.* London: Lions Publishing House.

Worden, J.W. (1982) *Grief Counselling and Grief Therapy.* New York: Springer Publishing Company.

CHAPTER 7

Grieving Together
Helping Family Members Share their Grief

Jess Gordon

Introduction

In this chapter I hope to offer an introduction to bereavement counselling with families, expressing ideas gained from my work with bereaved families in the Northampton Child and Family Consultation Service and also from my two years as consultant and trainer with our local branch of the national charity Cruse – Bereavement Care. Much excellent material on helping bereaved children and their families is provided in the Cruse – Bereavement Care training manual (1993).

A family bereavement can come as a surprise as well as a shock, even when the death has seemed inevitable. Most of us would agree with the American writer Emerson (1803–1882) who wrote in his Journal: 'The event of death is always astounding', and his words remain valid for our generation. Unfortunately, the subject of death could be described as our last taboo, now that we have learned to be more open about sexual matters. To cope with a family bereavement, ideally children need help both from their family and from their school (see Capewell 1994 for a comprehensive overview of how schools can help children after loss and trauma).

Discovering our Own Family Patterns of Grieving

I have found that a helpful way to prepare for bereavement counselling is by studying our own family experiences of bereavement. I make use of the geneogram in my work with families (Lieberman 1978; Marlin 1989) as an aid to understanding the family composition and the significant family events, including all the bereavements and other losses experienced. In thinking about our own losses, a good way to start is by drawing our own geneogram, focusing first on the losses we suffered in childhood and then updating it to include losses in our adult years. Finally, in recalling our memories of how our parents grieved we can consider whether we can identify the messages about how to cope with grief that our parents handed down to us, either in their words or in their behaviour.

In Figure 7.1 the twelve-year-old girl's older brother had died seven years earlier, a major bereavement for the whole family. The parents had also suffered the miscarriage of their first child and they had each lost one or both parents since their marriage, so they had a wide experience of bereavement. The family 'messages' about how to cope with grief remembered by the girl and her ten-year-old brother in their adult life were not to show any sad feelings, not to talk about their sadness nor about the people who had died, but to get on

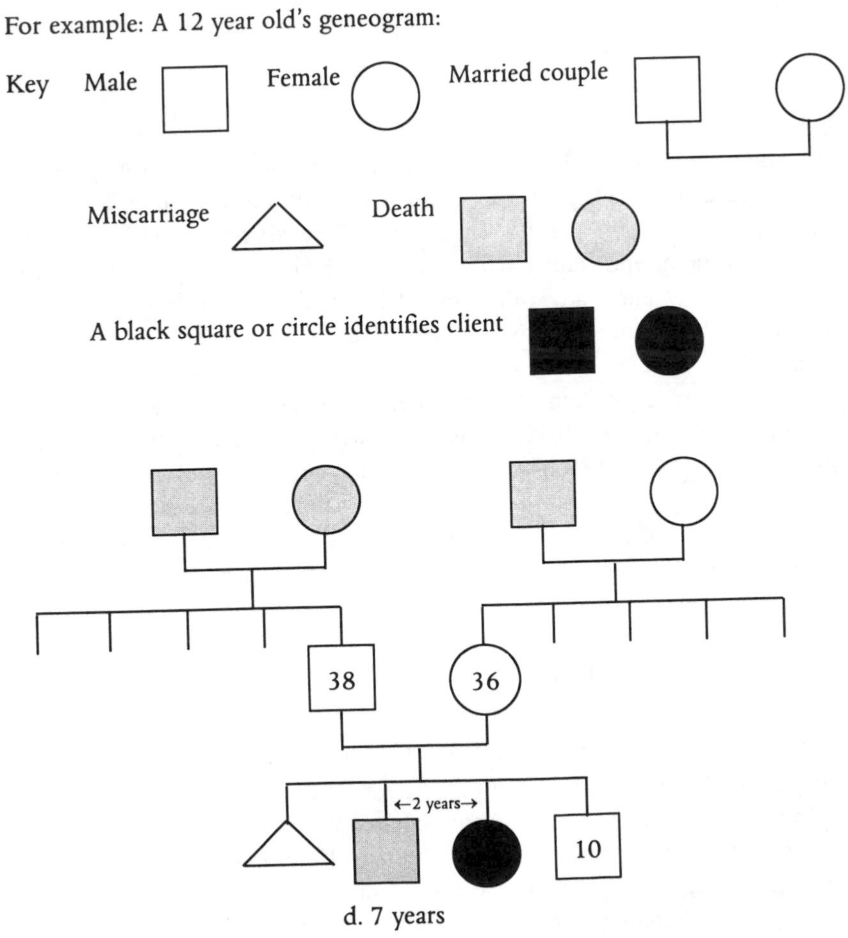

For example: A 12 year old's geneogram:

d. 7 years

Figure 7. 1

with living as if nothing had changed. I have found that these are not uncommon messages that parents hand down to their children. Moving on in time, consider that same child thirty years later, recently widowed, and overwhelmed by her feelings of grief for which she felt totally unprepared. No one had told her it felt like this. If in her childhood her parents had been able to talk with her about their own concealed feelings of grief then she might have been better prepared for the strength of her own reactions. She would still be helped by her parents' good example of getting on with life and making the most of her other relationships, so the other family messages would stand her in good stead.

My experiences of what I learned from my own family's responses to bereavement were similar to the example given. I also realize that I have needed to find my own ways of remembering my brother who had died as a child, without ever sharing these thoughts with my family.

In bereavement work with families, drawing up the geneogram is a quick way to find out what other losses the family has experienced, and in exploring these you may then discover valuable clues about how the family had coped and hence how they may now be coping with their recent bereavement. The family's rituals around death may be described. The family may also reveal their attitudes to loss in general, whether it is something to take in their stride or whether it has permanent sad effects on their functioning. For example, a mother may show acute distress when referring to the death of her own mother five years earlier, a sign that in this family old grief may be unresolved, making any fresh bereavement extra stressful for the family. Helpful and unhelpful rituals may be described. Examples of helpful rituals include the family planting a tree or a shrub as a memorial, and as time passes finding positive ways of marking the anniversaries with family occasions. Unhelpful rituals might include frequent compulsory visits to the grave or expressions of despair long after the death, or a room kept as a shrine to the dead person.

Some Family Messages about How to Grieve

Some common messages I have met in my work with bereaved families include the following:

- Just carry on as usual (back to school etc)
- Don't make a fuss ('Granny wouldn't want it')
- Grief is a private matter
- Children don't need to grieve
- Adults don't share their grief with their children
- Let's forget all about it
- It's morbid to talk about the dead or death.

As adults, if our family messages about how to mourn are inadequate to meet our emotional needs after a significant loss, then we are likely to flounder as we struggle to cope with our feelings. One hopes that if we explore our own experiences of bereavement in our childhood and become more aware of what helped and what did not, we can draw on this knowledge and be better prepared to help our own children and our friends after their bereavements. This understanding will also enrich our professional bereavement counselling.

The most common unmet need that adults recall from their own childhood experiences is the need to be told what happened and to learn the details of the death. Many adults have as children been excluded from the family talk, and have not been helped to find a way of saying goodbye to the dead relative or given a choice about whether to attend the funeral. Long afterwards both these issues can cause feelings of sadness and guilt about whether the 'wrong' decision was made at the time. A further wish often expressed by adults is that their parents had shared at least a little of what they were feeling and that they had talked more about the person who had died. Children need help to work out how to remember the dead person within the family and how to keep the memory alive (Stroebe, Stroebe and Hansson 1993 p.309). This is where family rituals can be helpful, especially the ritual of the funeral.

Can Children be Prepared for Coping with Bereavement?

The Funeral

It is now widely accepted that we all cope better with stressful experiences if we have previously had the chance to take part in a similar occasion, but one in which we are less intensely involved. Children are better able to cope with a personal loss if they have been helped beforehand to understand the concepts of death and its inevitability for all living creatures including ourselves. They also benefit from knowing about the natural after-effects of death and the practical reasons for having to dispose of the dead body. For example, in the case of funerals a child is in a better position to cope if he/she has attended the funeral of an acquaintance or distant relative before having to choose whether or not to attend the beloved parent's or a sibling's funeral. Such an occasion can give parents the chance to prepare their children and to answer any questions about the sad event without having to cope with their own overwhelming feelings of grief at the same time. It is also helpful if children have some explanation of what happens at the funeral service and where possible if they can visit the church before they attend their first funeral.

The Concept of Death

As loving parents we are tempted to protect our children from unhappy experiences whenever we can. However, given the inevitability of everyone being bereaved at some stage in life, perhaps we should consider how to help our children cope with such unhappy experiences rather than try to protect them. We need to use any opportunity to help children to develop a concept of death. For example, the death of a pet can allow the child to see the stillness of the dead body and how the pet is changed in death. If the child has some understanding of why the body has to be disposed of then the parents' explanations about the need for the burial or cremation of the body will make more sense. Perhaps this sounds morbid, but consider how cruel the burial service can seem if the child imagines that the dead person's body remains intact, like Snow White in her coffin. When adults use the death of a pet as an opportunity to help their children begin to learn about the physical changes after death, then children may begin to acquire some basic knowledge which will help them to understand the necessity for the burial or cremation when a relative or friend dies.

As a child I can remember visiting the home before her funeral of a girl I had not known well; I remember being surprised to be asked did I want to see her. I must have agreed for I have a clear memory of the girl looking very pale and 'different' in her satin-lined coffin. After this experience I had no illusions that she was not changed by death. I do not remember being distressed by the experience but I was left with a clear idea that the 'person' I knew was no longer there. I had come to believe that the opportunity to see the dead person in their own home is now very rare, but I have recently heard of two examples where the dead child's body has been returned home before the funeral and young friends have been invited to say goodbye in familiar surroundings. It is to be hoped that these are not isolated examples. Worden's first task of mourning (Worden 1991) is to accept the reality of death and it is believed that the opportunity to see the dead body helps in this process. We know that even pre-school children can understand the concept of death if they are helped in this way (Dyregrov 1994). The alternative is to leave the child with feelings of confusion, uncertainty and guilt that may prolong the process of mourning. The experience of seeing the dead body may banish some of the child's magical yearnings, a common one being that the person is not really dead. Dyregrov (1994, p.176) gives the moving example of his own four-year-old son's sad experience of realizing once he had seen his playmate's dead body that he could never again play with him; until he saw the body he could not accept this idea.

Bereavement Work with the Family

In the Northampton Child and Family Consultation Service the reasons for the referral of a bereaved child can be varied and sometimes neither the referrer nor the parent(s) can see the link between the child's presenting behaviour and the preceding bereavement. Examples might include a child's behaviour problems at school some months after a family bereavement, or a deteriorating attitude to school work. In a pre-adolescent the presenting problem may be of bed wetting or of soiling. An adolescent may be defying parental authority and becoming increasingly out of control; others may be apathetic and reluctant to go out with friends. As described below, at any age various somatic symptoms may also be a presenting feature. We try to help the parent(s) see the possible link between the child's symptoms and the family's earlier bereavement and only then will it be possible to convince the family that bereavement counselling may be helpful. Of course appropriate time and attention should be given to the child's presenting symptoms. Sometimes the parent is seeking help or support because of the family's distress over the bereavement and then it is easier to negotiate several sessions for this work, the number varying with the family and how much they can cope with at that particular time.

Assessment

This may take one to two sessions. I find it helpful to start by drawing the family's geneogram as already described. Most families enjoy doing this, and in the process the worker can often gain valuable insights into how the family functions. For example, it becomes clear how much the children know about their families, how the parent(s) and children communicate with each other and what respect each shows for the other in the giving of the information. Some parents speak for their children while others encourage them to work out the family relationships and everyone's ages for themselves, only helping out when necessary. If the family atmosphere is strained it may be difficult to gain the family's co-operation in drawing their geneogram at the initial meeting, but this in itself is an indication of the level of stress in the family on that day, or of the family's dysfunction. Other information may be offered to shed light on this stress and the factors causing it. If there have been several deaths, say in a road traffic accident, it may be too painful for the family to do their geneogram, but a tentative outline can be started by enquiring about the relatives and friends they see regularly, or the people they can call on for support.

Interventions with the Bereaved Family

Family work needs the active co-operation of the parent(s). Time is well spent in listening to their own assessment of what help they need and what outcomes they hope for. The parent's own stage of grieving is also relevant; in the early stages counselling may need to start slowly with the focus at first on support for the family or help with the presenting problem.

My aims in working with bereaved families are first to assess the family functioning, including the family's strengths, the warmth of the relationships and whether there are any other major stresses, and then to assess the impact of the bereavement. I try to explore the unique meaning of the loss for each family member, and how sensitive the family is to each other's feelings and needs. Some families benefit from being seen individually, followed by a whole family session for some sharing. Two counsellors may be required, especially if the parental needs are intense, for example after a death by suicide, with one counsellor to work with the parent and the other with the children. I find a helpful format is for individual sessions to take up to half an hour, then a further half hour or more for the whole family, so that one and a quarter to one and a half hours needs to be allowed for each session. Younger children, or older ones who do not easily express their thoughts or feelings in words, may prefer to draw or paint or to communicate their feelings in play. Relevant children's books can be useful at all ages to help a child feel less isolated, and books can also be used to help families explore painful issues (e.g. see Hollins and Sireling 1989).

The process of bereavement counselling with families may have to be modified but it is essentially the same as in individual work. First the worker needs to build a good relationship with the family, taking time to begin to understand how the family was before the bereavement and to learn about their separate and joint interests. The geneogram can help in this and details of family friendships and interests can be included on it. The worker needs to gain some understanding of the family's previous routine before the bereavement and whether this has yet been restored either in part or in full. The bereavement and its meaning for the family then needs to be explored together with the specific changes that have followed the loss. These changes may be causing the children extra stress and unhappiness. For example, after the death of a father the family may have to move house with a change of schools for the children. In some cases the children may have had to cope with months of family disruption because of visits to a sibling or a parent in hospital and they may now want to express their feelings about this. Any specific symptoms connected with the death, for example nightmares or intrusive thoughts, will need appropriate attention and treatment.

The details of the death should be explored, often at first with the parent only, to learn what the children have been told and about the parent's feelings and wishes concerning the sharing of this information with the children. This can be difficult after a traumatic death, for example the suicide of a parent, as the impact on the surviving parent may be so great that no one has been able to talk about the death. If this is the case, some idea needs to be gained about how much the children may have learned at second hand, from relatives or visitors or even school friends. Here the parent's need not to talk about this painful area may be in conflict with the children's need for clarification. Dr Dora Black (Harris Hendriks, Black and Kaplan 1993) has described in her work with traumatized children however young they are, their need to make sense of what happened to the dead parent before they can accept the reality of the death and then begin their grieving. It is hard in such circumstances for the relatives or carers to discuss these distressing details with the children; a good option is for the carers to allow the counsellor to explore with the children, together or separately, to find out what they do know, and then with the carers' permission to fill in any gaps in their knowledge. This last part is best done with the carers present so that the children are relieved of the burden of keeping secrets. It is hoped that, once this has happened, more open family discussion will take place at home. This can be followed up in the next session; some families will have been able to continue talking together with much relief all round but others will have to keep the topic closed between sessions and the work will thus be slower. The relatives or carers may require help to be convinced that their children would benefit from knowing what happened. People who work with bereaved children have no doubts about how important it is to fill in these gaps in the child's understanding. If we do not help children make sense of the event then they will have to rely on their own guesses and their imagination, which allows enormous potential for distortion and for the development of unnecessary fears and distress, including feelings of guilt. The facts are often less frightening than the child's fantasies. We can probably all remember events from our own experience that prove this point.

In family bereavement counselling a specific feature is that the death is experienced by each family member in different ways, and each loss is unique. The child's stage of development affects how the child experiences the bereavement at the time and with each stage of development the loss may have a fresh impact on the child, who will then need a further chance to talk over any new concerns.

Families can be helped to explore the uniqueness of everyone's loss. One way of doing this is for everyone in the family to make a list of what each misses most and to share these lists with each other. Amongst the items on the lists there will be tasks that the dead person carried out and which another family member may be able to take over, for example reading bedtime stories. There will, of course, be many things that no one else can do – be the special mum, or the little sister – and in the sharing of these sad details of what each is now missing most and that no one else can replace, the family is drawn together in their grieving and in their shared memories of what was special about the dead person. For a much loved parent the full list of what everyone misses can be enormous. The following brief poem by Steve Turner (1987) captures for me the essence of these sad feelings:

After You'd Gone

No one

Like you.

That then

The pleasure.

That now

The pain.

When the family is able to share their feelings of grief with each other, acknowledging the sadness of everyone's loss, some healing of the pain is begun.

Education about Bereavement

Education concerning the process of grief is an important part of working with bereaved families. Many adults as well as children are helped to hear that grief takes time and that intense feelings may continue for what seems forever, for example long past the first anniversary. Education regarding the fresh impact of the various anniversaries may help prepare the family to bear them, without the additional stress of not understanding why they are once more feeling such pain. Education on the grief process can also offer the hope that although the loss can never be made up the intensity of the sad feelings does decrease in time, and that it will then become more possible to remember the whole of the lost relationship, the happy times as well as the sadness of the loss.

Memory Books

Children can be helped to remember by creating their own memory books. These are especially important for younger children who can begin to suffer intense distress when they realize that they are 'forgetting' the dead parent or sibling. Photographs taken with the parent or sibling will become invaluable as a perpetual memento of that time spent together, of which the child may retain only the haziest memory.

I have found that many adults bereaved in childhood say that they did forget the dead person, especially if the death was never discussed in the family. The repression of intense feelings of grief is likely to contribute to future unhappiness.

Negative Feelings

Some families need help to accept that their negative feelings, their anger and irritability, are a normal part of the grief process. Anger can lead to family divisions between the adults with the destructive projection of negative grief feelings on to close relatives, friends or institutions, such as the church or the medical profession. Young parents after the death of a premature child are known to be vulnerable to the breakdown of their relationship after weeks of shared stress. The family needs help to recognize these angry feelings for what they are, a natural part of the process of grieving. They can be helped to recognize their anger by talking to each other about these feelings which may present as irritability or open anger and will probably be more obvious to the rest of the family than to the angry individual. Such discussion can lead to a better understanding of each other's needs. The result of facing this anger or irritability and supporting each other through it can be a greater closeness for the family in their mutual grief. This is infinitely better than the distress and isolation that results when angry feelings are acted on. As everyone knows, bereavements can be the cause of bitter family disputes that are difficult to heal and may last for years

Common Themes for Bereaved Families

1. For the Parents – Learning to Understand How Children Communicate

(i) HOW CHILDREN COMMUNICATE BY DENIAL

Adults can find it painful to recognize and acknowledge the intensity of the grief that children experience – even professionals taking part in the children's bereavement groups (see part 3) are overwhelmed at times by the feelings described and shown by children of all ages.

In family work I have often observed how even very young children try hard to protect their parent(s) from the knowledge of their own distress and confusion, in their efforts not to upset them further. They can also find effective ways of diverting the parent(s) from grieving by positive or negative behaviours, depending on what works in their family. It is often these behaviours aimed at diverting the adult that bring about a referral to our Service, especially if the parent(s) then comes to believe that such behaviour shows the child does not care and is not grieving.

> An example is of a father, nine months after the traumatic deaths of his wife and daughter, who complained that his ten-year-old son would not talk about his dead mother and sister and was also refusing to go within sight of the local churchyard where his mother and sister are buried. When seen on his own the boy talked freely about his losses, saying he was 'thinking all the time' about his mother and sister but he hated to see his father cry so he tried to avoid any reference to the tragedy in the hope of keeping his father's mind off the subject. During our work it was possible to negotiate ways in which father and son could share their grief with each other, at first within the context of our sessions and then by setting tasks for them at home with time-limits, for example five to ten minutes only. This met the boy's need not to be overwhelmed by his own feelings or his father's, as he might be without a time limit on their discussions. Gradually the son began to cope more easily and his father learned the value of setting aside very short periods of time for talking. The father also began to arrange activities together after their discussions and these activities became a healthy enactment of building their new life together.

I have met many bereaved children who are adamant at first that they do not want to talk about their bereavement. However, it is usually possible if children are given individual time by an experienced worker to encourage them to express some of their thoughts and feelings. For a young child this may be via play therapy or for a child of any age through art work. For many children the opportunity to talk away from their parents is all they need to begin to sort out their own experience of bereavement. Given such help children can usually become more open with their families about their grief feelings and more ready to listen to each other. In their individual sessions children sometimes express feelings of guilt about the death and it is then often possible in the family sessions to explore these feelings and it is to be hoped that family members will strive to relieve each other of any unnecessary burdens.

(ii) HOW CHILDREN COMMUNICATE BY PHOBIC AVOIDANCE

The phobic avoidance of a room or objects associated with the dead person is not uncommon. This may be the adult's problem presented as the child's, for example:

> One eight-year-old girl had to walk past her dead brother's bedroom to get to her own room; her mother said she was worried about her daughter's behaviour because she deliberately looked away from the brother's room and never went into it. However, our discussions revealed that the mother also had difficulty in coping with this room, which she had kept unchanged and unused; she often sat alone there, turning the room into a shrine to her son. Gradually, as mother was able to make some changes in the room and as she began to cope better herself the daughter's 'problem' disappeared.

> Similarly the clinginess of a child can meet the parent's own needs and make it difficult for the parent to discourage the child's over-dependence – an example might be of a ten-year-old sleeping with a widowed parent regularly for some time after the death, with the parent making no attempt to encourage the child to return to his/her own bed.

(iii) HOW CHILDREN COMMUNICATE BY SOMATIC COMPLAINTS

Children in any type of distress, including bereavement, may express their feelings in physical symptoms. For a bereaved parent such symptoms in their child can raise enormous anxieties, especially if the death was due to illness. It is important that the family doctor recognizes this not unnatural anxiety and takes the child's symptoms seriously and makes the appropriate examinations and so forth, before offering reassurances if there is no evidence of organic illness. Bereavement counselling with the family can have a dramatic effect in reducing the number of somatic complaints once attention is given to the underlying emotional needs.

To give two examples:

> A boy of ten was referred with several months' history of soiling only at home. His father had died two years earlier after a long illness with

bowel cancer. In our discussions it emerged that the children had not known that their father was dying and their mother was too distressed after her husband's death to talk about him. In our meetings it was possible to listen to the mother and the children separately and then to help them for the first time to talk with each other about their bereavement. Within a few sessions the mother and the children were more relaxed with each other and they all said they felt closer, and the children were able to talk more freely about their father. Gradually the son's soiling stopped.

A more common situation is illustrated by the thirteen-year-old girl whose school attendance began to deteriorate as she complained of headaches and stomach upsets; she was also putting on excessive weight. She was an only child whose father had been killed at work in an accident six months earlier. Her mother had given up her part time job and rarely went out; however, she became concerned about her daughter's deteriorating school work and requested help for her. In our sessions both mother and daughter talked about their own grief and the daughter surprised her mother by also expressing her anxiety about mother being at home so much on her own. It became possible for them both to see the link between mother giving up her life outside the home and the daughter feeling the need to stay at home with her. It was easier at first for each to see that it was not good for the other to withdraw so much from former activities. Gradually, both mother and daughter took the difficult early steps back to a more normal life-style, each being motivated by the wish to help the other. The daughter lost her somatic symptoms fairly quickly. With her mother's help and the help of a sympathetic educational welfare officer and her form tutor she resumed her interest in school and her school attendance improved. Mother found another part time job and they both began to go out again socially. Slowly they began to develop their new life together without father.

(iv) HOW CHILDREN COMMUNICATE BY BEHAVIOUR PROBLEMS

These are a common reason for referral to our Service. However some adults find it difficult to see the link between the family bereavement and the child's unwanted behaviour, especially if the adult believes the child is not very concerned about the death. In this situation the confidence of the parent(s) needs to be gained for bereavement counselling to be acceptable. If one child is scapegoated then the parent(s) may not see the need for the other 'good' children to be included in the family sessions. The counsellor needs to explain that children often communicate more freely with the support of their siblings, who in turn can be very helpful in family sessions in interpreting the so called 'naughty' behaviour. It often emerges that the referred child is not unique in being naughty but is more often noticed for it. Another reason to include all the children is that they have all been bereaved but some children cope by suppressing their anxieties and distress, especially if a sibling is gaining attention by misbehaving. The quiet ones may also need help.

An example of behaviour problems:

> A nine-year-old boy was in trouble at school for bullying some smaller children and also for swearing; his angry reactions when his teachers confronted him got him into more trouble. The boy was the eldest of four children whose father had committed suicide nine months earlier after an untreated depressive illness. The children had not been told directly about how their father had died. In our family work it became apparent that somehow all the children had gathered the facts about their father's death, sometimes during family rows. Mother in time allowed father's suicide to be discussed openly and it was moving to see the effect on the children. Previously they had all been restless and easily distracted; they became still and listened to each other and they all became calmer. This change has been maintained and the referred child is also calmer in school.

2. For the Children – Feelings of Insecurity After the Death of a Parent

(i) THESE CAN EMERGE AS SEEMINGLY **INSENSITIVE QUESTIONS** SUCH AS:

'Will you die?' to the other parent or close relative

'Who will look after me if you die?'

'Will you get me a new mummy/daddy?'

'When will you marry again?' or 'when will Granny marry again?'

These questions can be pointers to what is worrying the child but this is not always obvious to the individual grieving mother or father! Children need to discuss their worries, especially those concerning their own security, such as who will care for them if the surviving parent is ill or were to die. Often a parent believes their children 'know' about the plans, for example for them to live with an Aunt and her family, if the worst did happen. However, even an intelligent recently bereaved fourteen-year-old may need to hear this again and for the discussion to be ongoing, preferably including the named relative, before this particular anxiety may be put to rest. The surviving parent will, one hopes, do this at the same time as giving assurances of having no intention of dying for a very long time.

Multiple losses are the sad experience of some children and this can involve major changes for them of home, school, and even family if the child has to be fostered. After such changes most children need to feel secure and confident with their new carers before they can cope with grief work.

It is hoped that any bereavement work would involve the new carers. The memory book and the life story work as described in other chapters are an important part of the bereavement work with these children. To add up an individual child's losses in terms of scores for life events (Johnson 1982) can given an indication of the level of the child's losses over and above the initial bereavement, and the weight of emotional distress the child is bearing. Every effort should be made to maintain as much continuity as possible for the child regarding school, contact with relatives and so forth., to reduce the risk of any unnecessary losses.

(ii) CHILDREN'S INSECURITY AFTER THE DEATH OF A SIBLING

Questions around 'Will I die too?' are common and can be presented as somatic symptoms. At any age children are helped by having a clear understanding of how the brother or sister came to die. It is usually possible for the surviving child(ren) to be given assurances that the illness will not affect them too. The grieving parents need help not to become over protective.

A more subtle anxiety after the death of a sibling is contained in questions around 'Would you love me more if I died too?' or 'You loved (the dead child) more than me'. Such questions or statements suggest that the surviving children may be feeling left out and need to be reassured about their own unique value in the family. Family bereavement work can be helpful here in affirming the special place of each family member and the importance of everyone.

If there were many hospital visits before the sibling's death the surviving children may have been deprived for some time of their normal family life. When this happens, parents can help by expressing their regrets about this and by admitting that they are all missing out, with assurances that family life will return to as near normal as soon as possible. It may be hard for parents to share their fears about a sick child with their other children, but if they can it helps the rest of the family to feel included and it also prepares them for any outcome, including death. After the death of a brother or sister the surviving children need to be reassured that they are loved just a much as the child who died; they will begin to believe this when the parents resume their former family routine including some of the children's activities that may have had to lapse, such as swimming, time for family friends and so forth.

(iii) ONGOING REALITY ISSUES FOR THE BEREAVED FAMILY

After the death of a parent there is usually a significant change in the family's finances, occasionally for the better but usually for the worse. When the mother dies the father may use his work as a way of coping with his grief; the experience for the children is then of being without their father for most of the day and having to adjust to their new carers who may not know how to help them in their grieving. Fathers who stay at home avoid this problem but they may suffer from feelings of isolation and lack of support.

When the father dies the mother may be more available for her children, but some mothers have to take on more work to compensate for their reduced finances. Children can then worry about the over-burdened widowed parent having to go to work and come home to do the chores. If the parent can involve the children in helping according to their ages they will feel that they are contributing.

(iv) TRAUMATIC DEATHS

Traumatic deaths present major problems in adjustment for both children and their families, as when one parent kills the other, which usually means for the children the immediate loss of both parents with the surviving parent in prison. These children, together with their carers, are in need of bereavement counselling but the carers may be too distressed or burdened to consider such an offer. The family carers are often the grandparents, who need support in coping with their own bereavement and with their shock and anger over the circumstances of their loss. They have to adjust to their new relationship with the children now that they are responsible for them. This subject is fully covered in the book *When Father Kills Mother* by Harris Hendriks, Black and Kaplan (1993)

(v) FURTHER ADJUSTMENTS

Later adjustments which may precipitate further grieving have to be made when a new partner joins the family after the death of a parent, and when there is a new baby after the death of a sibling. Such events may precipitate episodes of intense grieving in the children which they often show in disturbances of behaviour or with physical symptoms, as described above.

Issues for the Professional/Bereavement Counsellor/Family Friend

(1) Is Bereavement Counselling Harmful?

A frequent question that presents in various ways and can undermine or even block bereavement counselling is whether such work does help or whether it might make matters worse. Both professionals and parents ask this question fearing that such 'help' may give bereaved children unpleasant thoughts that they do not already have.

Research provides some answers to these doubts. The Harvard Child Bereavement Study reveals that children one year after the death of a parent were struggling internally to make sense of the death, and still had a strong sense of the presence of that parent (Stroebe *et al.* 1993 p.311). Our clinical experience gained from listening to children suggests that they do not find bereavement work harmful and that most say they feel better for it. We see them grow in confidence as the work proceeds. This positive feedback encourages us to continue to offer help to bereaved children and their families.

After a family bereavement we know that children benefit from being listened to and having their feelings acknowledged and above all from feeling loved and valued, and being helped to feel secure in their family relationships. Like adults they are confused by and afraid of the family experience of death and like adults they need to be able to share their confusion and fears. Family work provides the opportunity for children to feel less confused and anxious and to gain reassurances about their family's concern for them.

(2) The Type of Help Needed

In our Service we try to keep an open mind about the needs of the bereaved. We offer combinations of family work, small bereavement groups for children of the same age-band, also some individual work for children and adults, to try to meet the wide range of needs that we encounter.

(3) The Timing of Bereavement Work

There seems to be no ideal time. We are not able to offer crisis intervention help except in a limited way. Fortunately, in Northampton adults can be offered support fairly quickly by the various local charity organizations for the bereaved. We find that support immediately after the bereavement can best be offered by such crisis services or by those professionals involved with the family before the death. Outreach work has been shown to be of value (Black and Urbanowicz 1987) but the resource implications are enormous and beyond our own Service.

We find that at whatever stage the family comes for counselling some of the bereavement work can be undertaken, but it is likely that further help may be needed at different stages of the family's adjustment to the death. The individual child has to make fresh adjustments with each developmental stage.

Conclusions

The value of family work is seen when family members can talk directly to each other about their sad feelings, sharing their confusion and their longings, and when they develop more confidence in how to help each other and in their own unique place in the family. The counsellor can provide the support of an experienced guide in this territory previously unfamiliar to the family. We can offer the family the assurance that others have learned to bear what now seems unbearable. Some families gain support from their religious beliefs and this framework is helpful for children if allowance is also made for the expression of everyone's sad feelings and an admission that no one 'knows' exactly what happens after death. It does help children if adults can admit to some uncertainties.

A useful metaphor in bereavement work is of a family sharing an unwelcome and difficult journey into unknown territory with each person needing the support of the other. Most people feel that a shared journey is safer than travelling alone. Adults have their previous experiences to draw on but they also need to be alive to any new experiences on the journey. This metaphor allows for even the youngest child to make important contributions that help the whole family on the journey, for example as on any family expedition by finding a vital direction, track and so forth, which the older members may miss. Similarly, in family bereavement work the youngest child can help everyone stay on the right track if we can make the space to listen. Children can offer the family valuable insights into everyone's feelings and needs and uncertainties. They can also display their own special courage and vitality in getting on with life after the bereavement, which can set very helpful examples to the rest of the family. For most bereaved parents their love and concern for their family provide their strongest motivation to struggle on through the difficult early months and years.

Bereavement work can be very demanding emotionally on everyone involved. For the counsellor it can bring its own special rewards in the close relationship with the bereaved and in the privilege of accompanying a sad family on a part of their bereavement journey, seeing them resume some of their former activities and begin to have fun together again. Of course most families manage this journey without professional help and support, with only a small proportion seeking help.

In the process of coming to terms with grief and loss the unique place of the dead person within the family needs to be honoured. A child's birth-parent can never be replaced, and the memory of that person needs to be maintained within the family. Research now confirms the importance of this (Stroebe *et al.* 1993 p.311) Bereavement counselling can be seen as a helpful means of facilitating this process for some children and their families and especially for those families who have extra need for support.

It has been known for some time that the long term outcome for bereaved children depends not only on the loss but on the quality of physical and emotional care that they receive after a bereavement. When a bereaved family is under stress family bereavement counselling can make an important contribution to the emotional well-being of the child and family both in the present and for the future.

References

Black, D. and Urbanowicz, M.A. (1987) 'Family intervention with bereaved children.' *Journal of Child Psychology and Psychiatry 28*, 467–476.

Capewell, E. (1994) 'Responding to children in trauma: a systems approach for schools.' *Bereavement Care 13*, 1. Richmond, Surrey: Cruse.

Cruse – Bereavement Care (1993) *Supporting Bereaved Children*, Training Manual. Richmond, Surrey: Cruse.

Dyregrov, A. (1994) 'Childhood bereavement: consequences and therapeutic approaches.' *Journal of Child Psychology and Psychiatry Newsletter,* July, 173–82.

Harris Hendriks, J., Black, D. and Kaplan, T, (1993) *When Father Kills Mother.* London: Routledge.

Hollins, S. and Sireling, L. (1989) *When Dad Died.* Cambridge: Silent Books.

Johnson, J.H. (1982) 'Life events as stressors in childhood and adolescence.' *Advances in Clinical Psychology and Psychiatry 8.* California: Sage.

Lieberman, S. (1978) *Transgenerational Family Therapy.* London: Croom-Helm.

Marlin, E. (1989) *Genograms.* Chicago: Contemporary Books.

Stroebe, M., Stroebe, W. and Hansson, R. (1993) *Handbook of Bereavement.* Cambridge: Cambridge University Press.

Turner, S. (1987) *Up to Date.* London: Hodder and Stoughton.

Worden, J.W. (1991) *Grief Counselling and Grief Therapy.* London: Tavistock/Routledge.

Further Reading
Dyregrov, A. (1991) *Grief in Children, A Handbook for Adults.* London: Jessica Kingsley Publishers.

Gersie, A. (1991) *Storymaking in Bereavement.* London: Jessica Kingsley Publishers.

Grementz, J. (1981) *How it Feels when a Parent Dies.* London: Gollancz Children's Paperbacks (reprinted 1991).

Kubler-Ross, E. (1983) *On Children and Death.* London: Macmillan.

Parkes, C.M. (1986) *Bereavement.* London: Pelican (2nd edition).

Perkins, G. and Morris, L. (1991) *Remembering Mum.* London: Black.

Pincus, L. (1976) *Death in the Family.* London: Faber and Faber.

Part Three

Groupwork

CHAPTER 8

Creative Groupwork Methods with Bereaved Children

Margaret Pennells and Susan C. Smith

Introduction

Working creatively with bereaved children was a challenge to us when we decided to adopt a groupwork approach. It remains a challenge. However, we have learned a great deal over the last seven years and have gathered ideas from many sources, refined and adapted them for different age groups and invented new ones along the way.

When we began in 1988 there appeared to be little or no structured groupwork for bereaved children, so our initial task was to examine why we should choose a groupwork approach and then to set out our aims and objectives. This has been documented in detail (Dwivedi 1993) along with the organizational aspects of our work and our evaluation methods. Further examples of organizational issues appear in other chapters in this book and we cannot emphasize sufficiently how important it is to be fully aware of the groundwork necessary for running effective groups.

Our second task was to establish a programme with therapeutic methods that would guide children through the stages of grief and enable them to express their feelings appropriately. This chapter aims to describe some of the methods we have found to be helpful in this task.

Beginnings

The beginning of our therapeutic work is an important time for establishing trusting relationships and creating an atmosphere that will encourage open dialogue between ourselves and the group members. We use a number of trust building and icebreaking games to begin this process.

Food and Drink / Good News, Bad News

As our group starts after school and the children are often hungry when they arrive we begin each session with food and drink: this simply consists of fruit squash and biscuits or cakes but it is a symbol of caring and sharing that brings the children together as they help with the preparation and serving.

Whilst we are eating and drinking we have a round of good news and bad news with each person, including the group workers, sharing one good event and one bad event that has happened in the last week. Beginning in this gentle non-threatening way is a good way of fostering trust and openness within the group, and along with the following games, it acts as a preparation for the more serious work of the group.

Ice Breaking Games

We begin the 'getting to know you' process with games we have found in the *Gamesters' Handbook* (Brandes and Phillips 1990). Our first game is a ball throwing exercise where we throw a soft ball or cushion to another member of the group and say our name. The game then changes slightly so that the person who throws the ball says the name of the person to whom they have thrown it. This can continue for a few minutes or until everyone has a grasp of names.

We follow this simple exercise by pairing the children and asking them to interview each other, discovering their likes and dislikes. Various suggestions are made to start the children off. These may include mention of their favourite pop group, food, or colour, and how many pets, brothers/sisters they have. The group workers take part in the exercise thereby assisting in trust building. Approximately ten minutes are allowed for this exercise, as we have observed that the children often get side-tracked and restless if left too long. After the allocated time the children rejoin the larger group and 'introduce' their partner to the others, relating the information they have gathered.

The group workers then re-pair the children with different partners (thereby mixing the group further) to complete the next exercise which, as the questions are a little more revealing, is designed to extend self-disclosure. The children ask each other what their funniest moment was, their saddest moment, most embarrassing moment and what their ambition or wish for the future is. As before, they feedback to the large group the information they have gathered. We often find that the children say that their saddest moment is the time their relative died. However, some children do not feel ready to disclose such information at this point.

Use of Stories

Stories told to children not only capture their imagination but help them to identify with the characters in the stories. There are now a number of books for children on bereavement and bereavement issues. Some stories 'distance' the bereavement by casting the characters as animals who experience the same things as humans, for example *Badger's Parting Gifts*, (Varley 1984) and *Fred* (Simmonds 1987).

From the story the children can see how the animals solve their problems and it gives them confidence that they too can cope and manage their feelings. These stories also aid discussion and enable the children to express how their circumstances were similar/different to the animals in the story. Stories also increase a child's knowledge, and there are some useful books that tell of funerals, how to say goodbye and so forth. Such books include *When Uncle Bob Died* (Althea 1982), *Remembering Grandad* (Padoan 1987), and *Emma Says Goodbye* (Nystrom 1990).

In our group for children aged six to eight years we have based each session around a story or part of a story which takes the children through the grieving process.

Story Wheel

Children themselves can be imaginative and create their own story. The children can sit either in a circle with their backs to each other, or lie on their back on the floor with their heads towards the centre (this formation prevents distraction). Someone begins a story, for example 'There was a girl called Sarah...' then each group member takes it in turn to add a piece to the story. The story often turns into a bereavement situation giving the children a chance to express situations and feelings through the use of a third party or situation. This 'distancing' lessens the trauma of the situation and makes it more manageable.

Bambi Story

This bibliotherapy exercise is taken from the book *Bambi* (Salten 1928). It is the conversation between two leaves left hanging on a tree. They are wondering who will be next to go and what happens afterwards. To begin the exercise the group is asked to shut their eyes and to get comfortable, before the Bambi story is read to them.

Everyone is given a piece of paper and pencil, and asked to pretend to be the leaves in the story and to write a letter to the tree. On completion of their letters the children are asked to fold them in half and they are then collected up, shuffled and given out again, making sure that children do not get their own letters back. Each child then reads the letter they received and writes an answer to the leaf as if it were from the tree. When they have finished writing their replies the children are asked to fold the letters back so that everyone can see their own handwriting; then they retrieve their own letter with its reply. Time is then given for people to read their replies and to discuss the task together. This exercise helps children to look at unresolved grief reactions, the inability to say 'goodbye' and raises questions about after life.

Positive Recall

Bereaved children may have experienced prolonged periods of upheaval, resulting in much confusion and insecurity. This stress accumulates with the trauma of the actual loss until children are left feeling very miserable and somewhat negative about their world and the people in it. Even the prospect of attending the group can initially be viewed negatively as the child is anxious about meeting new people and worried about how painful the experience might be. It is often useful in working with bereaved children to begin by helping them recall happy memories of the deceased. This is less threatening than the more painful issues which can be tackled once a relationship, trust and confidence have been built up between the child and workers. Recalling happy, positive memories of the deceased also engages the child in the early stages of grief work when idolization of the dead person can occur. After the traumatic experience of a bereavement it is helpful for the child to 'hang on' to good memories and to treasure the good times they had with the deceased. This is extremely important where children have hitherto had a negative model of relationships (as in cases of abuse) where their positive memories may have been buried under unpleasant experiences. Encouragement and sensitivity will be needed to uncover these happy memories. Some children may feel they have no memories of the deceased, possibly because the child was very young when the person died, and they therefore cannot easily recall times spent with them. In such situations it can be useful to have siblings attend the same group, they may be able to provide information which will stimulate recall. With younger children recall can also be helped by reading to them a story concerned with positive memories of the deceased. We have used *My Grandson Lew* (Zolotow 1976), and *Badger's Parting Gifts* (Varley 1985).

Phototherapy

This is another technique which can aid recall in a positive form. Here children can cut out of magazines pictures of people that remind them of the deceased. This allows the worker to ask further questions about the pictures selected and gives an opportunity for the child to talk about the picture rather than the deceased person directly. For example, the group worker can choose features of the picture selected and expand on them:-

JANE: 'I like people with grey hair'

WORKER: 'Did you know anyone with grey hair?'

JANE: 'Yes, my Gran – she died. She was so kind to me.'

The child can go on to make a collage of a scene he/she wishes to create around the pictures chosen.

Link Object

Children can also be asked to bring a link object to a session. This may be something which once belonged to the deceased such as an item of clothing, jewellery and so forth, or a gift that previously was given to the child by the deceased. Often children choose to bring family photographs which can link with a happy memory. Whatever the object, it is likely to generate discussion and questions from both the workers and the other group members giving a further opportunity for the children to explore their feelings.

Use of Art

Art is a non-threatening tool which enables a child to explore and release feelings. The permanence of the object produced is one of the benefits of art therapy: it is a spontaneous creation and not subject to memory distortion (Rose 1988). Most children at some stage find language and verbal communication difficult, especially when it comes to the expression of emotions and feelings. Drawing and painting offers a very effective non-verbal means of communication. Art work also helps children express and test out numerous anxieties they may have about life, and overcome such concerns (Segal 1984). Most art therapy has been undertaken on an individual basis (Simon 1992) although art therapy for groups is becoming more widely known and used (Dalley 1993). In our group, art is used both for individual work and expression, as well as being presented as a group task.

Individual Tasks

(1) **Happy memories**: Following our exercises of Positive Recall (see p.144) it is helpful for the child to make their memories more tangible by drawing a picture of a happy time spent with the person before they died. This may be an outing, holiday or everyday occurrence which remains special in the child's memory. Some children may choose to use clay to sculpt a scene rather than to draw it.

(2) Children may be asked to draw a picture of **the day they were told about the death**: (we ask them to do this after showing them our video *That Morning I Went to School* (1993) which acts as a preparation and prompt for them to tell their own story). The drawings they produce are often vivid and contain what was significant from the child's perception of the situation. One child in our group, whose mother had collapsed and died on the street, drew a picture of the day it happened. The adults assumed the children upstairs had not known what was going on. Anna drew what she saw and the panic she felt!

(3) **Saying Goodbye**: Many children find themselves excluded from the events following a death. A gap in children's knowledge and experience is thus created. Children's last memories are often of seeing the person ill, dying or dead, then

visiting a plot of earth, rosebush or plaque. They may not have attended the funeral, been consulted or included in the choosing of a headstone or the inscription on it.

This issue is addressed by helping the children look at ways we say 'goodbye' to the deceased. They are given cuttings of the obituary columns from newspapers to read and discuss. They are shown poems written by adults and children, and after a visit to a cemetery or stonemasons, they are encouraged to create in paint or other art material, their own headstone for the deceased. The children are allowed to choose the headstone design and the words with which they would like it inscribed. A child's cultural background is important here as the rites and rituals surrounding burials will vary according to cultural and religious beliefs.

(4) **The Future**: Asking the children to draw what they think will be happening to them in a year's time and projecting themselves forward to five years' time is a helpful way to look at the resolution phase of grief. Children are able, through their art work, to realize that their life will go on and that they can survive the changes that a bereavement brings about. This exercise also helps children to acknowledge that the powerful feelings they have in the present, could lessen with time. The art work produced may also reveal anxieties and insecurities that the children have, such as not being sure who will be in their family in the future; for example someone else may die. Through this exercise the children, particularly adolescents, are helped to assess what has happened to them and how the bereavement and its sequelae may change the course of their future. One teenager from our groups realized as she drew her projection of five years, that her subjects for higher study would probably be different now her father had died. He had helped her with her maths and geography, but the bereavement experience was leading her to want to study psychology.

(5) **Colouring feelings**: Each child is given an outline of a body on a piece of paper and coloured pens which represent different feelings, for example blue = sad; black = fear and so on. They are asked to colour the parts of the body where they feel these feelings. A similar exercise can be found in Heegaard (1988). This exercise helps the children to identify where in their body they experience their feelings and what feelings predominate. One child in our group coloured the face and chest blue (sad) and the hands and legs, black (fear) saying he shook when feeling fearful; another child coloured the whole of the body red (anger) as he felt this was the main feeling with which he had to cope.

Group Tasks
(1) **The Death Mural**. This exercise requires a large piece of paper (about one metre square) with the word 'Death' written in the centre of it. The children are encouraged to draw around it the images and symbols they associate with death, for example angels, graves, ghosts, skeletons, churches, worms, crosses.

This inevitably gives rise to discussion about the more frightening aspects of death, the nightmares children may be experiencing, or their confused ideas surrounding what happens to bodies after death. Some children have related how they were taunted by others saying 'I bet the worms are eating your dad' or 'Your house will be haunted'. Many children report nightmares concerning ghosts and a few report actually being 'visited' by the dead person. The discussions that emerge help to lessen fears and gives rise to understanding of hitherto confused ideas. This is an opportunity for group leaders to note any problems that may be worked on at a later stage, for example the handling of difficult peer group situations (see Conflict Situations, p.151).

(2) **The Group Mural**. As an ending exercise for each session a group mural can be produced. Using a very large sheet of paper (or several taped together) we ask each child to depict what they feel about the day or the session. This can result in many and varied drawings and in the past have included rain, clouds, sunshine, angry scrawls and so forth. The drawings accumulate over the weeks, and a completed mural symbolizes their experiences in the group. It is photographed on the last session and each person receives a copy as a lasting momento of their attendance.

(3) **The Flower Mural**. A useful exercise for saying goodbye to the group when the programme is over is to draw the outline of a large daisy like flower having one petal for each group member. The children then draw on their petal something they feel they have worked through during the time of their attendance at the group and can now leave behind. We then use balls of coloured tissue paper to cover over what they have drawn, thereby leaving a brightly coloured flower in its place. This symbolizes that painful and difficult issues can be transformed into something positive. A group photograph of the children is taken with the flower collage, once again providing a lasting momento of the group.

Expression of Feeling

It is often difficult for children and young people to own feelings and to discuss them openly with others. In our group programme we use various methods to elicit these feelings and gently bring each child around to owning these experiences for themselves.

Loss Cards

To demonstrate that feelings associated with being bereaved can also be experienced in other loss situations, we help group members understand that we only have one set of emotions, and that we do not invent new ones for different situations. To develop this understanding we ask the children (usually

those over nine years of age) to pair up and brainstorm the feelings they might
have if they found themselves in the following circumstances:

(1) You are five years old and you are lost. What do you feel?

(2) You discover you are to move to Scotland in the morning with no
     chance to say goodbye to your friends. What do you feel?

(3) You are to captain your sports team at the county games but you fall
     and break your leg. What do you feel?

(4) You thought you were to play the lead role in the Christmas play but
     the part has been given to someone else. What do you feel?

The object of this exercise is to help the children understand that other loss
situations can generate similar feelings to those experienced at times of
bereavement, and that they may face such feelings and situations at any time
during their lives. As we use senarios rather than the individuals life events we
effectively remove the pressure upon them to relate their own experience.
However, it is impossible to do this exercise without putting something of
oneself into it and group members may in any case already have experienced
similar situations. This undertaking is a gentle lead in to self-disclosure done
initially within a pair rather than in a larger group. Finally, the spokesperson
for the pair then writes the feelings elicited up on a large sheet of paper to
which the other pairs contribute, gradually bringing the individuals together
into a united experience.

Brainstorming

The feelings that were elicited from the last exercise are used as a way of
producing a more extensive brainstorm. At this juncture we ask the group
members to get in touch with their negative feelings concerning the death and
being bereaved. As the words accumulate on the sheet of paper we draw
attention to the similarities between feelings in other loss situations and feelings
in bereavement: for example frightened, panic, anxious, alone and so on.
Another object of this exercise is being able to show the young people that
they have been able to cope with negative feelings and situations in the past.
These experiences can prepare them to cope with their current intense feelings
about bereavement.

Body Exercise

We have extended the brainstorming technique into the next exercise where we
ask the young people to visualize their feelings into objects. Initially this was
done to provide a further outlet for the expression of feeling; however, we
quickly realized that it also showed a connection between feelings and behaviour, and feelings and physical illness. Often a child's painful memories, fears,

confused feelings, and unexpressed emotions are held within and are not given vent in a positive way – this may lead to the feelings being expressed in a psychosomatic or bodily reaction, for example headache, stomach-ache, feeling sick, or pains in the legs.

From the brainstorm sheet prepared earlier we write each individual feeling on a card (approximately 15cm x 5cm) making sure there is one card per child for each of the feelings (i.e., six happy cards, six sad cards, and so on). We then spread these cards in piles around the floor. We ask the children to walk around the room and pick up the feelings they felt the most when they were first bereaved. Group members can choose as many feelings cards as they wish, and some collect one of each feeling whilst others are more selective. This part of the exercise symbolizes the 'owning' of feelings. The card is a tangible representation of their feeling and they have had to pick it up and carry it around with them. We then ask group members to choose from their cards the two feelings they feel the most and to explain these to the group. This encourages the children to focus for a short time on the most difficult of their feelings and often results in a deeper exploration of a particularly troublesome issue and the attainment of a better perspective.

The exercise is extended further by asking the participants to symbolize these two feelings in a drawing – turning these feelings into objects. For example, what would anger look like or be if it were a thing, what would depression be if it were a thing. This is another outlet for expression and, in addition, it gives the children a clue to the intensity of their feelings while making them more tangible. We often find that 'anger' is expressed as a hot fire or a roaring lion. Other examples such as 'confusion' have been drawn as a house with furniture on the ceiling. After the children have spent ten to fifteen minutes on the drawings we ask for a volunteer to lie on a large sheet of paper whilst someone draws around them producing a large body outline. We then ask group members in turn to place their feeling picture where they feel it the most in their body. Frequently the majority of feelings are placed either in the stomach area or in the head; however, there are times when they will be placed in legs, arms, hands or heart. This is done to demonstrate how feelings affect behaviour and health. If they are feeling angry and have placed their drawing on the feet or hands it might suggest why they kick or hit out at people, or if they place confusion in the head it might suggest why they suffer from headaches, or have problems with concentration or attainment at school.

This exercise breaks feelings down into manageable parts and then brings them together into a 'whole experience'. We find this most useful with children from the age of eight years upwards. It does not seem to be too difficult for the younger children to grasp but they often need some assistance to begin to spark the imagination.

Group Yell

A further way to release feelings is for the group to join together in a group yell (Brandes and Phillips 1990). We all form a circle and join hands, crouching down on our haunches. We take a big breath and begin to make a low humming sound, and as we unfold our bodies and stand up the hum gets louder and louder until we finally jump in the air raising our arms above our heads with our voices at screaming pitch. It is surprising how freeing this exercise can be, and the young ones love the chance legitimately to make as much noise as they can! The yell may be repeated two or three times for maximum effect.

Use of Drama

Drama is a creative technique which involves the acting out of problems, conflicts and relationships (Stephenson 1993). It is essentially play guided by the worker and gives an opportunity for children and young people to *experience* rather than just discuss. Self-discovery is often gained by seeing a situation brought to life, and less verbal children often find the use of drama particularly useful.

Acting out a Funeral

This exercise is useful for the group workers to explore myths amongst the members of the group who have not had the opportunity to attend a funeral. We have asked many groups to participate in this exercise and we never cease to be amazed by the number of children who confuse a burial with a funeral. They often have no real idea about the ritual that takes place before a coffin is finally buried. More often now we find the deceased will have been cremated and the children do not always know that a service of some kind takes place beforehand.

Initially, we ask the children to devise a play about a funeral using dressing up materials and a toy such as a teddy or doll. They then perform their play for the group leaders. A discussion follows about the different elements of their enactment and sometimes this results in the children wanting to re-think their drama and re-act it in the light of new information gained during the discussion. For example, one child was not aware that hymns may be sung and prayers said. Other children have said they did not know what a hearse was or that flowers were sent.

This exercise is also useful for children who have been to a funeral, to share their knowledge and thus help those members of the group who have little or no experience. It provides these children with a sense of contribution to the group by using their own expertise instead of that of the group workers.

Conflict Situations

Another area where drama can be effective is in looking at problems caused by peer reactions, such as teasing and unkind remarks. Situations like these often result in the bereaved child retaliating and ultimately getting into trouble with teachers. They may also find themselves getting into conflict situations at home with a parent or care giver when emotions run high and there is a difference in expectations of one another. This can result in arguments and punishments which the child (rightly or wrongly) feels are unjust. We use role play to act out such situations, asking the group members to create alternative endings which might give them increased control over their actions and ultimately over the outcome of the situation.

Sculpting

'Sculpting' as a technique was developed by Frederick Duhl (Duhl, Kantor and Duhl 1973). Its essential feature is that family members can be placed so that they represent aspects of the family's relationships and dynamics. This technique was used mainly in Family Therapy (Barker 1986), but we have adapted it to illustrate changes in families following a death. Relationships and alliances are easier to understand as they become three-dimensional and are acted out in a neutral environment. Sculpting is a particularly powerful medium to use with teenagers who can more fully appreciate the concept of the 'still-life', but it is also effective with children from approximately nine years of age.

Each child is asked to 'sculpt' their family using the other group members to play the parts of mum, dad, siblings etc. The players are positioned in a 'freeze frame', behaving as they would have done before the death occurred. For example, Peter's mother enjoyed being in the kitchen cooking. Therefore Peter placed the young person acting as mother at an imaginary cooker to the left of the room with a smile on her face. Dad was always watching TV, therefore the child acting as dad was placed in a chair some distance from mum. This process continues until all the members of the family are positioned. The group workers also join in but do not necessarily take the adult roles and could easily find themselves playing a two-year-old with temper tantrums! The child whose family is being 'sculpted' is asked by the group leaders whether the participants look happy, sad, ill, whether they were close or distant, got on well or not and so on, until a real feeling of the family, however it existed, can be experienced. Each player is then asked what they feel being that person and these contributions are discussed. The group leader then asks the person who died to leave the tableau and the child to re-position everyone according to the changes in their role. For example, when Peter's mother died, dad took over mum's jobs in the kitchen and Peter watched TV instead. Group members are all asked again how it feels to be that person. It is at this point that the child may become aware for the first time how the surviving parent or sibling feels about the changes in the family. They are hearing someone else's perspective instead of their own.

The person playing the deceased is also asked to speak and some comments have been:

'I didn't want to die and leave you.'

'I'm sad you are all fighting now I have gone,'

'I'm sorry to see how sad you all are.'

Again the child is helped to see a new dimension, as they may not have considered how the deceased would view having to leave their family.

The last part of this exercise is to ask the child how they would want their family to be in the future. Once more the players are moved around, perhaps displaying how arguments can be resolved and members of the family grow close together again. Sometimes the opposite occurs with the young people wishing to remove themselves from the family altogether or maybe a co-habitee is removed and the deceased replaced. A discussion takes place as before, about how each member feels and whether or not this outcome is achievable. The reality, of course, is that the deceased cannot return and how the young person deals with this is also discussed.

Use of Music

Music can set the scene for using the imagination. It helps the listener to explore and discover the inner self and is a venue for emotional release. Its healing power has long been recognized (Alvin 1966). The music needs to be unfamiliar, soothing and relaxing so that imagery and projection can occur. There are now a number of relaxation and mood music tapes which are commercially available (e.g. New World cassettes and Inner Harmonies).

Fantasy Journey

This is a guided fantasy using quiet background music. The journey is always framed in a positive mood and consists of a meeting with the deceased. Although we aim for this to be a happy meeting leaders should be aware that this exercise can evoke powerful and sad memories. The children are prepared for this exercise by getting them to relax in a warm, dimly lit room. They can do this by sitting comfortably or by lying on the floor in a circle with their heads in the centre. Gentle, soothing relaxation music is played while the leader takes the group on the guided fantasy. The journey starts by getting group members to place themselves in a favourite, happy place such as the countryside, the seaside, their bedroom and so forth, and to become aware of the sights, smells and sounds around them. Then the leader introduces them to the fact that someone, in the distance, has appeared in their scene, and as this person gets closer and closer they realize it is the person they know who died. They happily greet the deceased person and a conversation takes place, and perhaps questions are asked. However, there comes a time to say goodbye and the participants need to be prepared for this. The deceased person walks away into the distance and disappears. The children are then made aware again of the room they are in and they gradually open their eyes bringing themselves back into reality.

This exercise helps children to look at any unresolved issues – it gives them a chance to say what they would have liked to have said to the deceased, to ask questions and perhaps gain reassurance that 'all is well' both with the deceased and with those left behind. Some children find this exercise very sad as it confirms in them the fact that their loved one is dead. This task is part of actualizing the loss and is therefore a very important step in the process of the group work and in moving the children on to another stage of grief.

However, it may emerge that some children are not yet ready to move on. One teenager said 'I stopped doing the fantasy journey in my mind because I realized I was not yet ready to say goodbye to my dad.' Another said 'I felt bad at the awful way I had behaved since my dad died, I felt he knew what was going on and in my fantasy he talked about it with me. I knew he wouldn't like what I was doing now and would be disappointed in me.'

Additional Uses

Music may also be used as a background to art work. Soft music can be played while the child draws a picture of heaven, peace and so on. Children can use percussion instruments to help them express suppressed and hostile feelings, for example using cymbals, drums and tambourines, after a discussion about anger.

Education

Although education has not been stressed as an aim in bereavement work (e.g. Worden 1991) we feel that for children this is a vital element to help them pass appropriately and effectively through the stages of grief and mourning. In working with bereaved children in a group setting, the gaps in their knowledge, their fears and confusions become apparent and these issues are addressed by the following exercises which we call 'Educational Visits'

Visit to a Cemetery

As some children have not taken part in the ritual of burial, they often hold confused and ambivalent feelings as to what a cemetery is. This outing is most useful for children age six and upwards who have been excluded from the funeral or those who find it difficult to visit the grave of their deceased. However we find it less necessary with teenagers as they are more frequently included in the rites of passage.

Before embarking on such a visit parents'/carers' permission is obtained and the children are prepared by setting the visit in an educational context. This means choosing a cemetery that is unknown to the children and therefore would not be associated with their own experiences of visiting a grave. The children are provided with worksheets, a tool which enables them to roam freely around the cemetery and to examine the various stages of internment and the headstones. The worksheet contains various questions such as, how many different shaped headstones are there, what was your favourite epitaph, what was the oldest or newest grave seen. Inevitably many questions are raised by the children as they go round, and many of their fears and fantasies can be resolved. One child in our group thought that she was treading on the dead person and did not realize the body is buried several feet underground. Some children may find the thought of this visit difficult as cemeteries can be portrayed as frightening places that are associated with ghosts and vampires, or are linked to the children's fear of the unknown and their fantasies about what has happened to the deceased's body. This exercise may help these children as we encourage them to come with the rest of the group but do not pressure them into entering the cemetery: a group worker can remain apart at a short distance with the child/ren and use the opportunity to discuss why they have these fears and fantasies.

Visit to a Monumental Mason

A visit to a monumental stonemason can be a very exciting and worthwhile trip which expands children's knowledge and experience. They can be shown all the different stones used in the making of a headstone, the different shape they can take (crosses, books, and so on) what can be put on them (pictures, photographs) and how the lettering is put on the stone. It is helpful if the children have the chance to see not only how this is done by computer, but also shown the art of chipping out the letters. The visit also serves as a prelude to encouraging them to design on paper a headstone for their deceased person, as again, the choice of a headstone is something in which children are rarely involved.

Cultural Aspects of Bereavement

A cultural approach to bereavement brings a richness and valuable experience to the lives of children. It is possible that the group itself is composed of children from different ethnic backgrounds. Whether this is so or not, it is of great educational value to learn how other cultures approach death and bereavement and to gain an understanding of their rites and rituals. However, this may need discussion with some parents who may not wish their children to be exposed to the views of other faiths. We believe that it is important that no one doctrine, religion or culture is imposed on the group and provide a wide educational approach to the children, who learn that there are various views on death and after-life, and how one can grieve and mourn. As well as drawing on the personal experiences of group members, the use of books about different cultures is useful, especially those with illustrations (e.g. Williams and Ross 1983).

We use photographs of graves, burial places and so on that we have collected on our trips both at home and abroad. The children find these fascinating and they are stimulated to ask lots of questions.

Use of a Question Box

A question box is left out during each group session for children to write down any questions they may have and to put them in the box anonymously. At some stage in the group (usually about the middle of the programme) we open the box and the questions are read out. A debate usually takes place drawing first on the thoughts and ideas of group members. Questions are asked, such as:

> 'What happens to the body after you're dead?'

> 'Is there an after-life?'

> 'What is a cremation?'

> 'What is meant by suicide?'

Once the group have tried to answer the questions, the group leaders may need to provide some education on the chosen topics, discussed in a way that children's misunderstandings, misconceptions, fears and fantasies are cleared up. Sometimes the group leaders will need to be honest and say that they do not know the answer, or that there is no one clear answer as people have different ideas and views. Respect for differing cultures and religious beliefs needs to be integral to the group ethos if children are to be helped to learn to respect others while their understanding and knowledge develops.

Videos

Use of the media also provides education for the children. Children learn from watching and observing others, hearing what they say and seeing how they solve problems. When we first began our groups, we tried to find suitable video material that would help the children understand what others in a similar situation had been through. We could, however, only find material of adults talking about their bereavement experiences. This bore little resemblance to what the children themselves experienced. We therefore made our own video material which has been available publicly since 1991 when it also won the Social Work Today Award. The two videos, *That Morning I Went to School* and *Childhood Grief* come together with a booklet 'Guidelines For Working with Bereaved Children' which can be bought or hired separately or as a pack. The video is divided into sections with topics for discussion being easily identifiable.

This video material is useful both in the group setting and may also be useful for class-room viewing and discussion. Topics covered include how do children get to hear about a bereavement, what feelings do they have, should children attend funerals.

We find that showing the video to the children in the group helps them to tell their story, as they can often identify with the children presented.

Endings

Ending each session is as important as ending the entire group experience. It became obvious to us at a very early stage that we would need to structure the end of particular sessions to avoid the children leaving the group feeling unsupported or distressed. Free time to run about, play and socialize with the other members is important but special attention should be paid to particularly emotional sessions. The presentation of a game to liven things up if they are subdued or one to quieten them down if the session has been a lively discussion or role play is useful. The *Gamesters' Handbook* (Brandes and Phillips 1990) is a useful source of ideas and the children themselves can be inventive too. It is always much more difficult to play games with teenagers; they often feel self-conscious and that its 'just for kids'. We have found a good way to unwind is to use *relaxation techniques*, sometimes accompanied by music. We spend three or four minutes taking the group members through an imaginary sequence, for example:

> Imagine you are in a meadow and walking towards a stream, you sit on the bank and put your bare feet into the water and as the stream flows it soaks away all of today's troubles and upsets...

> Or: Imagine you are on an escalator going up and when you reach the top you are in a completely empty room where you sit in the middle, you think of all the unpleasant, unhappy things that have happened today that you would like to leave behind; fill up the empty space with these thoughts.

These exercises can be embellished as you go along and we are sure there are many variations which practioners may choose to use. Before beginning the actual journey it is important to set the scene by asking the participants to close their eyes, relax and regulate their breathing. It is equally important to bring group members gently back to the here and now before ending the exercise, again focusing on breathing and perhaps the sounds and smells of the room. These exercises can be useful when sleeping is a problem or when a young person is particularly stressed. We have found that, on the whole, these exercises have been well received and we have often provided a typed selection of them for the group members to take away when the group ends.

Table 8.1 Groupwork Exercises

Stages of Grief	Exercises	Age Range
Shock	Use of stories or Story Wheel	6–8 years
Numbness	*Bambi* story	9+ years
Disbelief	Phototherapy	All ages
	Link object	All ages
	Drawing happy memories	All ages
	Fantasy journey	9+ years
Anger	Use of video	All ages
Guilt	Brainstorming	All ages
Denial	Feelings and Body outline	8+ years
	Group Yell	6–11 years
	Death Mural	All ages
	Loss Cards	9+ years
	Use of Music	6–11 years
Yearning	Question Box	All ages
	Cemetery Visit	6–11 years
	Monumental Mason	9+ years
	Acting out Funeral	6–11 years
	Sculpting	9+ years
Acceptance	Use of Poems	9+ years
	Conflict situations – role play	6–11 years
	Epitaph/Headstone design	All ages
	Projections of Future	9+ years
	Group Mural	All ages
	Flower Mural	6–11 years

Other Exercises

	Relaxation	12+ years
	Icebreaking Games	All ages
	Support package	12+ years
	Workfolders	6–11 years
	Cultural aspects	All ages
	Food and drink	All ages
	Good news/Bad news	All ages

The relaxation exercises form part of the *support package* we provide. This consists of work sheets taken from *Good Grief* (Ward 1993) and poems, epitaphs and other writing by young people. For the younger group members we provide folders which contain the artwork and writing they have completed throughout the programme. These are taken home at the end of the group as a memento of their time in the group and they can be shared with parents or carers if the child wishes.

Summary

We have selectively used the methods we have described in age appropriate programmes. We do not use all of them all of the time, but we have found it effective to have a diverse selection which enables us to be flexible in our approach. For example, not all six- to eight-year-old children will respond in the same way and we alter our programme accordingly, varying the method to suit the needs of the group. The following table (Table 8.1) can be used as a guideline for the reader to select an appropriate exercise according to either the age range or the stage of grief the children may be going through.

You may find that you wish to try an exercise designed for one age group, with another age group. The guideline is simply that, and we encourage you to be creative with these tasks, perhaps adapting them for use in individual work with children and young people. No matter which exercise you choose the overriding philosophy is that the children are given a safe outlet for hitherto unreleased feelings or emotions.

We have found working with children using a groupwork approach stimulating, rewarding and enjoyable, even if at times a little difficult and emotional. It has been a privilege to journey with the children through their painful bereavements, and they have taught us much about their world of grief.

References

Althea (1982) *When Uncle Bob Died*. London: Dinosaur, Collins.

Alvin, J. (1966) *Music Therapy*. London: John Barker.

Barker, P. (1986) *Basic Family Therapy*. London: Collins.

Brandes, D. and Phillips, H. (1990) *Gamesters' Handbook*. Cheltenham: Stanley Thornes.

Dalley, T. (1993) 'Art psychotherapy groups.' In K.N. Dwivedi (ed) *Group Work with Children and Adolescents*. London: Jessica Kingsley Publishers.

Dwivedi, K.N. (ed) (1993) *Group Work with Children and Adolescents*. London: Jessica Kingsley Publishers.

Duhl, F.J., Kantor, D. and Duhl, B.S. (1973) 'Learning space and action in family therapy: a primer of sculpture.' In D.A. Bloch (ed) *Techniques of Family Psychotherapy*. New York: Grune and Stratton.

Heegaard, M. (1988) *When Someone Very Special Dies*. USA: Woodland Press.

New World Cassettes, 'Music for Relaxation and Inspiration', Paradise Farm, Westhall, Halesworth, Suffolk, IP19 8BR.

Inner Harmonies, 182 Southfield Road, Chiswick, London, W4 5LD.

Nystrom, C. (1990) *Emma Says Goodbye*. Oxford: Lion.

Padoan, G. (1987) *Remembering Grandad*. Italy: Happy Books.

Rose, E. (1988), 'Art therapy – a brief guide.' *Adoption and Fostering 12*, 1, 48–51.

Salten, F. (1928) *Bambi*. London: Jonathan Cape. (Glasgow: Collins, 1946.)

Segal, R.M. (1984) 'Helping children express grief through symbolic communication.' *Social Case Work 25*, 10, 590–599.

Simon, R (1992) *Symbolism of Style*. London: Routledge.

Simmonds, P. (1987) *Fred*. London: Puffin Books.

Stephenson, C. (1993), 'Use of Drama'. In K.N. Dwivedi (ed) *Group Work with Children and Adolescents*. London: Jessica Kingsley Publishers.

Varley, S. (1985) *Badger's Parting Gifts*. London: Picture Lions.

Video (1991), 'That morning I went to school', and 'Childhood Grief', Margaret Pennells and Sue Smith.

Ward, B. and associates (1993) *Good Grief* (Vol.1: *Exploring Feelings, Loss and Death with Under Elevens*. Vol.2: *Exploring Feelings, Loss and Death with Over Elevens and Adults*). London: Jessica Kingsley Publishers.

Williams, G. and Ross, J. (1983) *When People Die*. Edinburgh: Macdonald.

Worden, J. William (1991) *Grief Counselling and Grief Therapy*. London: Routledge.

Zolotow, C. (1976) *My Grandson Lew*. Surrey: Windmill Press.

CHAPTER 9

Sharing Experiences – The Value of Groups for Bereaved Children

Jenny Baulkwill and Christine Wood

Introduction

Groups for adults are of established value in bereavement care even for individuals who are coping well. An opportunity to share experiences in a group situation on one or two occasions can be very beneficial. Having had experience of running such groups we felt a similar approach might be helpful for children. Through our own individual work with bereaved children, we had become increasingly aware of the isolation commonly experienced by them. The overwhelming nature of grief, often so all consuming for the surviving parent, may allow little opportunity for emotional experiences to be shared. Bereaved children have rarely had any significant contact with other children in similar circumstances, apart from their own siblings. Often this heightens feelings of vulnerability and separateness from their peer group, exactly when peer identification is beginning to emerge most strongly.

This knowledge prompted us to explore the potential gains of providing a group of children with the opportunity of sharing difficult and different feelings together. Our belief was that a group could provide a safe setting in which to address their bereavement issues.

Setting Up the Group

In selecting participants, we decided to target children of families already known to the social work department at the Hospice, using information from our data base. We agreed to identify children where the parent had died in the past year, either as an in-patient or at home, under the care of our hospice nursing team. Initially, we proposed an age range of eight to twelve years old. However, in order to accommodate requests for older siblings to attend we have increased this to thirteen years on occasions. In group-work practice it is usually considered inappropriate to include family members in the same group. Parents, however, were anxious that we should not exclude brothers or sisters and our groups included several sets of siblings. Our experience so far has shown this not to be a problem.

Our approach to parents required careful consideration and forethought. All parents or carers were sent a letter asking for permission to contact the children and explaining the purpose of the group. The invitation to the children states specifically that they would be meeting and talking with others whose mother or father had died within the last year. This gave us a pool of approximately eighteen children for each group of whom around 50 per cent accepted the invitation. The invitations were designed by one of our colleagues with artistic skill and reply slips and stamped addressed envelopes were provided. It seemed important to give the children this sense of choice and control.

Practical Issues

Our staff group has consisted of two social workers, two volunteer bereavement counsellors and more recently an art therapist. This has allowed for the needs of each child to be addressed individually during some of the exercises and has contributed to the 'safety' of the group. It became clear that artwork played a very significant part in the exploration of the children's feelings and our professional art therapist has been able to develop this further in recent groups. We also required the assistance of our departmental administrative staff at each stage of the planning.

We decided to hold the groups on a Saturday, during the school term from 11.30am until 3.30pm. From our previous experience it had been difficult to choose a day in the holiday period which would allow all the children to attend. Our hospice volunteer service arranged transport for some of the children.

The groups were held in the Day Centre at the Hospice which offered a spacious venue with a large sitting room, adjoining art and craft room and excellent kitchen and toilet facilities. The self-contained nature of the premises provided a comfortable and safe setting. It was also helpful to have plenty of physical space, to allow for the release of excess energies. The exclusive use of the premises helped to create an environment free from distractions, as the Day Centre is separate from the main Hospice and has its own entrance. Although some of the children remembered visiting their parent in the Hospice this did not appear to cause them any distress.

The Hospice garden and fish pond held clear memories for some of our children and had been a sanctuary for them during a very special time in their life. They needed somehow to re-visit this. One child whose father had been cared for by our Home Care sisters wanted to see their offices and clinic room. The children were therefore offered the opportunity of visiting these areas again if they wished.

Catering

Cold drinks to which children could help themselves were provided throughout the day. Lunch was very much a communal activity with the children involved in preparation and serving. Food was kept simple with a variety of choices; any dietary requirements had been sought when the invitation was sent. The proximity of a kitchen was very helpful, although picnic food could be organized outside if weather permitted, or orders could be telephoned to the local pizza parlour!

Devising the Programme

We devised the programme from a range of activities, some already familiar to the staff group and some taken from Marge Heegaard's Facilitator Guide (Heegaard 1988).

The general pattern of the group was as follows:

- To welcome the children and make them feel comfortable.
- To help them feel part of the group and get to know each other.
- To acknowledge their bereavement and explore what had happened in their family groups.
- To further assist an expression of their feelings using artwork.
- To share experiences together and normalise their feelings.
- To help them leave some of those feelings behind.

Welcome

The children were met at the main entrance and taken up to the Day Centre as they arrived. We used a white board at the entrance to the Day Centre to write up the children's names; this served as another means of welcoming the children. Each child was given an individually decorated name badge and the staff members also identified themselves with badges.

The children were offered drinks and biscuits and we attempted to create an informal relaxed atmosphere, with radio music playing in the background. Initially, the children presented as anxious and unfamiliar with their surroundings, so individual attention was important at this stage. In trying to engage the children we talked about holidays, home and school life and other general topics.

Introduction to the Day

In the introduction to the day one of the group leaders welcomed the children. In a very clear, simple statement the group leader acknowledged the reason for inviting the children and the purpose of the day. This message was reinforced with three group rules, which we had adapted from Heegaard (1988):

GROUP RULES

MOST TIMES ARE FOR TALKING AND SHARING

THERE ARE TIMES TO BE QUIET AND LISTEN

IT'S O.K. TO CRY AND O.K TO LAUGH

Figure 9.1 Our illustrated version of the rules for the group based on the suggestions in Marge Heegaard's 'Facilitator Guide' (1988).

(1)   There will be time for talking and sharing.

(2)   There will be time for listening and being quiet.

(3)   It is OK to cry and it's OK to laugh and have fun.

The rules were written up and illustrated, (see Figure 9.1) and were explained by the group leader and remained clearly displayed throughout the day.

After this brief introduction, we quickly moved into a game to learn each other's names. Forming a circle and using a large soft ball, we threw the ball to each other. The person throwing the ball said their name and the name of the person to whom they were throwing. As we all became familiar with everyone's names, the throwing gathered momentum. This physical activity immediately released some of the tensions present and helped the children to relax.

The next activity involved adapting The Barnardo's (1992) game *All About Me*. This is a board game designed to be played with a child and adult, using questions to encourage children to talk about their feelings. The questions range from relatively easy topics to allow the child to build up trust, to questions relating more directly to feelings. Prior to the session, we preselected suitable 'safe' questions including subjects such as school, holidays, favourite foods and so forth. We did not use the board but placed the cards in a pack face side down. Then throwing the dice in turn, each player counted out cards according to the number thrown on the dice, the last card serving as the question. The time allowed us to go round the group twice, after which the group had to remember something about each individual.

The children responded well to the familiarity of using a dice and cards. The format of the game allowed each child to participate equally so that even the most withdrawn children had the opportunity to share something about themselves. It was also encouraging to observe the older children naturally helping any younger children who were experiencing difficulties reading the questions. One of the most revealing remarks came from Robert (age 13). His question card said 'If I had a time machine which time zone would I like to be in'. In answer to this he said very openly that he would like to go back to when his Mum was alive. Without us having to be directive, therefore, the children were all grounded in the material they had come to discuss and develop.

Family Trees

This involved each child in creating their own family tree. The children were provided with a large sheet of white card with the outline of a tree drawn on it. In the middle of the room we placed several bowls containing different coloured, shaped and textured buttons. During the preparation stages we had selected the buttons and separated them into different colours.

One of the group leaders demonstrated the process involved by developing her own family tree which was pinned up on the wall. She started by selecting a button for herself, placing great emphasis on the importance of doing this first. Buttons were then selected for each family member and placed on the tree as she felt appropriate. This included placing any significant family members who had died. We also encouraged the children to include friends and any pets. The children launched into this exercise with great enthusiasm. Many of them were familiar with the concept of drawing family trees and we encouraged them to use whatever style they preferred.

As the children developed their family trees, much discussion about the nature of family relationships naturally occurred. The high ratio of staff to children was particularly important in encouraging this process. Each child needed some individual help and it was highly beneficial for them to share their information with an adult who had experience of bereavement work. It was significant where the children placed themselves on the tree in relation to other family members. Why the children had selected a particular button and where they placed the individual members raised issues about the changing dynamics within the family since the parent's death.

The children demonstrated a high level of imagination and concentration throughout this session. The siblings worked separately from each other, only displaying some interest in looking at their sibling's tree towards the end of the session. One pair of siblings independently chose a small transparent button for their baby brother, who they had first seen in an incubator, after he was born prematurely. It was interesting to observe some of the children changing their choice of button for the dead parent as they talked about their relationship with them and the difference their death had made in the family. Lisa began by choosing similar buttons for both her Mum and Dad. Then after some deliberation she selected a more decorative button for her Mum who had died. As she introduced other members of the family and talked about them, her Mum's image and identity remained the focus of her attention. Jason expressed a great deal of anger towards an aunt and uncle, where there had been a major breakdown in relationships following the death of his mother. The expression of this anger led him to delete his aunt from the family tree. This activity seemed to be a truly therapeutic experience, allowing the children to share a whole range of feelings about different relationships.

At the end of this exercise, we did not share any of the information in the large group. We asked the children to push their family trees with the buttons under the chairs around the edge of the room. The children had expended a lot of energy and we felt it was important to preserve the trees in their completed state. Many of the children wanted to select a special button from their tree to take home at the end of the day.

Lunchtime

We found lunch to be a very important part of the programme and it often lasted longer than we anticipated. The exuberance of the children indicated a release from the emotional tension of the previous activity and they needed time to relax and recuperate. By this stage we found that the group interacted well and the children offered an enormous amount of support to each other. It was of great benefit to have the space available to move into another room for lunch. The children were very hungry and this needs to be taken into account when catering is arranged. We normally allow 45 minutes for lunch.

Artwork

The art therapist gave only a very brief introduction, asking the children to remember why they had been invited and what they all had in common. She was anxious not to impose any particular themes or risk pre-empting the children's real feelings. She talked generally about the difficulty of having mixed up feelings, linking this experience to the death of one of her parents but without giving any specific examples.

She then provided each child with a piece of paper cut from a large roll. The paper was measured up against each child and cut to their individual height. The therapist introduced this idea as a way of suggesting to the child that their piece of paper represented themselves. The children were encouraged to choose any colour of paint, use brushes, fingers and hands and generally to be as messy as they wished. The children worked with enormous intensity and concentration and often in absolute silence. At the end of the session they put their paintings on the floor and were asked if they wanted to make any comments. In contrast to most adult groups very few of the children wished to say anything. Perhaps this was an indication of the difficulty children have in verbalizing intense feelings.

Most of the children drew very busy pictures full of energy and using very bright colours. Lisa's picture was entirely purple. She started off just using her hands covered in paint and swirling the colour on the painting. She later said it had started off as something else but had turned into a butterfly. Maria's picture resembled a child crying with large black footprints all over it very carefully drawn. She had written the words dad and dead on different parts of the picture. This picture was an amazingly powerful image. Robert's picture was totally different from the others, perhaps reflecting the depth of his sadness and the fact that he was considerably older than the others. He had chosen very pale colours and at the bottom of the picture was a figure in a coffin surrounded by yellow angels with crying faces. He was very sad at the end of the artwork session and we felt he was struggling with his feelings in front of the younger children. The therapist closed the session by acknowledging the expression of a lot of different feelings in the paintings. Only one child wanted to take her picture home. We reassured the other children that their pictures would be kept in a safe place.

It was clear that this session had accessed some very powerful feelings for this group of children and it seemed appropriate to ask them to share individually a little of what had happened to the parent who had died. They were gently given the opportunity to do so within the group which by now seemed to provide a safe setting for all its members.

Mystery Suggestions Box

We asked the children to think back to the time when their mother or father had died. We formed a circle and each child was provided with paper and pencil. In the middle we placed a decorated shoe box. We asked them to write down something that had been helpful and something that had been unhelpful following the death of their parent. They folded their two pieces of paper and posted them in the mystery box. In turn each child then picked out a piece of paper from the box, read what was written and we discussed this in the group. Many of the children's topics were similar, but their views differed. A variety of topics arose.

How the Death was Handled at School

> *'A few weeks after my dad died my whole class had to be told about it and my teacher made me tell the class. I would have liked it if the teacher told the class.'*

Figure 9.2. One child's response to how the death was handled at school

This topic was of enormous importance to the children. William only wanted his best friend to know but his teacher told the whole class without asking him. Ben perceived his teacher as being sympathetic because her own husband had died. Many children expressed anger at the result of unhappy experiences at school following the death of their parent. Most would like to have been consulted but never were.

Funeral and Flowers

Many of the children had attended their parent's funeral. Jason spoke very movingly about his decision to view the body of his father following the death. He said he had had to insist on doing this as it was against his mother's wishes. He felt it was one of the things which had really helped him most and thought all children should be asked if they wanted to do this.

Special Presents

The children were not impressed by adults who had given them special presents, especially if this was an effort to make up for poor relationships in the past. All the children had some insight into this subject and expressed some very sophisticated opinions.

Anger

Anger was expressed about adults who said 'be brave' and 'look after your Mum/Dad.' They felt this made them feel very confused. They also resented adults who said 'I know how you feel.'

Expression of Emotion

The expression of emotion, particularly crying was discussed at length. William felt it was wrong to cry in front of those very close to you. On exploring this it seemed he especially meant his mother. Ben, on the other hand felt that crying was good. It was important to him that people outside his family cried as well as he saw this reflecting on the status and importance of his father who had died. Anne felt that her Mum had been too young to die and this seemed very unfair (see Figure 9.3).

> *'I think it helps to cry so it takes all the anger out of us. My Mum died of cancer in 1993 on July 24th which was 12 days after her 39th birthday. That is very young to die at.'*

Figure 9.3. Anne's poignant comment on her mother's death

This was a lengthy exercise and the children were very tired at the end of it. We were pleased that so many of them felt able to participate enthusiastically. Those who felt less able to take part in this seemed to listen intently and so shared in the experience.

Endings

At the end, we acknowledged clearly how important it had been to share different and difficult feelings. We thanked the children for participating and helping each other. We also recognized how helpful their contributions had been for our own understanding of their situations and for other children who might experience the death of a parent. We either ended with a relaxation exercise using a guided fantasy tape or by reading some appropriate poetry. The poems varied from ones about pets to those about memories which were taken from a book called 'I Like This Poem' edited by Kaye Webb (Webb 1979).

Special cakes and drinks were provided at the end of the group while we all said our goodbyes.

Discussion

'We have to learn to cope with the loss of our professional confidence, to share what we do not know as well as our knowledge and above all we have to learn to be ourselves.' (Barbara Monroe, Director of Social Work, St Christopher's Hospice, unpublished)

We had been aware for some time that the knowledge base for much of our practice in working with children was very scant. The group facilitators had a theoretical knowledge of children's bereavement with some expertise in working on a one-to-one basis. Most of our work with children, however, was done through adult members of the family and the group provided us with an opportunity to hear opinions and experiences directly from the children themselves.

Working with children involves a certain element of risk. We were certainly aware of our lack of confidence as the staff team began to think and plan for our groups to help bereaved children. As social workers with many years' experience of working with individuals and families there was a surprising amount of anxiety involved in planning the project for such a vulnerable group as bereaved children. Feelings of risk were high on the agenda – the twin issues of protectiveness and fear of making things worse were never far away. We had felt compelled to respond to a need we recognized in the families of our hospice patients and from direct requests from bereaved parents for help for their children. Working with children also arouses considerable emotional pain. Allowing adequate time for planning the programme was crucial and thorough preparation helped to allay some of our anxieties. We had time to build trust and establish good support within the staff team. This was a necessary foundation for sharing our own emotional pain in the planned feedback sessions which were held following the groups.

Paying particular attention to detail and timing also proved critical. The successful recruitment of children for the group depended on our initial approach to parents and carers. Their support and encouragement was of great importance. This meant, however, that the groups were to a certain extent self-selected and the children mostly came from families where communication was already open. It was essential to ensure that each child was personally welcomed on arrival and escorted to the venue. With some of the children arriving at varying intervals, this required careful co-ordination. The practical issues, including the catering arrangements and assembling the materials used for the activities, also needed much forethought and preparation.

The balance of the programme has, we believe, been achieved through the combination of the various activities. In designing the format, we were keen to develop an approach which naturally integrated the individual child into the group setting. We perceived it as important for each child to establish their own identity and to feel comfortable with themselves. The family tree exercise proved invaluable. It provided an important foundation for the exploration of family dynamics, allowing each child to examine their own identity within the context of changing relationships and circumstances. In some children, this process helped to build self esteem, resulting in an increase in confidence. Creating their family trees allowed the children to exercise their own degree of choice and control. The children had total freedom to dictate who they included on their tree. This power of self determination was instantly reflected in the vast differences between the trees produced by the siblings in the group. Although, the children worked on their family trees individually, doing this as a group activity helped to sustain their attention.

Introducing the different mediums of self-expression helped to provide both continuity and variety to the day. The artwork session proved another creative means of accessing the individual child, within the group. The simple technique of cutting the piece of paper to represent the height of the child, conveyed a powerful message in itself. The children were effectively released to express their own unique feelings at a deeper level. The intensity of concentration and the absolute silence reflected the children's absorption into their own inner worlds. It was significant that the children did not want to comment on their paintings. As far as they were concerned the paintings portrayed all that they wanted to express. It was also, perhaps, an indication of the difficulty children experience in verbalizing the very intense feelings within themselves. Yet, it was important to acknowledge some of the emotions contained in the pictures and to accept the children's work without any judgement or comparison. Reassuring the children that their work would be kept in a safe place gave them the possibility of leaving behind some of their more difficult feelings. This session was well placed in the timetable. The lunch time period had helped to release some of their physical energies and after working on their painting, the children were well prepared to share their experiences and feelings together. The suggestion box provided the ideal vehicle for this to happen. Maintaining anonymity helped the children to express freely some very difficult feelings, which had already been accessed through their paintings.

From the groups we have run, refining the balance and pace of the programme has been an on-going process. Whilst it has been important to have a clear structure, some flexibility in timing and the ability to respond spontaneously to the different needs of each group has also been a necessary requirement. We were surprised that the group members were able to relate to each other in a very short space of time. The death of a parent was common ground for all and quickly acknowledged as such by the group. We felt it had helped greatly to state this in our initial approaches to both parent and child. The children needed and were willing to talk about their feelings and experiences and the group seemed to provide a safe forum for this. We were aware of the importance of giving the children a chance to talk outside the family circle and apart from the surviving parent. The sense of responsibility towards the surviving parent was very strong. The groups have provided us with a means of delivering bereavement care directly to the children and we feel it has also been a means of support for the surviving carer or parent.

The fundamental success of the groups has lain in clearly stating at the outset the reason why the children had been invited and the purpose of the day. This required a clear, directive approach, combined with some courage on the part of the group leader. It is readily acknowledged how hard it is for adults to talk to children about death. Sometimes, it may help parents to rehearse difficult conversations beforehand. During the groups we have run, it has been noticeable how much bolder we have become in directly addressing the issues of death and dying. The group rules gave permission for different feelings to be expressed, and provided an important model for the day. Consulting the children about their views validated their own experiences as important and meaningful. Again, this helped some children, particularly those articulating feelings perhaps for the first time, to develop their self-esteem. It was encouraging to observe the children confidently exchanging their own opinions on the issues raised. The fact that it was their agenda and they were controlling it, with only minimal intervention from the group leaders, also served to promote an open discussion.

The children appeared to find the group an appropriate setting in which to discuss the feelings surrounding the death of their parent. Our initial anxiety about raising this in a group environment proved groundless. Their comments were thoughtful and pragmatic and they were sensitive and generous to each other. It is evident that there is much scope for making further efforts to address the needs of bereaved children. The provision of groups on a regular basis could be a useful addition to other methods.

References and Resources

Barnardo's (1992) *All About Me.* Board game. Barkingside, Essex: Barnardo's.

Heegaard, M. (1988) *When Someone Very Special Dies – Facilitator Guide.* Minneapolis, MN: Woodland Press.

Webb, K. (ed) (1979) *I Like this Poem.* Harmondsworth, Middlesex: Puffin Books.

CHAPTER 10

Camp Winston
A Residential Intervention for Bereaved Children

Julie Stokes and Diana Crossley

Introduction

'Winston's Wish', a grief support programme for children, was initially launched in Gloucestershire in October 1992. Working in a Palliative Care setting in a busy District Hospital it became clear to us that there were very limited services for children whose parents or siblings were dying. A visit to child bereavement centres in the USA and Canada funded by a Winston Churchill Travelling Fellowship highlighted many different ways of helping bereaved children. Winston's Wish, a grief support programme for six- to fourteen-year-olds was created to meet the needs of children and young people in Gloucestershire following the death of someone important in their lives. Winston, the bear who cares (Figure 10.1), is its symbol, mascot and guiding spirit.

Based at Gloucestershire Royal Hospital, Winston's Wish, a registered charity, is jointly funded from statutory and voluntary sources. The programme is led by Julie Stokes, Clinical Psychologist and a small professional, multi-disciplinary team from health, education and social service backgrounds. The programme is supported by a much larger team of trained volunteers.

The service attempts to respond to the individual needs of bereaved children and their families and has a number of aims:

(1) To organize a service which can offer an intervention to **all** children bereaved of an immediate family member, with the intention of reducing the risk of psychological and somatic problems in later life by

- having open access to the programme

Figure 10.1

- offering a range of clinical services including individual work, group work, and residential camps
- adopting non-pathological criteria for inclusion, i.e. the child does not need to be experiencing 'problems'.

(2) To increase a child's knowledge and understanding of death by

- establishing their current beliefs and knowledge base
- providing opportunities to ask medical professionals questions about illness and death.

(3) To increase awareness and understanding of the grieving process by

- enabling children to meet others with a similar experience
- normalizing emotional reactions
- providing verbal and non-verbal mediums to 'tell the story' of what happened.

(4) To promote open communication within the child's family by

- offering similar interventions for children and their parent(s)

- reassuring parents about the benefits of open discussion with their children

- providing parents with the skills to help them support their child.

(5) To respond to the individual needs of each child and it's family enabling them to continue their lives in a meaningful way by

- providing a comprehensive assessment

- offering a range of interventions to accommodate individual needs

- conducting service evaluation and audit.

This chapter will aim to give the reader an insight into the development of weekend residential camps for bereaved children, one of a range of services provided by the Winston's Wish Programme. At the time of writing (July 1995), 161 children have attended a total of five camps.

Camp Winston

A two-day group for twelve children was piloted in 1993 and evaluation results (Hardy 1993) indicated that a more effective intervention may have been achieved by making the group residential. Plans were therefore made to run Camp Winston at a rural Youth and Community facility (the Wilderness Centre) in the Forest of Dean. The camp is run by three co-ordinators (members of the core team) and approximately 20 trained volunteer team leaders. It is a residential intervention for 25 to 28 children. Although each camp costs in the region of £3500, families are not charged as it was felt that for some, (e.g. those with a low income, or those with more than one child) the cost might prohibit their child/children from coming on camp. Families are informed that if they would like to make a donation, it will be used to help finance the service, although ordinarily the costs are met through statutory funding, voluntary contributions, fund-raising activities and income generated from training and consultation.

Assessment

The philosophy behind the Winston's Wish programme is that it is a non-pathological service, based on principles of health promotion and the prevention of complicated grief reactions in later life. Thus, all children (aged six to fourteen) who have been bereaved of a parent or sibling can be routinely referred to the programme. It is not necessary for a child to be presenting with any specific behavioural or emotional problems. Referrals are therefore taken from a variety of sources and at present the highest number of referrals come from parents (17%), teachers (13%) and school nurses (12%). Following referral, the family is sent information on the programme and offered a home visit to complete a detailed assessment. Using a structured interview and standardized questionnaires, we aim to find out as much information as we can about the family and their situation, together with looking at how the children have understood and coped with the death. During the assessment, the assessor spends time with the parent(s) and child(ren) separately. The assessment process is seen to be an integral part of the programme and is essential in engaging both the children and their parent(s). This is particularly important when it is a residential intervention that may be offered, usually to a widowed parent, who may be struggling with their own experience of bereavement. Depending on the outcome of the assessment process, children and their families are linked into an appropriate part of the clinical programme. For the majority of children, 'Camp Winston' will be the first point of entry to the Winston's Wish programme. However, if a family were coping with a particularly challenging loss (e.g. suicide or murder) they might be offered an alternative intervention prior to attending camp, for example the opportunity of attending an after school group. In such a group all participants would be learning to cope with the specific issues raised by 'socially difficult deaths'. Occasionally some individual work may also be offered in order to get a family to the point where they feel the camp would be a useful experience.

Figure 10.2 Table to Show Ages of Children attending Camp Winston

Age	%
6 and 7 years	28
8 and 9 years	30
10 and 11 years	19.5
12 and 13 years	19.5
14 years	3

Figure 10.2 shows the age range of children attending camps. Because the camps can accommodate a large group, there is usually an even age distribution. The children are then divided into five age-related 'bear' groups:

- Pooh Bears (5–6 years)
- Paddington Bears (7–8 years)
- Honey Bears (8–10 years)
- Yogi Bears (10–12 years)
- Huggy Bears (13–14 years)

The membership of each group will vary depending on the chronological age and developmental stages of children attending each camp. Dividing children into groups in this way allows small group work to be achieved at an appropriate level.

Of the children referred to the programme, 40 per cent have come to camp to remember their father, 22 per cent to remember their mother and 20 per cent to remember a sibling. The remaining 20 per cent have usually experienced a multiple family bereavement. The types of death are categorized into sudden (55%), expected (31%) and suicide (14%). Of the expected deaths, 64 per cent are related to cancer and of the unexpected deaths 33 per cent are caused by road traffic accidents and 11 per cent are due to heart failure. Thus as suicide is essentially a sudden death, an overwhelming number of families referred to the programme (69%) are coping with sudden death.

Invitation to Camp

Children are invited to attend Camp Winston by letter approximately three weeks before the camp is held. The letter outlines some of the activities they will do at camp and a kit list of the things they need to bring. Parents are invited to attend the Parents Group which takes place at the same time at a nearby location.

Parents' Group

Preliminary evaluations have indicated that the development of a thorough programme for parents was essential for the children's programme to be really effective. By providing a parents' programme it is possible to reinforce the messages of camp, provide support and information in a non threatening environment, and allow parents to learn from each other. Thus, a two-day non-residential programme has been developed. Many activities offered to parents are similar to those experienced by the children, for example the candlelight ceremony, salt sculpture. This has proved useful in helping all family members share the experience of attending camp when they return home together. The parents' group also addresses the issues/skills involved in parenting children who are coping with grief, for example a child whose behaviour has become more challenging, as well as surviving as a lone parent. On the Sunday morning the Programme Director attends the parents' group. Parents are given the opportunity of understanding what their children have been doing on camp and also what parents might expect of their children when they go home. For example, some children may not want to tell a parent what has happened at camp immediately and it is important not to pressurize children and important that parents do not feel rejected. More detailed feedback on individual children is available over lunch, when a team leader from each bear group joins the parents' group.

Clearly, a whole chapter could be written on the importance of adopting a family approach with any children's service; however, in this chapter we are focusing specifically on the camp experience and will therefore not describe the parents' programme in further detail.

Preparation for Camp

The volunteer 'team leaders' (20 people) who have all undergone training and vetting by social services arrive on Friday evening. In addition to the team leaders there are three camp co-ordinators for the children's camp and two co-ordinators who organize the parents' group. After a shared supper the team leaders divide into their bear groups and discuss the children they will be working with throughout the weekend. They plan how they might facilitate the small group work during the weekend, and consider issues which may be important in order to maximize the child's experience of camp. There are usually three or four team leaders allocated to each bear group and the core team members who completed the home assessment are available to advise them if they have any queries about the children.

It is important to note that the camp intervention is not seen as 'therapy' in a traditional sense; thus, it can be argued that fairly minimal information is actually required by the team leaders. Often detail relating to family 'pathology' (e.g. alcoholism, prison sentences) only serves to overwhelm the team leaders and detracts from the underlying assumption that grief is a 'normal' process. Thus, as it is a bereavement that brings the family into the programme, it is felt that this should not be confused by a range of other pre-bereavement factors which usually cannot be resolved on Camp Winston.

Camp Winston – Day One

Registration and Introduction

An hour is given to welcome the children and their parent(s). When they arrive, children are told which bear group they have been allocated. In most circumstances, siblings are in different groups, as often they will not talk openly in front of each other. Separate groups allow them to say as much as they like in small group sessions, yet share the common experience of attending camp, which can bring them closer together. They are then given their Winston name badge, which is a Winston Bear holding a coloured balloon. It is explained that the colour of the balloon denotes the person who they have come to remember. For example, a blue balloon indicates the death of a father. Children who have experienced more than one bereavement are given the opportunity to have a badge with several relevant coloured balloons, or a badge with a balloon to represent the person they would specifically like to remember at camp. All personnel involved on the weekend wear badges, thus the children can readily identify that most of the team leaders have also experienced the death of someone important in their lives and they can recognize those who have experienced a similar death. Care is taken to involve the parents in the registration process, as they are often anxious at the prospect of leaving their children. Attention is also given to checking dietary or medication requirements identified during assessment.

The team leaders gather around the registration desk, ready to make contact with the children when appropriate. The team leaders are introduced and they then take the children to collect their Winston sweatshirt and choose which bed they would like in their allocated dormitory. At this juncture, parents are invited to see the sleeping arrangements or to say goodbye and go to their own camp, which is located a mile away. Children seem to settle very quickly, excited by the prospect of what is in store at 'Camp Winston'. This sometimes allows them to be quite dismissive of the 'separation anxiety' shown by some parents. Thus care is given to ensure that each child takes responsibility for saying goodbye properly before a parent leaves and are reminded when they will meet up again the next day.

The children bring a photo of the person who has died which is displayed on a 'We Remember Them' board, alongside team leaders' photographs. This helps children to focus on why they have come to Camp Winston and also prompts many discussions.

Camp Activities

Welcome to Camp

At 10am the group convenes and everyone is formally welcomed by the Programme Director. It is explained that Camp Winston is a very special place for children and young people who have experienced the death of someone important in their lives. The aims of camp are identified and some of the forthcoming camp activities are briefly described. In addition to the statement 'it is all right to have fun', it is also clearly explained that there are rules and boundaries concerning behaviour on camp. Team leaders then break the ice by performing Winston's welcoming song. After this, the children are read a short illustrated story which tackles grief from a child's perspective (Powell 1990). Following the story, each child and team leader is asked in turn to say their name and who they have come to camp to remember.

Winston's Wilderness Challenge

After a short snack, 'Winston's Wilderness Challenge' begins. Winston challenges the children in their bear groups to complete five activities. The activities, (including archery, wall climbing and puzzle solving) are designed to promote a sense of team building, trust and self-esteem for both children and team leaders. It is at times, physically challenging and great fun (Figure 10.3). Care is taken to select activities which can be completed by six-year-olds, as well as

Figure 10.3 Wilderness challenge

the older thirteen- to fourteen-year-olds and this outdoor activity is usually rated one of the high points on camp by children of all ages.

After each challenge is completed, the group are given an object (e.g. a toy car, a toy hospital) and at the end of the challenge groups are invited to construct a story utilizing the six objects. This allows them an opportunity to begin to tell their story using safe metaphors. Although the children have the choice to construct a story that does not relate to death, they often do incorporate their experience of death. This may well be a reflection of the careful home assessment process which clearly lets the child know that Camp Winston is a place where children go to understand more about death.

Small Group Work – 'Telling the Story'
After a barbecue lunch (during which there is scheduled free time for team games and informal chats) the groups reconvene for the first of two 'small group sessions'. How these groups operate is very much determined by the children's wishes and their stage of development. The aim for the first session is to create an environment which enables the child to tell **their** story of what happened as **they** understand it. The older groups may often choose to simply explain verbally what happened; however, the younger children will usually use a variety of non-verbal mediums, for example paint, collage, puppets, or clay to tell their story. As children create their art work they are encouraged to explain

how and **why** their relative died. During this process team leaders will try to identify any issues which may benefit from clarification. These issues are then written down and posted (anonymously) in Winston's Post-box to be answered in the 'Questions for the Doctor' session which takes place later that afternoon.

Questions for the Doctor

One of the key aims of the weekend is to provide education on all aspects surrounding a child's experience of death. Children have important questions which often go unanswered. In addition, in the absence of reliable information they formulate their own (often erroneous) conclusions concerning medical and spiritual issues. Many children are confused as to **what happened, why it happened** and **what happens next**. The absence of such information can complicate their grieving process.

The children assemble in the group room and are introduced to Winston's doctor. He is an experienced local GP. The personal qualities that are important in selecting a camp doctor include:

- an ability to relate medical terminology in plain English, using child-friendly (and if possible, humorous) metaphors

- someone who will abandon their white coat and other medical 'armoury'

- someone who is comfortable with death and who generally accepts that medical science has its limitations

- someone who is comfortable with saying 'I'm not sure…' and engage in an open discussion with one of the camp co-ordinators who joins the doctor in facilitating the session

- someone who can respond to additional, impromptu questions from the floor and is at ease talking to a large group of children.

Many questions have been asked during the five camps which are broadly divided into five categories:

(1) Factual Medical Information

By far the greatest number of questions (69%) that children ask the doctor are about medical issues – treatment, medication, hereditary conditions, pain for example:

- What is cancer?

- What is a heart attack – will I die from one too?

- If I have the HIV virus and I pass it on, does it mean I don't have it anymore?

Many questions also seek to demystify treatments:

- Why does morphine make you see things?
- What is radiotherapy?
- Why do they have computers in ITU?

Alternatively some of the questions seek to understand the complexities of medical practice – how doctors work. Behind such questions are often unresolved dilemmas regarding blame.

- Why can't doctors make all people better with chest problems?
- Why did the doctor give mummy too much medicine?
- Why didn't the operation work on her heart tubes?
- If the doctors had known earlier that my dad had cancer, would they have been able to save him?

Such questions are obviously challenging and need to be handled with respect, honesty and sensitivity by the doctor.

(2) Emotional Issues

Another group of questions relate to emotions and fears rather than specific medical issues, for example:

- Why are some people nasty to us when someone special has died?
- Why do some people cry and some not, even when they both knew the dead person?

One of the basic principles behind Winston's Wish is that children should be able to understand the variety of feelings that people have when someone important has died and the reactions of other people around them. They learn that it is OK to feel sad, to be angry, to cry, to laugh, to have regrets and that all these feelings are a valid part of their grieving.

(3) Searching for an Explanation

The third category of questions centre around the child's search for an explanation. The questions are varied and are often related to a child's level of cognitive development and how this relates to their knowledge of and understanding of death, for example:

- Why do people die?
- My brother died in a car crash, some of the other people in the car didn't die, why did my brother have to die?
- Why do doctors get it wrong and let my dad die?

(4) Issues Relating to Suicide

The fourth group of questions can be categorized into issues generated from a person 'choosing' to die:

- Why do people want to commit suicide?
- If people are depressed, why can't they ask for help from family and friends, instead of killing themselves?
- How do car fumes kill a person?

(5) Spirituality

The final category identified surrounds spiritual questions. In such situations it is obviously important for the doctor (and indeed all camp co-ordinators and volunteers) not to adopt any particular religious stance. It is more helpful to generate a selection of alternative answers. The child will then usually choose the answer that best fits their cultural and family beliefs, whilst recognising that other explanations exist.

Spiritual questions have included the following:

- Where do people go to when they die?
- If people go to Heaven, can they see you all the time? (i.e. Can Mum see me even when I'm misbehaving?)
- Will people ever come back?
- What do you eat in Heaven?
- Why do people have to be buried or burnt?

For whatever reason, whether it is the child's own knowledge of death, the desire to protect the child, or the child jumping to erroneous conclusions – it has become increasingly clear that children (like adults) need to understand and make sense of significant events in their lives and 'Questions For the Doctor' opens the door to this process.

The significance that children attach to this session is reflected in their ability to sit and listen to the doctor. Because of the younger children, it was always envisaged that such a session should last about 45 minutes to one hour. However to-date, the children have always been keen to continue and are happy to listen for at least 90 minutes.

Candlelight Ceremony

After supper, we hold Winston's candlelight ceremony. It is a simple ritual which allows participants to connect with some of the feelings of deep sadness that may rarely surface. Each child and team leader are given their own hand-crafted Winston candle and it is explained that Winston likes to light a candle on special occasions to remember people who have died. Sometimes he remembers funny events, sometimes difficult memories, sometimes happy times and also sad times. It is explained that one of the beliefs that Winston holds is that it is 'all right to cry'. One by one, everyone is invited to light their candle and given the option to say 'I'm lighting my candle for…and the thing(s) I would like to remember about them are…'

Most children do choose to say something; however, occasionally the younger children may whisper their message to a team leader who will then repeat it to the larger group. It is very important (as with all the activities on camp) to provide a sense of safety and choice so children do not feel pressurized to speak. Eventually, when all the candles are lit, some music is played which gives time to reflect on the feelings that have been aroused (Figure 10.4). Plenty of tissues and physical comfort are available throughout the ceremony. The fact that team leaders also participate in the ceremony can provide a useful role model for children who may not have seen adults cry.

Figure 10.4 The candlelight ceremony

One by one, each candle is blown out and the ceremony reaches its conclusion. The children are encouraged to keep their candles, as they may then decide to light the candle on important occasions, for example birthdays, Christmas, anniversaries. Children can also choose to light their candles to mark important personal events, for example one boy decided he would light his candle each year to mark the beginning of the fishing season as this was an activity he had always shared with his dad.

Although the candlelight ceremony is emotionally draining for all who participate, it has proved to be a remarkable release for many children. It has also been observed that within half an hour of the ceremony ending, children seem to have the capacity to distance themselves from their sadness and 'get on with' the rest of the evening's activities. It is very impressive and encouraging to all the adults involved to observe the robust coping strategies with which children are equipped. It has consistently been observed on all five camps that the candlelight ceremony provides a transition point on camp and that afterwards the children are noticeably more relaxed and calm.

Camp Winston – Day Two

The Anger Wall

There are many emotions and feelings following the death of someone close, but some are more easily expressed than others. Perhaps one of the more difficult feelings is anger. On camp this feeling is acknowledged by the use of 'an anger wall'. Children are invited to think about what it feels like to be angry and to think about events, behaviours or actions in connection with the person who died that have made them angry. These targets on which their anger is focused are represented in words, for example 'The Doctor', 'Drugs', or visually as pictures, such as two cars in a crash. They are then attached to the wall and clay 'bombs' are made and thrown at the targets (Figure 10.5). Children are encouraged to throw the clay bombs repeatedly, releasing energy by shouting or screaming at the same time.

Figure 10.5 The anger wall

It is important that children create a constructive end to the session, as anger can sometimes be viewed as a negative emotion. Thus, children take some clay and are encouraged to make it into a model of something connected with the dead person. For example, a ten-year-old who lived with a violent father until he died suddenly from a heart attack, created a model of her father watching his favourite television programme. She placed herself on a separate chair also watching the programme and recalled it was one of the few times she felt safe at home. During the model building, positive and non-harmful ways of coping with angry feelings are discussed. For example, when people are feeling angry they can help express that feeling by drawing a picture about the thing they are angry at and then tearing it up, or writing about it in a diary.

Creating a 'Salt Sculpture'

This group activity involves children identifying five memories/objects/behaviours and so on that they associate with the person who has died. Colours are used to represent each item, for example 'smile' may be represented by yellow. Piles of salt are then coloured by rubbing in chalks and the different colours poured into a small jar in various combinations of their choice. Spectacular salt sculptures are easily created and the exercise can be completed efficiently by all age groups. Salt sculptures form three-dimensional representations of memories about a person who has died. From different angles the sculptures are different – just like people – who at certain times might display certain characteristics more than others. This can be particularly helpful when children have difficult memories about their relatives and they can see that sometimes things were worse or better than others.

Small Group Work – 'The future'

After a mid-morning break, the children assemble into their groups for the second small group session. The focus for the small group session on the first day was 'telling the story of what happened', whereas on the second day the focus is on 'the future' and how life can continue following the death of someone important. The two small groups essentially mirror a model of bereavement proposed by Stroebe (1994). The model identifies the need to focus both on the past (loss orientation) and on the future (restoration orientation). In facilitating this session family sculpts are often useful, particularly with the older children.

Obviously there are some children attending camp who may have been very recently bereaved (three to six months), whereas for others the bereavement may have taken place some years ago. Consideration must therefore be given to children who do not feel ready to consider a future without the dead person.

Memories

Although Camp Winston is only a two day residential event, the children and camp volunteers become close friends very quickly. For this reason and the desire to provide a positive experience of saying goodbye, the greater part of the afternoon concentrates on memories and preparing to say goodbye. Throughout the afternoon parallels are drawn between saying goodbye at camp and saying goodbye to someone important who has died. Children complete memory sheets which together with their photograph and autobiographical information, explain who they came to camp to remember, favourite memories of camp and wishes for the future. These are collected, copied and collated as a Memory Book for presentation at the Bearduation Ceremony later that afternoon.

Research has shown that bereaved children need to be given opportunities to remain connected with the person who has died (Silverman and Worden 1994). On camp children are presented with a memory bag. It is explained that the bag can be used as a place to keep important things to remember about the person who has died. Each bag contains a smaller bag of three stones. It is explained that the stones represent memories. Some memories still hurt and have sharp edges (rocky rocks), some either do not make us feel anything or are more difficult memories that have become less painful (smooth pebbles) and others are very special memories (polished gemstones). Children generally find the metaphor useful and easy to understand. The session leader gives examples of memories that might be rocky rocks, for example feeling guilty because I told the person I hated them before they died. Memories that might be smooth pebbles could be having breakfast with Dad, and precious gemstone memories, opening our Christmas stockings in bed with Mum.

Since this session is the last time the children and volunteers will be together as a group (without the parents) this is acknowledged and the group takes time to say its goodbyes. This is a vitally important part of the process. Originally, when the goodbyes were left to the end (as happened on the first camp) some children acted out and were angry and dismissive of their parents for taking them home. In later camps this process was not observed and children and parents seemed enthusiastic about reforming as a family unit.

The Bearduation Ceremony

This is a very important point in the camp process. It marks the reuniting of parents with their children and formally acknowledges the achievement of families participating in Camp Winston. The ceremony starts with the children and team leaders performing Winston's Welcome song for the parents. Parents are very proud to see their children sing this song, which is sung to the tune of Joseph's Coat of Many Colours (with permission). The Parents' Co-ordinator and Programme Director give a short talk to 'bridge' the events which have taken place on both the child and parents' camp. The importance of 'families' needing to work together is reinforced.

The 'Bearduation' itself is essentially a simple graduation ritual. It is based on identifying achievements, 'moving on' and marking the occasion by giving the children their own Winston Bear to provide a tangible connection with their experience on camp. One by one each child is introduced; they are then invited to receive their Winston Bear and Memory Book (Figure 10.6). 'Winston' appears (this time as a life-size teddy bear – who is available for hugs and paw shakes) only at the Bearduation. The actual appearance of 'their bear' has proved enormously important for younger children on camp. Winston only appears at this time marking the importance of the family's achievement symbolized at the Bearduation Ceremony.

Figure 10.6 Bearduation

The Balloon Ceremony

Immediately after the Bearduation, families are invited up to receive helium filled balloons. Each family receives a bunch of balloons, representing each member of the family. In the afternoon children and their parents have written two messages on a balloon label – one a message to the person who died and the other a wish for the future. The family then attach their labels to the balloons.

Outside, all the families and team leaders assemble for the balloon release. The Programme Director thanks everybody for taking part in Camp Winston, and as the group says goodbye, the balloons are released. A large red balloon (belonging to Winston) is also released and this effectively leads the way for the other balloons. The ceremony seems to work on a number of different levels; children often attach tremendous significance to the prospect of their message connecting with the dead person, whereas parents have often commented on the need to metaphorically 'let go' of their grief and begin to construct a different life for their family (Figure 10.7). This marks the end of camp and all families leave the centre by 5.30 p.m.

Figure 10.7 Balloon ceremony

Debriefing of Volunteers

Participating in Camp Winston is a physically and emotionally draining experience and debriefing of volunteers is paramount. This is completed in three ways. First, team leaders meet in their groups to briefly record any concerns they may have about particular children and/or parents. This information is then processed carefully after camp by the Co-ordinator of the Clinical Programme. Volunteers are thus reassured that any appropriate action will be taken and that they are no longer responsible. Second, after a brief period of 'clearing up' the whole group (i.e. parents and child team leaders and camp co-ordinators) then assemble and are invited to share a memory from camp. Finally, volunteers have supper together continuing to reflect on their experience of camp.

Follow Up

Using information recorded at the debrief session that includes information for each child about how they coped with camp, friends they made, things they learnt, enjoyed or found difficult and concerns that may need further work, a follow up procedure is carried out. In the week after camp the Co-ordinator of the Clinical Programme writes letters to each family and the person who referred the child to the programme. These letters summarize how the child coped with camp, any problems they may have had and further interventions that may be offered if necessary. It is proposed, that in addition to these letters, families are contacted by the member of the team who carried out the initial assessment so they discuss the family's response to camp and answer any outstanding questions or queries.

Evaluation

Since the late 1980s accounts of interventions aimed specifically at bereaved children have been published (for example Black and Urbanowitz 1987). The need to carry out research in this area is of paramount importance and it is unethical to introduce a service without finding out if it does good or harm (Murray Parkes, in press). It is only recently that research on clinical interventions involving outcome measures has been undertaken. Despite the complexity and difficulties of this task it is only by collecting information and measurements to assess the effectiveness of the programme that service providers can be sure they are achieving their objectives and aims. In addition, by evaluating the service the information we collect can be used to develop the service in the most appropriate way.

It would appear from anecdotal feedback of children and parents that Winston's Wish is providing a highly valued and quality service that is deemed to be meeting their needs. However, anecdotes and opinion can only be used as short term expedients and reliable knowledge from methodologically sound surveys and studies is necessary (Twycross and Dunn 1994). For these reasons a research budget was secured and a programme of service evaluation carried out. To date two camps have been evaluated (May 1993 and March 1994). Parents and children were visited at home and a semi structured interview completed. The results of the evaluation show

Children benefit from the programme
Children's behaviour changed as a result of camp in a positive way
Children were more open and more settled
Children's understanding of death increased
Communication levels within the family improved
Children were helped to cope with their relative's death

It would appear that the programme is effective in normalizing the process of grieving. Children are aware that they are not alone and that there were other children like themselves. They realise that it is OK to show their feelings and to talk about how they feel.

Parents Said About Their Children:

'He's a completely different person. In the car he was talking all the time. He's been so quiet since the death, it really brought it out, I was able to talk to him as well. Before camp he had never talked about it.'

'They are a lot better in themselves, meeting other children in the same situation really helped. They've really settled.'

'He's a lot more open, he wouldn't talk about it much before and he doesn't wet the bed so much.'

'There are no more nightmares or tantrums.'

'It's not only me that's noticed the change, everybody has.'

'It was like something had been laid to rest.'

March 1994, Service Evaluation

Children Said About Camp:

'The doctor's questions helped me to understand.'

'I learnt how to cope with it, I don't just remember the sad times... I remember the fun times. I used to cry every night, now I don't. I felt it was my fault, now I understand.'

'I learnt about what happened to others, you knew it wasn't just you.'

'I learnt it's all right to talk about it and it's not always a bad thing to cry.'

March 1994, Service Evaluation

Parents Said About the Parents' Group:

'It's lovely to meet people, you are searching for people in the same situation as yourself, you don't feel you are the only one.'

'I found it did help. Everyone was at different stages, it made me realize there is life after. After two days you've shared everything with these strangers, it all comes out naturally...we all had tears and cried on each other's shoulders at some stage.'

March 1994, Service Evaluation

Conclusion

Winston's Wish is still a very new and developing programme. The service staff are highly motivated to developing new and innovative ways of working with bereaved children and their families. Although still in its infancy, it is committed to furthering knowledge through evaluation and audit, the results of which are used to influence the type of service provided.

The loss of a parent during childhood is a profound psychological trauma that can threaten the child's social and emotional development. We firmly believe early intervention at the time of the death can help children avoid some of the difficulties they might encounter if they are excluded or do not understand what happens when someone dies. Bringing children and parents together who have experienced similar bereavements seems to reduce their sense of isolation and they learn a great deal from each other (Figure 10.8). Camp Winston provides children and their families with a few more resources which we hope will help them along their journey through the grieving process

Figure 10.8 Together

References

Black, D. and Urbanowitz, M.A. (1987) 'Family Intervention with Bereaved Children.' *Journal of Child Psychology and Psychiatry 26*, 467–476.

Hardy, N. (1993), *The Effectiveness of Doing Grief Work with Children: An Exploratory Study.* Submitted to the Department of Psychology, University of Plymouth in partial fulfilment for the degree of Doctor of Clinical Psychology (unpublished).

Murray Parkes, C. (in press) 'Guidelines for Conducting Ethical Bereavement Research' *Death Studies.*

Powell, E.S. (1990) *Geranium Morning.* Minneapolis, MN: Carolhoda Books Inc.

Silverman, P.R. and Worden, J.W. (1993) 'Children's reactions to the death of a parent.' In M.S. Stroebe, R.O. Hansson and W. Stroebe (eds) *The Handbook of Bereavement.* London: Cambridge University Press.

Stroebe, M.S. (1994) *Helping the Bereaved Come to Terms with Loss: What Does Bereavement Research Have to Offer?* St George's Mental Health Library Conference Series. London: St George's Hospital.

Twycross, R.G. and Dunn, V. (1994) 'Research in Palliative Care: The Pursuit of reliable Knowledge.' National Council for Hospice and Specialist Palliative Care Services, Occasional Paper No. 5.

CHAPTER 11

Group Work with Bereaved Children

Anne Harris and Sally Curnick

Introduction

In this chapter we hope to describe the work that we have undertaken with children who have been bereaved predominantly of siblings who have died from cancer. It will contain our experiences and the lessons both good and bad that we have gained during five years of running these groups. It is in no way meant to represent a blueprint or instructions for group work. This method has worked well for us in our setting – everybody needs to find a method that works best for them in their individual setting. We have chosen to use puppets as a means of communication with the children, and as another medium through which they could express their feelings.

Background

The group was started in response to repeated parental concerns about problems they were experiencing with their healthy surviving children. In keeping with Sabbeth and Leventhal (cited in Davis 1993), they were reporting behaviour problems, manifesting in jealousy, guilt, poor school performance and increasing anxiety. As a result of the stresses already present within the family, the parents did not appear to have the emotional energy to deal with these issues, were becoming polarized from their children and were perhaps compounding these difficulties.

We found ourselves spending more time engaged in individual work with bereaved children who were expressing wide ranging yet similar experiences. These children had been involved to a greater or lesser degree with their dead sibling's treatment and had a wide ranging level of understanding of the illness that had ultimately caused the death of their sibling. They were all isolated within their local peer groups, and were expected to be functioning within school and their local community without the acknowledgement of their recent trauma. Their local communities were flooding the bereaved parents with sympathy and concern, but frequently the bereaved sibling appeared to be pushed aside. The fact that he or she had also lost a brother or sister and was grieving appeared almost forgotten.

A common response of bereaved parents, particularly those who have had long-term contact with the hospital, is one of several bereavements – not only has their child died, but they have lost the close contact and friendships that they have made within the hospital. It seemed logical, therefore, to assume that surviving children also experienced this sense of loss, but were perhaps without the words to express it.

We decided that we would start by bringing together a group of younger bereaved children for a trial meeting to see if it would be an appropriate means of working with a few bereaved children, and to see if any common threads and experiences emerged.

Initial Planning

During the planning phase of the first group we met with colleagues from the Department of Family Psychiatry to plan a loose agenda and discuss various areas of concern to us. Initially we met with a consultant child psychiatrist and social worker attached to the Family Therapy Team. They were experienced in running groups with children, although not with bereaved children, and we felt that they would be an appropriate source of support for us during the planning phase. They were invaluable in helping us clarify the aims that we had for the group: that we hoped to support normal grief, and to offer the children an arena in which they could safely explore some of their feelings. They were also able to act as a sounding board as we discussed various concerns.

Setting

It took us some time to find a venue that we considered suitable for the group. We eventually chose the group room within the hospital, a large room with scattered cushions and multi-coloured lights that the children could use as they chose. The room was away from the main hospital and was in an area with which the children were not familiar. We considered this to be important, to mark the group as something new for the children, not tagging onto something that their brother and sister had previously done. Given that a common complaint of the children was that when they were on the ward everyone knew their parents' and their sibling's names but nobody seemed to know their name, it seemed that to start afresh was making a clear statement.

Initially we discussed the idea of the group with bereaved parents, but the invitation was sent directly to the bereaved child. Again this seemed important in marking it as being 'their' group – a bereaved parents' group was already running, and it was important for us to differentiate the two. We met with considerable resistance from parents; paradoxically, they had been asking for help and support with their children, but when offered they were reluctant to become involved. We made it clear to all the parents that what happened in the group would be entirely confidential within each group, and that we would not be offering any feedback to the parents – although the proviso was left that the children could feed back to their parents if they wished.

This was a major cause of parental concern and resistance. There was a distinct feeling that while their (the parents') feelings and confidences were to be respected – those of the bereaved children were family property and could and should be shared. We spent time discussing with our supervisor our very strong feelings that the group should be kept confidential. We were relieved to find that he shared and supported these feelings. It certainly gave us the courage to stick with our convictions.

We decided that we would make four the youngest age that we would accept into the group. Although according to Lansdown (1985) by four years old children do not yet have a concrete and adult understanding of death, we felt that by this age the children would be able to function independently from their parents, and we believed they would be old enough to articulate their feelings, fears and beliefs surrounding the death of their siblings.

Perhaps the most important statement that we made about the group when we were in the planning stages was that we were not setting them up as therapeutic groups – that we intended them to help bereaved children through their normal grief. We are firm in our belief that childhood grief is normal, to be expected after a death, and needs to be supported.

We also expect that most children will proceed through the passage of grief without significant problems as long as they are allowed to give vent to their feelings in a supportive environment. We made it clear to anyone who wished to refer a child to the group that we were not in a position, nor did we have the expertise, to run a therapeutic group. This was also made explicit to the parents – it was important to reinforce to the parents that we did not consider their surviving children to have significant difficulties in grieving but that, as with bereaved parents, children did want and have a need to talk about their siblings and to re-live the time leading up to and immediately after the death. We acknowledged that it was often painful for the parents to support their children at this time and we were hoping to offer that opportunity.

Group Structure

We decided that we needed a loose formula for each group. It was felt that each group should set their own group rules, but that confidentiality was the one unchangeable rule. We made it clear to each group that we would not be relaying back to their parents the discussion or content of the group, but if they chose to tell their parents about the group then that was acceptable. We wanted to start with some general warm-up games, ones that would build a group identity and let the children identify common threads and experiences. We started with 'Name Train', a lively game which has group members standing in a circle. One member agrees to start being the train and they go round the circle then step in front of a group member, unknown to them – they say 'I'm a name train and my name is...what's your name?', the other person answers and joins the front of the train – this carries on with the entire train announcing their name each time a new member joins the train. This has several benefits as an introductory game: it is fun and the children enjoy it; it is also non-threatening in that no child is put directly on the spot; and as they have to move about the room in a chain it enables them to release energy and discharge the tension that builds up prior to the start of the group.

We then move on to try and focus the group on their common experience. We used the game 'Fruit Salad' which involves all group members in sitting in a line with one member being the caller. The object is to ask children who have something in common to change places. The group can be as gentle or as searching as required – we usually start with some obviously shared statements such as 'everyone who is wearing socks' change places, 'everyone who had breakfast today' change places. Moving onto more personal statements as the games progress 'everybody who had a brother or sister die', change places, 'everyone who has been to a funeral' change places. If the caller says 'fruit salad' then everybody changes places.

Different group members take it in turns to be the caller as they choose. The game has several advantages – the caller has the opportunity to manipulate the statement as the group requires – it can be left as general or made as specific as seems appropriate. It is also totally uncompetitive. When the game starts, younger children in particular fear that it is going to be a form of musical chairs with a chair being removed each time – once they realize this is not the case they appear to relax into it. As it is a pre-requisite of the group that any adult involved with the group must join in, the children get particular pleasure in watching adults struggling to their feet and panting around the room!

After the two warm-up games we offer the children drinks and while they are eating and drinking we ask them to draw pictures of their house and who lives with them. This has a dual purpose, it calms children down and gives us the opportunity to gauge their perception of their altered family. Many children will continue to draw their dead siblings, choosing to explain later that he or she may not be there in body any more but that they remain a part of the family. Children will also often draw their dead siblings who underwent amputation as having their missing limbs returned to them, explaining that it upsets their parents too much to consider them as 'imperfect in death'. When the drawing is completed each group member is invited to explain to the group who they have drawn and their role within the family. Obviously this requires a degree of self-disclosure on the part of the adults present but it helps to draw the group closer together.

Puppet Work

We decided prior to the first group that we wanted to give the children another medium through which they could express their feelings. We felt that in particular the first group may feel inhibited in talking about their experiences; it should also be acknowledged that we had considerable anxiety about our ability to spark discussion and to lead the group. We decided to use puppets as our chosen method of communication; we hoped that the group members would see them as safe toys and that they would enhance articulation and help them talk through their feelings. We accept that displacement of feelings can often be used as a defence mechanism but in keeping with our policy not to run the group to strict therapeutic guidelines we did not feel that we had any need or indeed right to challenge the group member's defence. We were aware that this could lead to accusations of our promoting their denial state but we did not feel that this is a valid accusation and that the merits of offering the children a new channel of expression would outweigh the possible disadvantages.

Choosing the puppets that we would use within the group was a difficult task – we decided that we wanted a mixture of nice and nasty puppets to give the children a wide variety of choice. As we planned to ask the children to portray events within their family by using puppets we wanted to avoid having only cuddly friendly puppets, but equally did not want to lead the children by having only ferocious animals. It was important to have a mixture of easily identified characters, a police puppet, a witch, a crow and also characters that could be anything according to the child's imagination. Initially we used puppets that were available within the hospital; since then we have gradually added to our supply, buying whenever we find suitable puppets. We had decided that we would divide the group into two or three sub groups and asked the children to do 'a play' for us about a topic, either about something very sad that had happened in their family or about going to a funeral. We decided that we would keep the topic fairly loose and that we would not expect the children to stick to the storyline that we had given them. The children all had free choice of the puppets and could use as many as they wanted. We would make a stage for each show and then each group would watch different shows.

Without doubt the use of puppets has been an immense success within the group. The children have found them easy to use and have expressed a wide range of emotions with them. Children who have not been able to articulate their feelings have found that the puppets have offered a safe voice for them. In one of the earliest groups we ran, two seven-year-old boys were playing with puppets, one boy picked up a crocodile puppet and told us it was leukaemia, the other boy picked up a puppet and said he was the doctor and was going to kill leukaemia. He hit the crocodile puppet about the head and then turned to the rest of the group and announced he had killed leukaemia as that was what doctors did. He turned to walk away; however, the crocodile puppet grabbed the doctor puppet by the neck and threw the puppet across the room saying you 'can't kill cancer, cancer kills your whole family'. For the little boy who was portraying the leukaemia puppet this was undoubtedly his reality. Since his brother's diagnosis he has had to change from main stream to supported education, his parents' marriage was failing and his brother had a long and difficult phase of illness at home. Since his brother's death the seven-year-old had become increasingly withdrawn and reluctant to talk about his brother. If asked as himself how he had felt about his brother's illness and death he would have found it difficult to communicate; however, the puppets offered him a safe surrogate to release his own pain. This was without doubt one of the most moving scenes we have ever experienced and served to reinforce our beliefs that children, if given the support and opportunity, will find their own answers to their many questions. If we accept that children quickly pick up on the adult feelings of uncertainty and fear and as a result stop questioning and sharing thoughts, then the puppets act as 'the perfect adult'.

Initially, parents found the use of puppets difficult to accept, thinking that we were cranky, or merely playing games with their children. However, an eight-year-old child summed up the use of the puppets within the group when I returned him to his parents. He said 'I like the puppets, they are my friends, I tell them things that no-one else understands'.

Closing the Group

After the puppet show we planned to calm the group down before all going out to lunch to mark the closing of that day's group. We planned to play 'sleeping lions' – asking all the group members to lie totally still and quietly on the floor with one person being appointed to watch and put people 'out' if they moved. We hoped that this would succeed in de-roling the children and would also ensure that the activity of the group would remain within the group room. According to established theories of group work it was important to close the group with a significant event, therefore all the children were invited to stay for lunch before we took them home. The first group were offered the choice of venue for lunch and unanimously chose McDonalds!

The relaxed atmosphere at lunch enabled the children to unwind and chat freely amongst themselves and to complete any group business that they considered unfinished. The original intent was that the children would be collected from the restaurant; however, in practice we delivered many of the children home. This offered the opportunity to chat on a one-to-one basis and to address issues that seemed to be concerning the children. It also gave us an immediate feedback with the children usually asking when they could next come to a group and telling their parents that they had enjoyed themselves.

On-going Groups

While each group is seen as a one off, each particular grouping of young children will meet on approximately four or five occasions. During subsequent groups we continued to use the puppets for further exploration of their feelings and enabling them to deal with the issues that concern them. They are often used as a means of facilitating communication with their dead sibling. Children very often appear to have unfinished business which the puppets enable them to resolve.

We help the children explore some of the issues with which they have been struggling, and help them see that they are still loved and wanted in their own right. We accept that children will come to terms with their feelings of grief in their own time, and that it is OK for them to move on without their deceased sibling. An important lesson learnt in the group is that it is OK to be happy, it is not a pre-requisite of bereavement to be miserable all the time, and that within the group we laugh and have fun. We do not minimize the strength of their sadness or their grief but do promote their feelings of joy and happiness without the guilt which children may experience within a home that is actively grieving.

Parents are made aware that their surviving children can come to more than one block of groups, although in practice very often children do not feel the need to return when the natural cycle of one group is finished.

Problems Experienced Within the Group

When we first established the groups we were unprepared, and upon reflection, possibly quite naive about our expectations and the outcomes we were anticipating. Without doubt this meant that we were unprepared to deal with some of the problems that occurred.

Confidentiality

An accepted group rule is that the group should remain confidential. As this was the established norm within the bereaved parents' group it was clear that we would need to offer this courtesy to the children we were inviting. As mentioned, this initially caused problems amongst the parents. Many parents appeared to consider the suggestion of the group to be an advanced parent and toddler group, that they would bring their children to the group and then sit around the edge of the group room and wait for the duration of the group. Obviously this would have removed any vestige of confidentiality and could not be allowed. Without doubt there have been children who have not been allowed to participate in the group because their parents could not accept the confidentiality ruling. We were aware that there were instances of parent and child groups running side by side with both groups coming together for a mutual discussion at the end; however, we did not feel that that format would work for us.

We made it explicit at the start of each group that the content should stay within the room, but this guarantee led us into problems within the first few groups. A group member was extremely distressed throughout the group, choosing to hide amongst the scatter cushions and using a puppet to act as his voice at strategic points. However, it quickly became apparent that the child had marked suicide intent and was clear in the mode, time and place that he intended to attempt suicide. Clearly this presented an ethical dilemma. We would have to breach confidentiality in order to find him further expert help in dealing with his grief. It was clear that the welfare of the child was paramount, therefore after a long discussion with the boy he agreed that we could share with his parents his feelings of extreme distress.

We now make explicit the fact that the group will remain confidential unless we consider that after consultation with the child we need to disclose their feelings in order to further help them.

Despite the problems that we have experienced we consider that confidentiality must remain a prime group rule as within the groups children have disclosed feelings of anger and resentment towards their parents that they would certainly have kept to themselves if they felt that there was going to be any direct feedback within the family. We hope that giving the children the avenue to express these feelings goes some way to defusing their intensity and helps to reunite the family.

Group Saboteurs

Some children, as some adults, are not natural group members. Although the group is open to all bereaved siblings, natural selection means that many children will elect not to attend. However, some children have chosen to join the group but have, for a variety of reasons, not been able to deal with its content and have attempted to disrupt the other group members.

In our experience we have faced problems with children who have been bereaved a long time before their first group. We have been persuaded to include children who have had long-term entrenched grief and who do not appear to have had the opportunity to work through their feelings. It would appear that these children have established defences that they are not able to relax and that they are very uncomfortable amongst children who are able to face their feelings. As the group is not run to a therapeutic level, merely to offer a safe environment in which to discuss feelings, it was not an appropriate setting to work with children having marked difficulty in grieving.

The only solution that we have found is to remove the saboteur from the group and to work on a one-to-one basis with him or her. In order to achieve this we have always ensured that we have another room available and enough group leaders to allow the child one-to-one work.

As a result we are now much more prescriptive in our selection process prior to children joining the group, and will refer to other agencies children that we do not feel we will be able to contain within the group.

Family Group Membership

Initially, we decided that we would include all appropriately aged siblings in the one group and this appeared acceptable to the bereaved families. In practice, however, it caused marked difficulties within the group. It had the effect of inhibiting particularly the eldest sibling present who would then appear less able to articulate feelings – it is to be assumed that the same protective mechanism that prevents children from sharing their grief with their parents was operating in relation to protecting their siblings. On one occasion one child became very distressed during the group and found the shame (as she perceived it) of crying in front of her younger brother too difficult to cope with and she chose to drop out of the group. In other instances siblings have vied with each other to gain attention and have become increasingly disruptive within the group, or, yet again they feel that as siblings they are being viewed as a collective group and not as individuals in their own right.

It is now our policy never to mix siblings within a group. Although we accept there are some positive benefits in doing so, we feel that maximum benefit will be gained by children coming individually.

Mixed Group Membership

Initially, the group was only open to those who had been bereaved through childhood cancer. This led to accusations of us being 'diseasist' and further isolating these children. Therefore we have on occasions opened the group to children who have been bereaved, usually of a sibling, but with other causes of death. This has had both positive and negative outcomes – it helps the children see that children do not die only from cancer and that they are far from alone – however, the experiences of having a brother or sister die after unsuccessful treatment for malignant disease is very different to death from a road accident or sudden infant death syndrome, and it has caused some conflict within the group. Given our setting and experience, the majority of children come from the children's cancer unit, and this has led to other group members feeling increasingly isolated and as though their personal experience was unique.

On a purely selfish level, we found that opening the group meant that we were flooded with referrals with which we could not cope; sheer volume means that we are unable to offer a supportive group environment to all bereaved children in our area. For children who needed therapeutic input there are two groups run offering a service and we suggest that they are referred for assessment by the group leader.

Adolescent Grief

When we planned the first groups we did not envisage running a group for bereaved adolescents. We did not feel that we had the expertise to run the group; however, it became obvious that the adolescents felt very strongly that they wanted a meeting-place where they could meet others in the same situation. By excluding them from the group they felt further isolated and unimportant. We decided to run a one off group as a trial to see if we could meet the needs that were being expressed.

We felt that it would be inappropriate to ask the adolescents to follow the same formula that we used for the younger children. They were expressing very clear and individual needs – the developmental tasks of adolescents are difficult enough without having to deal with the task of grieving. The bereaved young people with whom we had contact were expressing similar grief to that expressed by their parents, but found it difficult to share this grief with their non-bereaved friends who were starting to abandon them.

The initial group was run purely as a discussion group, and was used to plan further meetings. As with the younger children, the adolescents were told that we did not intend it to be therapeutic, just an arena for them to use as they wished. This caused them great feelings of relief as they appear to have fantasies about what we would be asking them to do.

The first meeting was functional in terms of gelling the group; however, the members were clear that they did not want to sit around and talk in that format again. The adolescent group is now an extremely cohesive self-maintaining activity focused group. We meet regularly and the young people spend their time virtually without adult involvement discussing whatever is concerning them at the time.

Adolescents often appear to have put their grief 'on hold' while they support their parents, and/or a younger sibling, or having to grieve alone feeling unable to seek family support. With hindsight we were increasing these feelings of isolation that the bereaved adolescents were experiencing. To offer a group for them was to acknowledge the validity of their grief and to support and promote the normality of these feelings.

Supervision for Ourselves

We considered it of prime importance to arrange effective supervision for ourselves while we were running the group – we acknowledged that regular contact with distressed and grieving children could create or raise feelings of distress and anxiety within ourselves and that we would need a more experienced counsellor to help us.

We arranged sessions immediately prior to and following each group which gave us the emotional support that we required, but also a forum to discuss any child that was concerning us. As our supervisor was a member of the Child and

Family Guidance Service and Family Therapy Unit it was an excellent opportunity to discuss a possible referral further professional support.

We would argue that in order to be fair to the bereaved children with whom one works it is vital to arrange external support mechanisms for oneself to avoid becoming an emotional sponge to the grieving all around.

Conclusions

Running the group for bereaved siblings has caused us considerable stress over the last five years; however, we have found it an extremely effective medium for working with children dealing with their feelings of loss. Perhaps the best measure of this is the fact that children always want to return and ask when the next group meeting will be. The best praise was offered by a bereaved child when we took him home. He confided to us in the car that he had not really wanted to come but that his parents made him; however, he said with a tone of extreme relief 'It wasn't as bad as I expected, and I think I'll come again'. It should also be mentioned that during our most recent series of groups when we were out for lunch we met this particular young man again having lunch with his family. He strolled over to us in an extremely casual fashion, looked around and said 'you with more bereaved siblings then?', he looked at one of the group members and said 'I used to come on these, but I don't need them any more'. It was a rare moment of praise.

When we initially planned these groups we met with considerable resistance from our medical colleagues who felt that we were cranky and inviting trouble with which we would not be able to deal. However, it is a measure of their success and acceptance within the medical unit that the consultants will now say that they have set up and facilitate the running of groups to support bereaved children.

While we do not suppose that the group meets all bereaved children's needs, we hope that we go some way to enabling children to realize that although the death of a brother or sister is a tragedy, with help and support it need not be a disaster.

References

Lansdown, R. (1985) 'Re: development of the concept of death in children aged 5–9 years.' *Child Care Health Education.*

Davis, H. (1993) *Counselling Parents of Children with Chronic Illness or Disability.* Leicester: British Psychological Society.

CHAPTER 12

Using Drama in Grief Work

Penny Casdagli

'Neti-neti' is a Zen term meaning 'not this, not that' suggesting an idea of perfect balance. When I co-founded the Neti-Neti Theatre Company in 1987, I had no idea I would explore grief for such a long time and in so many ways. Grief is a process, often likened to a journey. Therefore, in this chapter, I would like to chronicle my Grief Project, which ran from 1990 to 1994, hoping it will provide information, support and practical ideas for young people and adults working on grief or working through their bereavement. I also want to show how extraordinary life is, if we will follow where it leads.

It is frequently thought that young people do not experience grief profoundly, or that if they do, being young, they will get over it quickly. Very often their bereavements are not recognized as such at all – for instance, the acute grief a child may feel when a pet dies or when he or she makes the move from Primary to Secondary School. There is therefore little provision for the support of young people through their griefs, less acknowledgement that the areas of death, loss and change are of great importance to them, and very few counselling services available especially for them. Young people are not prepared adequately through their education, both in school and outside it, for the fact of grief and its inevitability in all our lives. Time is meant to do all the healing. This may be because we, as adults, have not come to terms with grief ourselves, and think that what was 'good enough for us will be good enough for them'. But what are the effects of grief on young people, and how can we help them resolve it?

The idea for the Grief Project came out of my previous play about bullying, 'Only Playing, Miss'. In it, Eugene, who has missed several weeks of school due to his father's unexpected death, is bullied on his return by David Rant. Aggressive and disruptive, Rant, it is revealed at the end of the play, is also bereaved. Although he still talks of his mother as if she is alive, she died in his

204

first year at Secondary School. He has not yet accepted the loss or been able or helped to grieve. I noticed many young people were as moved by this parallel theme of bereavement as they were by bullying, and decided to explore further.

The educational consultant and therapist, Dr Pat Lister, a valued adviser on our anti-bullying work, told me that, in her experience, 80 per cent of the students she counselled who were engaged in the bully–bullied relationship, were also suffering recent acute bereavement. For me, she confirmed the link between 'disruptive behaviour' and unresolved grief.

If, in 1989 when 'Only Playing, Miss' was written and performed, bullying was a 'taboo' subject, then death, loss and bereavement and their effects on young people go on being another. While it is possible to suggest strategies to reduce or prevent bullying, nothing can stop bereavement and death. No-one can intervene between us and the fact of our mortality, inhibit the passage of time, nor banish the powerful effects of loss or change from our everyday lives. Particularly because of the AIDS pandemic, the increase in teenage suicide, and contemporary war situations, I felt it important to try to present the issues of grief in a play, and set that play within a school community. To this end, I started to realize that idea.

Neti-Neti worked multilingually, in order to be as accessible as possible. The languages most frequently used were English, Sign Language and Bengali. As much bereavement results from loss of country and language, the multilingual presentation of the play would add a resonance to its content. Work on any Neti-Neti project often involved many activities in addition to the central experience of the play to amplified and supported it, specifically careful research, workshops and interviews.

When the 'Grief' Project started in February 1990, I had very little except the idea, and a cutting from the Observer Newspaper of 18th February 1990 about the suicide of Alexander Moschini called 'The Boy Who Couldn't Change The World', and some poems written by a young bereaved girl, Joanna Chapman, called 'You Too Will Weep'. Some of these poems were to become part of the 'Grief' text.

In the New Year of 1988, Caroline Griffin, a co-founder of the Company and a teacher, was taking her 'A' Level English group one morning. Joanna and her friend arrived late, putting a note on Caroline's desk. It said Joanna was sorry she had not done her homework and her mother had died that morning after a long illness. Her friend had written the note because she did not feel up to it. Caroline's mother had also died some time before. At the first opportunity, she took Joanna into the corridor where they cried together. She later encouraged Joanna to write about her mother and a moving series of poems were the result. Here are two:

School

The day she died I went to school.
It should have been the last thing on my mind
and yet it seemed so important.
I knew that if I didn't go in that day
I probably wouldn't go in ever again;
there are too many memories there.

School hurts a lot.
I sit in the assembly hall
and remember her.
I remember the first time she came to look around,
the parents' evenings, concerts,
and the teacher she spoke to
the conversation she had
the way she sat
and the notes she wrote
her impressions of teachers, pupils and my friends.

Whenever I think of school,
I always think of her.

Innocence Lost Forever

People still think I'm innocent.
They seem unable to see
I lost my innocence long ago.

How could I keep hold of it?
I had to let it go.
I couldn't keep it
and nurse my mother:
prepare her meals
and administer her drugs –
helping her on and off the commode
pulling her knickers up and down
clearing her urine and sickness away
wiping clean her bottom and her face –
help give her a bedbath
and put her into a clean nightie.

O how can I go back
to when I was a child?
My mother combing my hair
and I looking up to her

would see her smile shining down on me
protecting me from all harm:
keeping me innocent.

I can't go back to those days,
but people still think of me
as their 'little innocent Jo.'

More of these poems, together with the play text and specialists' contributions, are to be found in *Grief: The Play, Writing and Workshops* (1992).

In April 1990, Thames Television's 'Help!' team, who had made two short programmes in 1989 about our bullying work, filmed three of Joanna's poems for their programmes on bereavement. Beautifully performed by Charlotte Moulton-Thomas and Angela Sims in English and British Sign Language, they were broadcast that July.

In September, the writing workshops with young people began. The first took place in a London Sixth Form Centre with a class not specially selected in any way for their connection to bereavement. I was astonished by the terrific response to the ideas put forward, and by the writings and improvisations that resulted. I finished the workshops feeling shaken and exhilarated: it seemed the issue of grief would be of interest to our audiences. Here are extracts from that workshop:

'My sister tried to kill herself about a year ago. The thing was actually seeing her blood, and I never could cope with that. I don't talk to her as much as I used to. I carried on with normal life. I went to school that day, got into a fight and went out that night.'

'On Wednesday I came down the stairs and my sister had poured a teapot all over her. And she stood in the middle of the sitting room. Her skin started peeling off as if someone was pulling at it...I didn't know how to help her. You got such a strong feeling inside you: go and help your sister, go and help your sister. But you can't. That gets you even more. Gets you by the neck and you think what's going on? You can't even go and help her because if you touch her it's going to be – a shocking experience.'

'My mother called me into a room. Me and my brother. And she sat us down on a double bed...so we could be together. And she showed us a letter saying that Daddy...died. I don't know exactly how I felt. It seemed to me my mother's face was one of the worst things.'

These workshops widened my definition of bereavement to include other areas of acute loss, not only that of death. I read these writings – a further selection can be found in the 'Grief' book (1992) – and Joanna's poems over and over again whilst writing the 'Grief' play. Many of their sentiments, words and ideas are in the play and fundamental to it. They also sustained me and gave me a focus during the times when the writing proved excruciating.

October saw a week-long 'Grief' workshop with actors, Suresh Vedak, the play's designer, Joanna Chapman, Dr Pat Lister and Peter Nicholas, one of the composers for 'Grief'. We read, remembered, talked and wrote; we improvised, made masks, researched into different cultures' perception of death, and learnt to jig and dance while Peter played his violin. De-briefing from grief work is extremely important. Even though at that time I was not fully conscious of this, we ended the week with our own ritual. This involved a fire in the adventure playground behind the rehearsal room, made with the permission of the Park Keeper, burning poems, writings and paintings, holding flowers and dancing to more music.

During that week, Ian Lucas, the Project's Assistant Director, first wrote about Eddie, his extremely likable friend who had died suddenly in his final year at school. Even at this early stage, I think most of us recognized Eddie's importance. Although the Eddie of 'Grief' bears no resemblance to Ian's friend, Eddie was the name we gave to the central, absent character whose death is the catalyst for the whole play. Perhaps we needed to invent a benign agency outside the Project to guide us through this subterranean maze of sorrow, and lead us out into the world again – a world which we would find both familiar and different, changed, as we were, by our experiences. Or perhaps I did. When Ian asked me if I would like to see where Eddie was buried, I agreed, although it was only in retrospect that I became aware of the significance of that journey to Coventry.

Ian missed the train, arriving at the station late, shocked by news of a friend's suicide. We took the next train. I did not understand just what the journey must have cost him emotionally for I was not, at that time, bereaved myself. We lit a candle for his friend in Coventry Cathedral. Next morning, in thick mist and frost, Ian and I laid flowers on Eddie's grave in the countryside.

On the last working day before Christmas, I visited John Hall and Giselle China at ChildLine. They helped me immensely. For instance, John said that in one sense every call received by ChildLine is about bereavement, not only of the obvious forms, but bereavement of trust, safety, of innocence and self. They showed me round their workplace. Through a glass panel, I watched the telephones being answered by specially trained volunteers. I was struck by the teams of supervisors always present in case a volunteer needed additional support and advice on a particularly difficult call. I realized then that the 'Grief' Project would need a supervisor to help us through any distress the Project might engender in those working on it. I was delighted when Pat Lister agreed to be that person. We all needed to draw on her wisdom, strength and common sense. I am personally enduringly grateful to her for, on New Year's Day, bereavement came my way too and I was devastated.

What had been distressing research became my world, and it was doubtful, because of the nature of the bereavement, if I would be able to work. It seemed ironic the 'Grief' Project should be threatened by the emotion itself. To have cancelled 'Grief' would have meant closing the Company, which seemed more exhausting and terrifying than trying to continue. My colleagues, friends and family supported me. Without them, I can not imagine what I would have done. I felt irrationally that this pain was my punishment for daring to approach the subject, and went on hoping that when the Project was over my life would be as it was before, on the last day of 1990, and everything would be all right again. Impossible this, but it has taken me a very long time to accept. I tried to express this complex and paradoxical feeling of hope and despair in 'Grief'".

Amy and Eddie are twins. He steals a motorbike and crashes it in a fatal accident. The play goes on to look at the effects of his sudden death on Amy, the surviving and lone twin, and his mother and friends. Amy, like many young people, finds herself unable to cry. Finally, towards the end of the play, prompted by the compassion of a kind stranger, these words burst out of her:

'Half of me has gone. It hasn't gone forever, but I will never get it back,'

and then she cries for the first time.

Many months before, I had agreed to devise a workshop play around the themes of loss with acting students from the Guildhall School of Music and Drama, and did so – somehow. This work took place in excruciating circumstances: war in the Gulf, extreme cold and snow, travel chaos, bomb scares and, within the group recent and acute bereavement in addition to my own.

One of the most valuable realizations of this time was that there were people that knew about grief because they had experienced it, and those that did not because they had not – yet. I identified this in the concept of the 'Grief Club'; those that were in it and those that were not. There also seemed to be a fear that grief was contagious, that if you hung around long enough with a member of the 'Grief Club', or talked about it too much, you'd get it too.

And there was no shortage of grief around. On 17th January, the first day of fighting in the Gulf, I was due to be interviewed live about the 'Grief' Project on BBC 2's educational programme, 'Clean Slate'. There was an ominous atmosphere in the building, high security and groups of listless people watching the bank of monitors in the foyer. The introduction to the feature on us was hastily rewritten: 'Now that war in the Gulf is a terrifying reality, many young people will have to face...' Our Project had taken on a new and unwanted relevance.

We were getting calls from educational psychologists working with the children of people in the Armed Services wanting workshops on grief. After much discussion with the Company, we decided we were not the appropriate organization to respond to these demands. One of the first questions a bereaved child will ask when a parent is killed is 'why?' We could not respond to that question positively. We started to prepare ourselves for the tour of 'Grief' to be a 'war tour'. We also knew from Muslim colleagues of the increased racism they were experiencing, and began to think about making the work safe for our Bengali-speaking actors.

The play's themes had begun to emerge clearly, although none of us was certain if and how they could be realized in the final text. Some of the points we wanted to cover were: grief's effects on a school community; the reactions of teachers and other adults; different cultures and their ways of looking at death; ideas of celebrating death; alternative rituals, including funerals and being allowed or not allowed to go to them; divorce, betrayal, and broken love affairs as griefs that commonly affect young people; how a bereaved person may lose themselves, by going missing or in forms of addiction and criminal acts; time and its significance in bereavement; the experience of twins and the lone twin; the invisibility of a sibling when a child dies; the loss of innocence and childhood in having to grow up overnight; the idea that only the bereaved can help each other and that the only 'real' bereavement is death. We wanted to show how important it is for young people to be listened to, and indeed to examine the whole concept of 'listening' which is so much more than any physical ability to hear.

In February, 'Grief's beautiful songs were written, some by Caroline Griffin, others based on Joanna's poems, and set to music by Peter Nicholas and Pule Pheto. Here are the words of the opening song which were sung in English, Sign Language and Bengali:

> Under the light of the cherry blossom
> in the beginning of Spring
> I remember the friends I've left behind.
>
> And in mid-winter
> when light-bulbs glow
> round the fruit in the market
> I wish I'd known my mother.
>
> Life – sometimes I see you moving
> changing before my eyes
>
> As a child, I watched the waves
> appear and disappear.
> I looked at the sand,
> wet in my hand,
> and threw it away.
>
> When I dive into water
> and it closes over my head,

I think of my sister –
think of my sister –
who was afraid of the dark.

Life – sometimes I see you moving
changing before my eyes.
Life – how can we go on singing
in a world so strange to us?

In March, I took all the research material, workshops writings, and the Guildhall version of the play, shut myself up in a room, and, hardly leaving it, finished the play two weeks later. Many people helped me through by writing to me and by phoning. I was fortunate enough to see a young woman, Kaye Dallimore, aged sixteen, on television, talking about the death of her brother. She had had a terrible time, particularly at school. This helped me with the part of one of the teachers in the play, Mrs Purdey, who takes Amy to an empty classroom, and before leaving her there in isolation, advises her both to cheer up and to have a good cry! Later, as one of our Grief Seminar speakers, Kaye made a powerful contribution to these post-performance discussions (transcriptions of these Seminars, 'Talking About Grief', are published by Neti-Neti). In the seminars, there was animated discussion of Mrs Purdey's role in the play. Should a teacher show her own feelings of grief? Why does her crying make Hazel and the other students so angry? Mrs Purdey is an example of an adult with unresolved grief; therefore, when she tells Amy, 'Time is a great healer', the young people in the audience, and most of the adults, know she is speaking of her hope, not of her experience.

I also read Sheila Awoonor-Renner's article in a newspaper about the death of her son. This informed the part of the play in which Eddie's mother, Mrs Walker, learns of her son's death from the police, and is taken to see his body in hospital. Watched by hospital staff through the open door of the chapel, she is not allowed to be alone with him, in case she does 'anything silly'. I also contacted the psychotherapist, Joan Woodward, a lone twin herself, who has researched extensively into this unique form of bereavement. Both Sheila and Joan contributed chapters to the 'Grief' book which beautifully unfold their stories in more detail.

Joan put me in touch with a lone twin who was prepared to speak with me. She happened to be someone I had worked with in a theatre many years ago. She talked to me freely, and was also sensitive to my grief, which had opened up freshly with the writing of the play. When I sent her the script, she replied with a postcard of a dolphin, with these words written on the back: 'Yes – it's very good. I would ring but I am crying too much. Hope rehearsals go well. Best wishes...' I was impressed, and continue to be, by how willing people were to contribute their experience. I think we often feel so disempowered by grief that if there is something we can do, we will. Casting also took place in this month. I was delighted when Charlotte Moulton-Thomas, the profoundly deaf actress, agreed to play Amy, the central part. It turned out, although this was not deliberate, that most of the cast were already members of this notional 'Grief Club'.

Rehearsals started in April. I have never laughed so much while working. The cast, all excellent, understood the issues, and were able to bring the play to life while learning the appropriate languages and songs. The hardest layer of the play to achieve was that it was performed by a cast of actors who were playing a group of bereaved young people who, in turn, played out their story – in order words, they were the 'Grief Club'.

There was hardly any personal recounting in rehearsals, although I did ask the actors half-way through rehearsals to do a piece of private writing about grief and their own lives. I wanted the performers to be able to examine their relationship with the subject in private, knowing no-one would ever read what they had written. This crucial exercise allowed them the protection of distinguishing between their experience and that of their character. They then could draw creatively on any emotional parallels of their own but without exploiting or exposing these experiences. It was only a play we were working on, after all, however important the subject matter might be.

In the event, two of the cast wanted me to read what they had written. One, whose father had been killed in car crash eleven years before, said how it had been almost impossible to stay in the room on the first day of rehearsals. She had wanted to give up being in the play, but now felt she had been helped by rehearsals, and was looking forward to the play opening. The other performer told me about his sister, who he thought about every day. She had died from a cot death when the performer was three months old. The performer had always felt neglected by his parents who were still unable to come to terms with their grief. He said they hoped his sister would be proud of him now. I bet she is.

During the rehearsals, we were made acutely aware of the lack of bereavement support for young people with disabilities. For some unknown reason, one of the large charities for deaf children put a mother of a profoundly deaf boy in touch with us. The boy had been in the same room as his baby brother who had died from a cot death. She was searching for a counsellor who could sign because her son was now so terrified he was refusing to go upstairs, in case the house killed him. We explained we were just a theatre company, but we were so appalled we were determined to try to help – this mother had been telephoning everywhere without success. Finally, after three days, we did find someone who lived in her area and was willing to counsel her son. We learnt how disabled children may suffer even more than their able-bodied peers. For example, hitherto deaf children had not even been able to call ChildLine – although in the Spring of 1992 minicoms, machines which allow deaf and partially deaf children and adults to telephone, were installed.

A young woman on work experience in the office was greatly moved when she read the play. Her name was Elizabeth Walker and she had a twin, Alan. The twins in 'Grief' are called Amy and Eddie Walker therefore, by strange coincidence, they shared the same initials: A. and E. Walker. Elizabeth talked to the actors about being a twin, in addition to her other work, which was a great help, especially to Charlotte, playing Amy.

I asked Pat to come and talk to the company before going on tour. We wanted to learn ways of dealing with young people full of emotions, coming up to the actors at the end of the play and expecting them, perhaps, to 'do' something about it. This was our fear, not a reality, for although many of our audience members cried openly during the play, this situation hardly ever happened. More commonly, the actors were encouraged and told 'That's my story. That happened to me.'

'Grief' opened successfully in May, 1991, performing in schools and theatres in London and nationally. Even though it was summer, the sun hardly shone once. BBC 1's 'People Today' filmed parts of the first performance while BBC1's 'Ipso Facto' filmed the last. Both were excellent; the latter, in particular, made by and for young viewers, broke new ground and gave empowering information in a relaxed and direct way.

We had prepared the schools for 'Grief' as fully as we could, suggesting that some students might not want to watch the play because of the own bereavement, and had asked schools to provide a staffed 'safe' room in case members of the audience needed somewhere quiet to go. Most schools co-operated with great sensitivity. However, there was an exception during one of our theatre performances. A young girl came out of a performance, with one of her teachers, saying she had a headache. I was in the foyer looking after Ouzo, Charlotte Moulton-Thomas's hearing guide dog. She stroked him, had a drink of water and said she felt better, but she stayed out of the rest of the show. Her teacher drew me aside and said, 'I could kick myself, this student is a truant. This is her first day back in school for weeks, and we brought her to see the play but I forgot her brother was killed in a motorbike accident some months ago. I didn't think.' This is exactly the story of the play but the teacher, who had read all our preliminary materials, had not made the connection until her student had walked out. The student rejoined the audience for a Young People's Seminar after the play, at which Kaye Dallimore spoke about how her school coped, or failed to cope, with her bereavement. I think the student got a great deal from what Kaye said. Her brother too had been killed in a road accident.

The responses of our audience of young people and adults were excellent:

'I was very impressed. The presentation challenged the students on many issues, though it remained sensitive and entertaining.'

'Excellent. I used the play for my tutorial with the group confiding their bereavements.'

'I felt at the end of the performance incredibly moved, as did many other people I knew in the audience. I feel my attitude to grief has changed – before, I would have taken grief as being a feeling expressed when a death has occurred – I certainly now have a great deal to think about.'

'After the play, my most needy student – who was sitting in the front row – dead centre – and who is of Asian descent, living in a children's home, with a terrible life story – rushed up. "That show was so brilliant. I'm glad you said to go. I felt really pleased when the lady who couldn't hear, wasn't she beautiful, said Eddie died five days ago. Well, my mum, she died five years ago, oh I was so choked, I put my head down, you know, felt like tears, but it was so good."'

The reviews in the media and newspapers were also full of praise:

'An accomplished, deeply moving, intellectually stimulating play called "Grief" covers more ground in 60 minutes than most and contains suspense, chuckles, discomfort and sadness.' – *Times Educational Supplement*

'An outstanding contribution to this aspect of the curriculum…both in its content and mode of delivery.'– *The Guardian*

'The play's insight furthers our understanding of bereavement and its effects on your daily life… It challenges traditional use of language in theatre…Neti-Neti are breaking new ground in the realm of young people's educational theatre and their creative use of languages, Sign and all, is a challenge which all theatre companies can learn from and take on board.' – *Spare Rib*

The 'Grief' Project went on developing. As well as special projects such as working with bereaved family groups at Liverpool's Alder Hey Hospital and with a whole school community in a London school where a student was murdered in a racist attack, my work with the Project has included:

- extensive research with young people and professional agencies such as ChildLine, Keeping Deaf Children Safe, and the Twins and Multiple Births Association
- experimental drama and writing workshops with young people, actors and other concerned professionals

- the national tour of the multilingual play 'Grief' in 1992, performed in English, Sign Language and Bengali

- participatory drama workshops with young people and in service training sessions with teachers, hospice workers and other professionals

- television appearance in programmes such as Thames T.V.'s 'Help!', BBC TV's 'Clean Slate', 'Ipso Facto' and 'Def II's Extra', and 'People Today'

- publication of the script and writings of young people in 'Grief' published by Neti-Neti

- the hosting and documentation of a series of seminars with audiences of young people, experts and adults, 'Talking About Grief', published by Neti-Neti

- numerous presentations at and participation in medical and voluntary sector conferences on young people, the family and bereavement, both nationally and internationally

- the publication of 'Grief: The Play, Writings and Workshops', (Casdagli, with Gobey and Griffin 1992) which also includes chapters such as 'The Grief of a Deaf Child', 'The Loss of a Twin', 'The Journey of Mourning from a Muslim Perspective', all testifying to the need to acknowledge and talk about grief

- the professional production of 'Grief' as a video, also in English, Sign Language and Sylheti/Bengali with the addition of a unique Sylheti/Bengali synchronized audio-cassette, both available from Neti-Neti

- an adaptation of 'Grief' by myself for BBC Radio 5 which was broadcast in two parts in 1992

- the organization of 'Approaching Grief', a practical workshop day for professionals and carers to explore the way art, drama and listening to young people can change the school ethos and help young people, especially deaf or disabled young people and lead towards change

- the writing of *Grief, Bereavement and Change* (Casdagli and Gobey 1994a), a photocopy-free resource containing five detailed drama workshops, including full guide-lines for work on loss, change and bereavement and the preparation of the facilitator

- the writing of *Grief, Loss and Bereavement: A Quick Guide* (Casdagli and Gobey 1994b), explaining how these sensitive issues can be approached positively and creatively, and giving clear guidance to those dealing with young people and their responses to grief within the school community as well as in the wider community.

I hope my description of the 'Grief' Project will act as an example of how drama, story and theatre are an effective and creative approach to this sensitive area of loss and bereavement in young people. Neti-Neti's 'Grief' Project is now complete. All of us who were involved have now left the Company to pursue and develop our work in different directions and with new Companies.

Masud and Hazel say in the play: 'Only those who have never experienced grief think that it comes to an end,' and I believe this to be true. But I have also learnt that grief is a process and a journey, and that we can be helped and even better, companioned along the way. Sooner or later we shall all grieve, whether we are prepared for it or not. Any work on grief is about life and how we live it. We need to help each other find some answer to the question in the opening song of 'Grief': 'How can we go on singing in a world so strange to us?'

References

Casdagli, P., with Gobey, F. and Griffin, C. (1992) *Grief: The Play, Writing and Workshops.* London: David Fulton.

Casdagli, P. and Gobey, F. (1994a) *Grief, Bereavement and Change.* Cambridge: Daniels Publishing.

Casdagli, P. and Gobey, F. (1994b) *Grief, Loss and Bereavement: A Quick Guide.* Cambridge: Daniels Publishing.

Part Four

Specific Client Groups

CHAPTER 13

Helping Families and Professionals to Work with Children Who Have Learning Difficulties

Judy Sanderson

'I did not know what to say to him. I felt awkward and blundering. I did not know how I could reach him, where I could overtake him and go hand-in-hand with him once more. It is such a secret place, the land of tears.'

The Little Prince. Antoine de Saint-Exupéry (1943)

Introduction

Children with learning difficulties do not exist in isolation. They have the same need for understanding, love and support in times of crisis and sadness as any child. They are not separate from the world and its effects. Their needs, however, can appear so overwhelming that, like the Little Prince, caring families and professionals can themselves feel disabled. This chapter is about empowerment. Its contents are practice-based and derive from work done over a number of years with bereaved children and families. The work was informed by a variety of theoretical models and illuminated by a willingness to use them creatively in response to individual need.

Children experience learning difficulties for many reasons – intellectual impairment, physical and/or mental disability or behavioural disorders. The latter may arise because an individual child has problems or because there is serious family dysfunction. Whatever their source, children such as these can present their families, their teachers and other professionals with a real challenge when existing problems are exacerbated by death, loss and bereavement. 'Taken-for-granted reality has shattered' Smith (1982), or, 'Things didn't use to be like this', Simon, aged four. They may not easily be able to deal with their problems or express their pain. Therefore the possibility of their needing additional help should always be considered so that they can be offered extra input and support as quickly as possible.

It is becoming increasingly recognized that we cannot (as Barbara Munroe has described elsewhere in this book) fail to communicate with children about what is happening in their lives – particularly where life events are powerful and significant for other family members. This can be especially true for children with learning difficulties who may already be more vulnerable to changes in family dynamics.

These children will be acutely aware of how pre-occupied parents have become, and may begin to show their own distress and confusion long before the expected death occurs. Clearly, the nature and closeness of the relationship between child and dying relative will be highly significant, but at no time should it be assumed that there is no awareness of what is happening however incapacitated a child. Where bereavement is predictable, work can be started at an early stage so that a child can be prepared for what is to happen. Pre-grief work done in this way can do much to help any child to adjust to a forthcoming death – or indeed any major loss, such as moving house or changing school. Where death is sudden, unexpected or violent, there will be no preparation or pre-grief work, and for children with learning difficulties, this sort of trauma can be especially devastating.

The value of helping children to address the issues around loss and death through pre-grief work became very clear to one teacher in a unit for children with learning difficulties. She has undertaken with her entire class some work which had been designed to help two children whose mother had died (this is described below). The teacher was both heartened and a little surprised when, some time later another child experienced the death of her grandmother, and coped fairly well. The child's parents and class teachers believed that the discussions and work which had taken place previously had been very helpful. As a result, this teacher concluded that work in the area of death and change was so important that in future all groups would address the topics. She acknowledged, along with a number of her colleagues, that there was a real temptation to protect the children in the unit because they were already vulnerable and less able to look after themselves. This teacher now feels that no child can be protected from the reality of death and that, if children are included rather than excluded from what is going on, they can cope with these life events far more satisfactorily. She recognized that the children in the unit would not always be able to go out and find truthful answers for themselves and that they needed opportunities to explore the issues in a safe and understanding environment, such as that offered by school.

Families, teachers and other professionals will each have a different view and understanding of the child, and so ideally should share their insights and observations. Co-operation at this point between all parties is vital, and whether this is possible before the child experiences the death, or afterwards, it will help to alleviate worry and provide comfort for the child or young adult.

Assessment

Considered holistic assessment plays a large part in achieving a better understanding of what needs doing, who might do it and how it could be done. All those close to the child have a contribution to make. Day-to-day observations and each individual's unique knowledge about the child's usual response and any changes that have occurred will help to create a fuller picture. Assessing a child and his/her needs is not a one-off procedure but a process that needs to be repeated at regular intervals. This will enable appropriate changes to be initiated as time goes on and a proper response made to shifts in behaviour and demeanour as they occur. In undertaking any assessment, full use should be made of existing records or anecdotal information. In addition, in attempting to understand how the illness or death is perceived by the child, a developmental perspective is both helpful and important. Children with profound difficulties certainly experience the effects of loss and bereavement, but will do so in a manner perhaps reminiscent of a much younger child. Methods already used in school, such as creative writing, painting, and the use of workbooks, will be familiar for both teacher and child and can often be adapted for work in this area.

Factors in undertaking an assessment need to include a family history and the background to current events.

How was the death experienced by the child?

- how were they told?
- were they present?
- did they see the body?
- did they go to the funeral?
- what was the child's relationship to the deceased?
- what changes have occurred as a result of the death?
- how, as far as it is possible to ascertain, have the changes affected the child?
- what are the current issues for those concerned with his/her wellbeing, whether at school or at home?
- how are others in the family coping?
- who appears to be able to offer the most help to the child?

Finally, and perhaps most important of all

HOW DOES THE CHILD SEE IT?

It is very important to ask – and to keep on asking. If they feel safe, bereaved children will tell us how they feel. The most profoundly disabled will show us.

Clearly assessment is complex, but experience has shown that it is time well spent. It cannot be hurried, and the gathered information can be shared and used to put together a package of support and help for the individual in question. It may be helpful to draw up a profile of the child, including a family tree and a description of the family circumstances. This could include housing, church membership, other supports in the community and anything else that could illuminate the assessment. For a more formal model of assessment that could be used by parents and professionals, the chapter on assessments and statements in Diana Kimpton's (1990) book *A Special Child in the Family*, is very helpful.

Each child, each family, each loss is different and must be handled with sensitivity. This does not mean that group activities cannot be very helpful, but they will vary according to the individual needs of each child and these can best be decided in the light of a full understanding of the circumstances.

Once as much information as possible has been obtained, then those concerned can meet to decide how to proceed. There is no one best way! Sometimes it is necessary to try a variety of interventions – but if they simply know that the task is being addressed, many children will immediately begin to feel more secure and less alone.

Interventions

How does this work in practice?

> 'Tell them and they hear.
> Show them and they see.
> Do it and they understand.'
>
> Ward (1993)

Peter

Peter, who had suffered severe brain damage in a road accident when he was six years old, was nineteen when his father died. Before the accident he had been a happy, bright and loving little boy. Afterwards he was profoundly disabled and had great difficulty coping with even the most basic tasks of daily living. His parents, Joe and Katie, managed to look after him at home, however, and he had attended a special school during normal term-time. When he reached his mid-teens, his father was diagnosed as having cancer and his parents reluctantly agreed that Peter should go into residential care. They hoped that together they could support him in this necessary move. As well as his father's illness, his mother was frail and going blind.

Initially, Peter found the move traumatic. His already difficult behaviour became more and more of a problem with episodes of violence and increased fitting. His inability to express himself verbally led to a lot of what was described as 'acting out' and his parents had to fight to prevent their son from being sedated. As Joe himself became more incapacitated with his illness, he and Katie wanted to try and prepare Peter for Joe's death. Those caring for Peter did not agree – fearing a repetition of Peter's original response four years earlier when he had demonstrated very disturbed and distressed behaviour at being moved to a residential setting. When Joe finally died, Peter was quite unprepared, although he had seen his father change from a strong, well-built man to an emaciated figure, confined to a wheelchair. Peter did not see his father after death, and because of his unpredictable outbursts, did not go to the funeral either. However, Katie felt strongly that he needed to know what was involved and arranged for photographs to be taken of her husband's body as well as of the funeral itself.

Katie told Peter herself that his father had died and that her own twice weekly visits would no longer be possible. Peter was puzzled and clearly did not fully understand either what 'dead' meant, or why his much-loved father no longer came to see him at regular intervals. In the weeks that followed, Katie became depressed and felt very unsupported in her efforts to help Peter. Her own visits were curtailed by a lack of transport and failing sight. Peter, as he realized his father was not coming at all and his mother only rarely, expressed a lot of anger. He regularly shouted and sobbed and became especially disruptive at mealtimes. He threw plates and food at other residents. He ate very little and slept only fitfully. Katie had fought many battles on behalf of her son and, seeing his distress, insisted that everyone get together to see what could be done. As a result, a careful process of assessment was initiated to get as full a picture as possible of what was happening in order to help Peter to deal with his loss and his despair.

This involved all those concerned with Peter's care – and in particular his residential key-worker. Katie shared the photographs that had been taken and the key-worker began to put together a book about Joe for Peter to look at and use. He already had a picture book of photographs and drawings which he used to facilitate everyday communication, and during the assessment staff had told us that since Joe had died, Peter had refused to look at any pages that had pictures of his father on them.

It was important for Peter that staff and family understood why he was exhibiting such difficult behaviour. His expressions of loss, abandonment and grief were certainly very challenging, but were understandable in the context of his father's death and Peter's inability to express his feelings easily. A supportive programme was arranged to help him. Regular times to look at the photographs were set aside, even though he found this very hard and could only tolerate it for very short periods. Special efforts were made to praise Peter for positive behaviour, and to offer him enjoyable alternative activities if he was disruptive. He had always enjoyed listening to traditional Scottish music with his parents, and so Peter was given a Walkman of his own with a special tape to play, on which his mother introduced many of the tunes and songs. These reminded him of the occasions they had listened to them as a family in earlier years. The music became very precious to Peter. It helped him to grieve and express many of his feelings. Sometimes when listening he would bang loudly on the table with the music and he obviously found this a great release as he sometimes laughed and sometimes cried. He visited his father's grave – both with his key-worker and with his mother. We also introduced a volunteer bereavement visitor to the family and he was able to take Katie on more regular visits to Peter so that they could spend time together. They were an affectionate family and these visits provided opportunities for physical contact.

Katie was able to let Peter see her cry, and this shared expression of pain seemed to help Peter himself to express his sadness in a more acceptable way. The bereavement visitor was able to offer a flexible link between mother and son. He took time to get to know staff, and showed a willingness to get involved with Peter in a range of activities. This enabled Peter to restart 'riding for the disabled' and his pleasure at the physical contact with his favourite horse was unmistakable.

Katie relaxed and began to remember the other things that helped Peter cope with difficult times: a furry hot-water bottle, whatever the weather; eating outside on picnic rugs where spills and cutlery were less of a problem. Peter gradually began to spend time with his photographs, including those of the funeral, and although quite a few were destroyed when he became angry with his Dad, eventually the book became a powerful source of comfort – often taken to bed. (Copies of all photographs were kept as it was anticipated that Peter might react in this way.)

He was encouraged to help in the garden and to get involved in physical activities as far as he was able, and whenever practicable he was given a choice of activity. Staff noted that for some weeks he almost always chose to break up lumps of soil, or on one occasion he helped to demolish an old wall. Later he enjoyed planting bulbs and watching them grow. Peter's key-worker was heartened and reassured by his responses. Once she understood that his very difficult behaviour was a result of his grief, she was enthusiastic about finding ways to help.

In talking to Peter, all the staff mentioned his father and always spoke of him as dead. As Peter did not really understand what this meant, they made the most of every opportunity to show him. In the garden for example, a dead worm and a live one!! One day in his residents' lounge – a dead budgie and a live one! Peter was not able to indicate how much he understood – but he was very interested and curious in comparing the two. Staff again acknowledged that previously they would probably have replaced the dead bird as quickly as possible to avoid upset. In this instance, they organized a funeral for the bird, to which the resident young people were invited, and which they later compared to the photographs Peter had of his father's funeral.

I have described Peter's experiences in some detail because I believe his is not an isolated instance. Initially his mother had been excluded from his bereavement care as staff did not want to distress him any further. She had not realized how bad his behaviour had become, and yet, once informed, had been able to offer many comforting suggestions. She had not wanted to be 'protected' in this way and was angry that Peter may have had to experience additional avoidable pain as a result. Peter's needs in dealing with loss and bereavement were the latest in a series of battles Katie and Joe had initially fought together on his behalf and it was very important to Katie that she could still make a contribution, following Joe's death.

In the beginning, many of those involved in Peter's care believed his limited understanding meant that nothing should be done to 'rock the boat'. They initially failed to recognize what Peter had observed, felt and indeed, understood – that something terrible HAD happened. Life for Peter had become far from normal. Months later, Peter continues to adjust to the changes he has experienced – and staff, although finding it hard, are beginning to try and help him understand that his mother, too, is getting old and is often unwell. Peter's bereavement visitor is staying involved for the time being, and is himself looking to extend his understanding of learning difficulties. He believes training in both areas will help him to be supportive, not only to Peter, but to others in the future with special needs.

Peter's learning difficulties were profound. Many other children were less disabled, but they may still need extra help in dealing with their experience of loss and bereavement.

Jenny and Ben

'Can I have a ticket to Heaven, please?'

Jenny and Ben were ten and twelve years old and attended the unit for children with moderate learning difficulties I referred to earlier. When their mother became terminally ill they went to live with foster-parents as their father was unable to manage to care for both his wife and his children's special needs. The school was aware of these events and initiated a case discussion involving parents, foster parents, teachers and an educational psychologist, to look at ways of helping. Before any pre-grief work could be started, however, Mum died unexpectedly. Initially Jenny and Ben appeared unaffected, but they soon became very disruptive, both at school and with foster parents. As a result, the school made contact with the local hospice for advice. Following joint discussions and an assessment, it was agreed that their foster mum would do some individual work with them at home, and the teacher would initiate some group activities in class.

A major problem, expressed by Jenny in particular, was why Mum had not told her where she was going and what heaven was like. I suggested that the class teacher might like to use Doris Stickney's (1984) book about water-bugs and dragonflies, not as a story read out loud, but as the basis for a group activity. It described the transformation of a water-bug into a dragonfly and the feelings engendered by the unknown as this occurs. The class all brought pieces of material to make the pond, the reeds and the surrounding landscape – even using sequins for the dragonfly's wings. At each stage teachers and children talked about the feelings and ideas that the story inspired. Jenny and Ben contributed a great deal to these safe discussions as they did not feel singled out. The finished collage was often used for the retelling of the story. It remained visible in the classroom and later in the hall, and a number of other children made the connection between the dragonfly and a deceased pet or relative.

The teacher and her classroom assistant decided to extend the discussions to include projects on cycles and change and to include death as a natural part of life. The children picked flowers and watched them fade. They planted bulbs – saw them flower, wilt and (with a little help) flower again. Because many in the class found waiting quite hard, activities were varied so that bulbs flowering at different times helped to reduce the waiting time for youngsters with a short attention span. Dried and silk flowers were compared with fresh flowers over a few days – with the children regularly touching and handling them to experience the differences. To explain burial and cremation, dry leaves were used. Crumbled with soil, they 'joined with the earth' as bodies do in a burial. Allowed to smoulder gently, the smoke 'joined with the air' as in cremation. It was clear that repetition was both helpful and necessary, and the classroom assistant once confided that she had probably used the collage as a story so often that it had become her answer to insomnia!

Many of the very good story books now available to help children experiencing loss can be used in a practical way too, and it is often worth trying books aimed for a younger age group when working with a group of children with learning difficulties. The book, *Badger's Parting Gifts* (Varley 1985) can be used as a way of building links with past and present, home and school.

Jenny and Ben both brought treasures that had once belonged to their mother to show the group. Both carried her photograph, Ben in a small wallet, Jenny in a locket. Both highly treasured gifts had been discussed with Foster Mum when the children had first been placed with her. Mementos such as these can be very comforting. In another family a grandmother, who had been very involved in the daily care of her grand-daughters, bought each child an inscribed bracelet. These two little girls had only slight learning difficulties, but like most children with no such problems, found the gifts very comforting.

Jenny and Ben's teachers also encouraged them to bring 'comforting things' to school. Other children joined in and the class talked about how nice it was to have these things whenever sad, angry or painful feelings came up for discussion. The treasured items were usually brought to school on Fridays, and there were many much loved teddies, old blankets, and even a baby pillow. The book *Good Grief,* Ward (1993), provides many suggestions for how children can feel safer and comforted.

Some of these ideas were used by Jenny and Ben's foster parents. They offered lots of extra cuddles, even though they were often rejected initially. They spent time using the little book *When Someone Very Special Dies,* Heegaard (1991) with both children, but adapted it to make it much more simple for Jenny and Ben to use. They kept in touch with the children's father and supported all the family in visits to the grave.

Comments the children made, such as: 'We'll go back to Mummy now, if you don't mind' indicated just how long is needed for a real understanding of what had happened to develop. Again the 'Water Bug' story was re-told. This time the children drew the story with crayoning to underline the reality that Mummy could not return. Opportunities were offered to express feelings of anger at the perceived rejection. Clay was pummelled, balloons were burst and during a brief two days of snowfall the children built, and demolished, a number of snowmen. These icy characters also experienced a lot of verbal abuse – against mum, dad and the foster-parents, but Jenny and Ben were allowed to shout and realize that it was all right to express strong feelings in a safe place. They needed many such opportunities and, like much younger children, needed the information repeated and, wherever possible, demonstrated, over and over again.

All children need clear, honest explanations within the limits of their understanding. For children with learning difficulties this is even more important. Children with special needs are even more likely to take things at face value. So like all children, they should not be told that granny, for example, 'went to sleep' and they need repeated reassurance that nothing they said or did resulted in anyone dying. Jenny and Ben, for example, were sure that they had been sent away for being naughty, and even though they did not indicate that they felt they had contributed to Mummy's death, they were often told indirectly that no blame could be attached to them, to make absolutely sure they did not feel responsible.

The value of consistency, and continuity, at school and at home cannot be emphasized too strongly. Again, it was Jenny who, having seen some live fish in the lake at a local park and packaged fish in the local supermarket, told her foster mum that the pig hanging in the butcher's was dead, unlike the ones wandering around in the children's zoo. All concerned felt that this was a tremendous realization for Jenny – but it had taken 18 months of regular discussion for this to be achieved. Many 'normal' children would benefit similarly; few get the opportunity, whether there are special needs or not. In Jenny's case, her foster mother had worked with her alone and with her teachers, including spending time in the classroom and on class outings.

Death is part of life and an understanding of it is possible within the normal curriculum. It can be introduced as a special topic when there is an urgent need to respond to a bereaved child. Addressing issues around loss can help, not only in bereavement but, as suggested earlier, in many of life's experiences. Children with learning difficulties may sometimes be more sheltered than most, but exposure to major issues can also be all the more difficult to deal with. At Acorns Children's Hospice, Birmingham, every effort is made to help parents and siblings come to terms with what is often an expected death. The support is offered by a multi-disciplinary team, working closely with other professionals involved in a child's care. Many Acorns children themselves have learning difficulties, and so close links exist with the schools or units where the children receive their education. Such links are invaluable and ideas are often passed on about ways communication with the children can be improved.

Acorns is fortunate in having a building in which to spend time with the children. The *multi-sensory room* is a safe place to explore and express, feelings. The *jacuzzi* is both fun and a source of warm comfort. Staff are able to work together, and where problems seem insurmountable, consultation and sharing often provide not only fresh ideas, but support. There is also a *special bedroom*. This is where children who have died can stay – often for as much as a week, prior to the funeral, and it is a place where parents and other family members are able to visit freely. It provides an absolutely invaluable opportunity to come to terms with the reality of death. Any visiting child going to the special bedroom, perhaps to see a dead sibling, will be very carefully prepared. They go with someone they trust and feel safe with. They are told that the deceased child will be pale, perhaps a little discoloured, and most of all cold. The children show interest and curiosity. Older children may cry and become distressed. All children take their cues from the adults caring for them. Many come back each day – touching or holding the dead child. They bring small gifts, stories and poems. They say goodbye – and can keep checking out the 'deadness of dead'. Some adults find this shocking. Our experience is that when handled with great sensitivity, it is tremendously helpful. No one, child or adult, goes there unless they themselves feel it is what they want. Sometimes families cry together and get angry together. As long as the children are not excluded, they usually cope very well. Nothing is worse than being left in the car whilst parents come in, only to re-appear with tear-stained faces. In such circumstances the children's imaginations work overtime. The special bedroom can be made to suit individual need and preference. It is non-denominational and used equally by families from all cultures and religious beliefs. Essential oils can be burned, and it has recently become possible to offer parents and children the comfort of aromatherapy from a trained therapist in a quiet room away from the bedroom itself.

The special bedroom is private and families also have the use of a small, equally private, sitting room. Drinks and food are provided as needed, and many families choose to sleep on the premises. Resources such as these are few at present – but where they exist they do offer a lot, especially to children with learning difficulties. The children's understanding is enhanced by being there and doing things. They can be involved in buying a 'special outfit' for their sibling, helping to dress them – even to help put the deceased child into a coffin before the funeral service. The funeral itself then makes more sense and is much less mysterious.

As Peter, Jenny and Ben have shown – doing can be far more helpful than talking by itself. Play materials can be normal everyday things – but can be extended to include special extras relevant to each child's circumstances. These include syringes (no needles), an oxygen mask, or bandages.

Children value and respond to honesty and to being included in family activities. Sometimes to help any child it is first necessary to reassure and support their parents, carers and teachers. Problems can and do arise throughout, and the level of input needed could become prohibitive. There are always constraints on time and resources and every professional has to be realistic about what is and what is not possible. In any case it is often better practice, and more effective, to support the parent or carer in doing the work. This benefits everyone as they share the task of dealing with the difficult feelings. It empowers the family rather than creates dependency.

The dearth of information about ways to help children with learning difficulties is part of the wider problem of addressing issues around death and bereavement. The best ideas are therefore often ones which are born of necessity. I have invented characters and situations 'on the spot' to deal with an issue which, if not dealt with there and then, might not come up again. For example, many of the toys belonging to bereaved children 'whisper in my ear', and very young children and those with learning difficulties will pay great attention to what has been said by Rosie, or Cuddles, or Bunny! My comments, by comparison, are uninteresting! This use of familiar toys as puppets can therefore be very helpful in showing a child that 'someone' understands their conflicting and difficult feelings. It is vital to recognize when any child has needs that go beyond the knowledge that we have. Perhaps behaviour is not manageable, either at school or at home. A child might be very withdrawn and unresponsive despite sensitive efforts to enter his or her world, or perhaps severe nightmares are a serious problem. Referral to specialists in child guidance, or child therapists is then of utmost importance. In any case it is often very helpful to keep other professionals, such as the family doctor, informed of what is already being undertaken.

Sometimes a whole community can acknowledge an individual death – 'celebrating the unique presence of each person'. In being open about death as a part of life, special assemblies, short meaningful ceremonies and group meetings all help. They need to reflect the cultural and religious beliefs of those involved – and this too is addressed elsewhere in this book.

There is a growing body of knowledge, and an existing wealth of ideas that can be imaginatively adapted. I have only been able to mention some of the ideas I have tried and worked with. Books such as those I have already mentioned and the further reading lists that they offer provide much more. Less obvious, but also of great value, are books such as Violet Oaklander's *Windows to our Children* (1978). She is inspired in her use of painting – describing ideas that make so much sense. Ideas such as 'paint things big to emphasize their importance' or the value of not giving too many instructions as to what to do with a lump of clay. She reminded me that working with clay, or music, or water can be a sensory experience – touching, feeling and sharing. She also said that although adults often tell children that it is rude to stare – that this is how they learn! For children with learning difficulties this can be really important; I laughed when she said that fortunately these children were often less inhibited.

Finally, I would like to encourage all those working with children who have learning difficulties to use all their skills and knowledge. I was previously familiar with the use of life-story books for children who were waiting to be placed for adoption. This adapted well to bereavement work. Current knowledge and secure practice can too easily be disregarded in a search for the 'right way'. All that might be needed is to use existing skills imaginatively, in a different context.

I would like to conclude with an invitation. Many readers of this chapter will have discovered other ways of helping these special children to cope with loss, death or bereavement. Please get in touch if you are one of them – next time, this chapter may be a whole book.

References

Heegard, M. (1991) *When Someone Very Special Dies*. Minneapolis, MN: Woodland Press.

Kimpton, D. (1990) *A Special Child in the Family*. London: Sheldon Press.

Oaklander, V. (1978) *Windows to our Children*. Moab, Utah: Real People Press.

Philpott, T. (ed) (1989) *Last Things – Social Work with the Dying and Bereaved*. Sutton, Surrey: *Community Care*.

Saint-Exupéry, A. de (1943) *The Little Prince*. London: Pavilion Books (1995).

Smith, C.R. (1982) *Social Work with the Dying and Bereaved*. New York: Macmillan.

Stickney, D. (1984) *Waterbugs and Dragonflies – Explaining Death to Children*. London: Mowbrays.

Varley, S. (1985) *Badger's Parting Gifts*. London: Picture Lions.

Ward, B. and Associates (1989) *Good Grief – Exploring Feelings, Loss and Death with Under 11s*. London: Jessica Kingsley Publishers (second edition 1995).

Suggested Reading

Heegard, M. (1988) *Facilitator's Guide for When Someone Very Special Dies.* Minneapolis, MN: Woodland Press.

Wilhelm, H. (1985) *I'll Always Love You.* Kent: Hodder and Stoughton.

Warden, W. (1983) *Grief Counselling and Grief Therapy.* London: Tavistock.

CHAPTER 14

Transcultural Counselling
Bereavement Counselling with Adolescents

Jan Wilby

Introduction

A school is a community in itself as well as a meeting point of many communities, cultures, traditions, values and beliefs. The amount of time, a minimum of six hours a day, which is spent in school means that the sharing which occurs between individuals and groups of people within the school system covers a broad spectrum of life experiences and concerns. If someone dies the resulting loss is like the effect of a pebble in a still pond. All aspects of our lives are affected and a significant part of that 'pond' is the school or workplace.

As a teacher counsellor I have spent a considerable amount of time counselling young people and adults within our school community following loss through death. A number of teachers are involved in counselling within Manning school and the transcultural model of counselling which I explain in this chapter is a developing approach. The staff have accepted counselling as an alternative approach within the pastoral system and have been involved in various training programmes.

My interest in the concept of transcultural counselling began during previous work as a Youth and Community Worker, but the learning is a continuing journey.

Transcultural Counselling is not about being an expert on any given culture, it is a way of thinking in which culture is understood, acknowledged, appreciated and valued. When applied to any particular area of counselling the importance for the counsellor rests in their awareness of their own cultural beliefs and attitudes, developing awareness of other cultures and being sensitive to the influences of culture during the counselling process.

As a counsellor in a multicultural society I need to be flexible. I need to be able to re-evaluate my counselling style and approach, to work consistently and continually on my cultural self-awareness in order to be an effective transcultural counsellor. I work from the base that all counselling can be considered 'transcultural' which, in this sense, means the interaction between people of differing cultures; the implication is of interactions crossing cultural boundaries.

Culture

The concept of culture has numerous definitions but essentially the fact that culture is learned and it is not innate has significant implications. We are all born into a culture and the experiences of those influences which are intrinsic in that culture affect the way we lead our lives, relate to other people and determine our futures.

D'Ardenne and Mahtani (1989) have found that the terms 'culture' 'race' and 'ethnic groups' are frequently used to express different ideas about a society, all of which can have very different meanings. They go on to say that people in general avoid terms such as race and class when they talk about culture because they are emotive terms and can bring out deeply held prejudices. I believe this to be true but I also believe that in any training or analysis of transcultural counselling the issues of race, class and gender are implicit in that process and cannot be separated. D'Ardenne and Mahtani continue to say that 'In common use, the term "culture" has come to mean any difference between one group of people and another' (p.4).

Transcultural counselling has been a major development in counselling over the past decade; this development challenges some of the accepted and traditional western counselling theories such as 'person centred' and 'behaviourist' theories. The traditional western patriarchal theories could be considered a form of cultural imperialism when they are simplistically applied to:

(1) people with clearly different cultural backgrounds

(2) people who personally live with cultural plurality.

The individual counsellor needs to explore his or her own culture so that they are constantly aware of their own beliefs and attitudes about life issues and through this awareness can respond appropriately, acknowledging the importance of culture in the lives of their clients. A useful approach is to use the model described by Don Locke (1992) who offers a range of questions which can increase self-awareness:

> 'What is my cultural heritage? What was the culture of my parents and grandparents? With what cultural group(s) do I identify? What is the cultural relevance of my name? What values, beliefs, opinions and attitudes do I hold that are consistent with the dominant culture? How did I learn these?' (p.2)

These and other questions suggested by Locke enable the counsellor to explore significant aspects of their own culture and enhance their sensitivity to others who may be of similar or different cultures. This sensitivity to cultural differences should help prevent ethnocentric assumptions that one's own culture or experience necessarily provides a valid baseline for understanding the feelings and behaviour of someone from a different cultural background.

Culture also determines our view of mortality and how we are prepared to face bereavement. It determines the rituals surrounding death, gives meaning to death and provides a structure through the rituals which in turn give some sense of security at a time of great distress and disorientation.

The bereavement counsellor needs to have an understanding of death within their own culture and be prepared to learn of other beliefs and practices so that the responses they make are appropriate. These are the basic premises on which the transcultural model of counselling is based. The effectiveness of counselling within the school system should be based on this model and the examples I will use have particular reference to the role which the school plays in the life of an adolescent who faces loss through death.

Manning school is a multicultural comprehensive school for girls which has an intake of some forty plus primary schools, therefore the students come from a wide range of social and cultural backgrounds. The ethos of the school is one of valuing the individual and there is a commitment to equal opportunities, anti-racist practice, gender and disability awareness. The pastoral system is an important part of that structure and enables the learning which is part of the equal opportunity policy.

Working with Adolescents

It is important that counsellors and teachers who are working with adolescents understand the particular difficulties which loss can cause at this time of life. Ellan Noonan (1993) describes adolescence as a period of transition, similar in many respects to bereavement, one which involves losing aspects of yourself and mourning that loss. Mood swings, anger, guilt, depression, impatience and impetuousness are all emotional states which are usual in bereavement and in adolescence. Her analogy of comparing adolescence with bereavement, as a stage in life when loss means facing a whole series of changes which have similar presenting issues, highlights one of the major difficulties for people whose parents die when they are still young.

A young person is already going through a kind of bereavement, losing parts of themselves and the people around them as bodies, personalities and through changes in relationships. A parent's death at the same time is a double blow; an additional loss and shock at a time of considerable change.

Rebecca Abrams (1992) tells her own story in order to help others understand. She says;

'Death is not in the scheme of things at this time of your life, it is usually premature and unexpected, it sets you apart from your friends, interferes with activities normal to your age and stage in life and places a burden of emotions, expectations and responsibilities on your shoulders that you are not at all ready for.' (p.xiv)

Case Studies

I have completed some research in our school with a few students who have experienced the loss of their mother through death. The students, with whom I worked particularly closely, were in my tutor group when the deaths occurred. I was their tutor and counsellor immediately following the bereavements and kept that role separate from the role which I adopted when doing research for my MEd a year later. One girl was particularly willing to participate as she felt that other people could learn from her experience.

Saria was a Muslim girl who had recently moved to this school. Her mother had been ill for some time and this had made school life very difficult for Saria. She said that she wanted so much to spend time with her mother and did not know how to explain this to anyone. Work was difficult as she had missed lessons but she seemed to settle well with a number of friends whom she had known for a long time. Saria's mother died in December. Her friends kept me in touch with her and I wrote to her, knowing that she would be going to Pakistan with the body as this is the tradition for many Muslim families. When she returned there was the opportunity to share time and feelings. The rest of the staff knew what had happened and were sensitive to her loss. A year later I interviewed her for the research. My main question was whether the school had been supportive and could we 'do better'.

In the Muslim community, the tradition is that everyone visits and supports a bereaved family. There is an 'open house' when people can go and share in the grief. This is common to a number of cultures and the effect is that grief is overt, acknowledged and shared. In school the peer group was supportive, knowing what would happen, confident that they could participate in the rituals, having previously been involved in these experiences as part of their cultural socialisation process. Saria said the school was as supportive as she could have expected. She valued the times when we had shared her grief, it was so important to be able to talk about what had happened, not just after the death but during the months of her mother's illness.

The comparative situation was when Jill's mother died, just before the beginning of the Autumn term. Jill was, Anglo African. She was the youngest of the family and lived alone with her mother. Her previous tutor had supported her through her mother's illness and continued this role when Jill returned to school directly after the funeral. There was no tradition which enabled time away from school but this is not unusual; many young people are sent back to their schooling immediately whilst the adults are coping with their grief.

Jill's father, although not part of the present family arrangements, was involved in discussions about her future. In her grief she rejected him and her African heritage, only seeing him as a provider of material needs. The insecurity which followed was very hard for Jill as well as trying to cope with school. Her grief surfaced one day in a lesson, which I was teaching. She slapped a Sikh girl who 'had looked at her'. The slap was a major insult in Sikh culture and the girl was concerned about that and how her parents would react. I was relieved of my teaching by the Headteacher and spent some time with the Sikh student who was very understanding about Jill's grief. The result of immediate space being created was that I could then spend some time with Jill so that bereavement counselling could take place. The remainder of Jill's school life was turbulent at times but a support structure meant that a number of people were there when needed. Her peer group also had a difficult time; they felt guilty talking about their mothers and felt very confused and anxious at times. For most of them death had never been an issue before; they had been shielded in their cultures from any real involvement.

Eventually Jill went to live with her mother's sister and we maintained regular contact with her aunt as well as giving appropriate support to Jill until she left the school.

The Implications for the School

A number of factors emerge from these examples. Primarily, we need to assess the response that a school can make. In cases like Saria's, the cultural norms of taking the body back to the home country means a significant absence which can lead to problems in academic courses. In Jill's case we needed to be prepared immediately and respond appropriately to the members of the family who consulted us.

There needs to be an understanding amongst the teaching staff that these students will need additional support on return to the school. The counselling approach is very helpful and can be used effectively as part of the supportive structure. When Jill was not able to cope in the classroom, the Headteacher immediately took over my teaching to free me for counselling. I also worked with the Head of Year who provided support and guidance on academic concerns and there was a high level of communication between all members of staff who were involved. The peer group also needed support and time was given to enable them to explore their feelings with me. As for any school-based counselling, consideration was given to the need for a quiet room and our school now has a Counselling room, away from the main teaching areas. Appropriate responses can be made if the bereavement is seen in a cultural context.

Death on the Curriculum

Children are often protected from the traumas surrounding death in the family. In a culture where younger members are included and socialized in the bereavement rituals of family and community, there seems to be a more confident approach. They are more sure of what to say and how to respond to the bereaved person and because of this can be more supportive. The over-riding motivation for the typical teenager, particularly in a school setting, is to fit in with peers. In groups where the friends are not as prepared to face the issue of death, they need support themselves in order to cope with the grief of their friend. In response to a request by a group of sociology students, I led a discussion on death. Their reason for asking was that they felt that it was an important issue and those who had been personally affected needed somewhere to talk and explore feelings freely and with confidence.

I have since introduced the issue of death as a subject for discussion in the personal and social education programme. The agenda for the course is chosen by the students from a range of issues and each group has asked for death to be on the agenda. The major impact that the lessons have on me, as the teacher, is that I am invariably impressed by the sensitivity of the students and the level of sharing which occurs. There is an appreciation of the input by students of differing cultures and real discussion about the meaning behind the rituals; for example, the cultural attitudes and choices made between cremation and burial. The religious beliefs are, in some cultures, the reason for the choice. Significant questions might be 'Does the soul leave the body at the point of death or at the cremation?' 'Does the burial mean that at some future time the body will be resurrected ?' I believe that by putting death on the curriculum one of the results may be a more assured attitude when they support friends through bereavement in school or in their communities.

Developing the Counselling Approach

My counselling role has developed in recent years with time allowed on the timetable. Many more students know about my role and are referred in a variety of ways but increasingly refer themselves or a friend. Individuals who know me have come to share their losses as well as bringing a friend later. With these younger students, the telling of 'the story', sharing memories and perhaps bringing a photograph of the deceased are ways in which they can begin to understand their grief.

When one black student came to see me because her Jamaican grandad died, we read the story *To Hell with Dying*, by Alice Walker (1988). The book is beautifully illustrated and written for a young person. The characters in the story are black and it was clear that my student could identify with it and found an element of peace in the story and the pictures.

It is useful to collect a variety of texts or pictures which can aid the young person in their bereavement. An example of this type of resource is *When*

Something Terrible Happens by Marge Heegaard (1991). These resources can enable the expression of feelings and help them to move on from the disabling sadness which is often the state in which they arrive, unable to cope with the normal school day. In a school, therefore, the counselling approach can include specific strategies for facing up to the needs of the bereaved person within the organisation. A significant part of these has to be the acceptance that grief does not disappear overnight, that the need for long term support is addressed and that the range of responses must match the needs of the individual with particular reference to their cultural selves. Death as a subject becomes easier to cope with when it is not left off everyone's agenda. The ongoing development of counselling responses continues to challenge those who counsel and that in itself means a support structure is needed for the counsellors.

Guidelines

I have summarized these points in the following guidelines which could be considered by any school so that we can ensure that the bereaved child has the facility to be supported and cared for during the school day.

- Young people tend to express grief in different ways of behaving. They act out their feelings and emotions. There needs to be awareness of these behaviours.

- All individual students may react differently to grief: withdrawal, aggressiveness, panic, anxiety, anger, guilt, fear, regression are all normal symptoms of grief. There is a need to be patient and understanding.

- Be aware that there may be denial of their feelings of grief and it may be months or years before the emotional reactions are shown. It is completely inappropriate for comments such as 'they should be over it now' to be made.

- Bereaved children must re-establish a new identity. 'Who am I?' becomes a major question and they need help with this. The counsellor or tutor may find themselves projected into different roles by the young person; for example, a parental role when it is report time or achievements are accomplished.

- If a student seeks you out to talk, be available and really listen. Arrangements need to be made for this eventuality but this can be an inbuilt part of the counselling system. At these times the bereaved child will need to tell everything about the experience of death and may repeat this several times on different occasions.

- Provide a quiet place which is private. This may be a room where counselling takes place or another space which the young person knows they can go to when they need peace and quiet.

- Giving a feeling of acceptance, warmth and if appropriate, a hug can give comfort when the hurt is surfacing. Be open and honest about feelings and enable questions to be asked and confidence built.

- Ensure that all of the staff are aware of the bereaved child so that inappropriate remarks are not made in the child's hearing. Everyone needs to be aware of who is counselling the child so that some of the time, as much as they need, the 'normal' school progresses. Many young people do not want to appear to be singled out and seen as different from their peers.

- Talk to the student's friends; they often need support as well. They need to talk about their feelings and be able to ask questions.

- Bereavement counselling does not necessarily take place in the immediate period after the death. If the death of a parent has occurred earlier in the young person's life, adolescence can be the time when deep held grief begins to emerge.

- Be sensitive to special anniversaries. For example, it is supportive to recognize that 'Mother's Day' or 'Father's Day' are difficult days for the child whose parent has died.

- All of these factors have a cultural context. Be aware of this, if you are unsure of the cultural connotations; make sure that any questions are open and therefore will not imply your own cultural bias.

Death is not in the scheme of things for these young people but the reality is sometimes very different. Schools have an important part to play in enabling a bereaved student through the process of loss and grief.

Summary

Transcultural counselling can only be effective if the counsellor is aware of their own culture and recognizes the importance and validity of raising their awareness of cultures which are different and similar to their own. Differences and similarities are sometimes not as apparent as one assumes. The bereavement counsellor is working with people who are, at that time in their lives, very vulnerable; therefore sensitivity to their culture is of prime importance. The beliefs, attitudes, rituals, and the meanings behind these, give a sense of order to the bereaved person when other things are in disarray.

There is one sure thing about life and that is death. This does not make sense to a young person who is experiencing that loss. The way we experience death is influenced by our culture. Every person is in different ways like all persons, like some persons and like no other person. The mixture of similarities and differences underlines the issues raised by transcultural counselling. For the counsellor today and for the future, the pluralistic nature of our society and the international mobility of people has implications for the counselling process.

All people and cultures are inextricably connected to each other and this connection will grow even stronger in the future. Our schools reflect the pluralistic nature of our society and increasingly schools have a vital role to play in the experience of the whole child.

The more overt the discussion about death and bereavement, the less the fear and mystique which surrounds it. In multicultural Britain different cultural groups, religious and non religious, have different rituals. We can learn from each other. The school has to recognize the range of experiences which will be brought by the students and be prepared to offer support when the experience is one of loss through death. Adolescence is a time of turmoil in most cultures and the additional stress of bereavement needs careful support and consideration.

References

Abrams, R. (1992) *When Parents Die.* London: Lett.

d'Ardenne, P. and Mahtani, A. (1989) *Transcultural Counselling in Action.* London: Sage.

Heegaard, M. (1991) *When Something Terrible Happens.* Minneapolis, MN: Woodland Press.

Locke, D. (1992) *Increasing Multicultural Understanding: A Comprehensive Model.* Newbury Park, CA: Sage.

Noonan, E. (1983) *Counselling Young People.* London: Tavistock and Routledge.

Rogers, C. (1951) *Client Centred Therapy.* London: Constable.

Traux, C. and Carkhuff, R. (1967) *Towards Effective Counseling and Psychotherapy.* Chicago: Aldine.

Walker, A. (1988) *To Hell With Dying.* San Diego, CA: Harcourt Brace Jovanovich.

CHAPTER 15

Managing Tragedy in a Secondary School

John Shears

The Setting

In life there are occasional moments that remain with you forever. Like many of my generation I can remember vividly what I was doing when the Manchester United football team plane crashed at Munich Airport. To this day, and as if it were only yesterday I can remember clearly the news flash that announced the assassination of John F Kennedy in 1963. Differently but with poignancy, October 21st 1988 will always be that sort of day and that sort of memory, because tragedy struck Streetly School, where I was Headteacher at the time.

But first, let me set the scene. I had been appointed to the school three years earlier and enjoyed working there, as relationships were good and there was a nice atmosphere. Streetly School is a Co-Educational Comprehensive School of 1100 pupils aged eleven to nineteen. It is located on the eastern edge of the metropolitan borough of Walsall, although in reality its links are as much with Sutton Coldfield and north east Birmingham as they are with the borough. The school's catchment area covered the above and was relatively prosperous, comprising what one would describe as middle class owner occupier housing. The school served a relatively professional environment giving the impression of an affluent suburb. As a result its pupil intake was above average and the school was popular and over-subscribed.

October 21st 1988 was the Friday evening at the start of the half-term week. At midnight on the day before, 20 excited children and two teachers plus one other adult had left Streetly for the experience of a lifetime – a week long cruise of the Eastern Mediterranean. Eighteen months of planning and much saving had gone into preparing for the cruise, and as the party boarded the coach at school it was clear that this was something special. The cruise was a joint venture with three Walsall schools – T.P. Riley, Brownhills and ourselves.

Families and individuals have given their full permission to be named in this chapter.

Staff and pupils were working together and even before the holiday had started there was an excellent rapport. With waves from parents and family an excited group left Streetly for a motorway drive through the night to Gatwick and an early morning flight to Athens.

As I write this my mind wanders to childhood memories of my own first school trip abroad. Such excitement, such laughter, such fun…yet sadly for Streetly soon to be tragedy and fear unlike anything most people face in their lives. From Athens the party was taken to the adjoining port of Piraeus to embark on the *S.S. Jupiter*, a Cruise Liner regularly used in the Mediterranean for school parties and at other times of the year, holiday-makers. The ship sailed from Piraeus in the early evening in good light and with a calm sea. Barely one mile out of the harbour, it was struck by an Italian freighter and it sank within twenty minutes. The collision occurred just as the children had gathered in the dining room to be briefed about the voyage, routines, safety and so forth. In one sense that was fortunate as the group was together and no one was in a cabin deep in the ship. Even so, there was confusion and some panic and despite an outstanding rescue effort which brought 472 persons to safety, two Greek seamen, a teacher from T.P. Riley School, Bernard Butt, and fourteen-year-old Vivienne Barley from Streetly school were lost, presumed drowned. No bodies were ever found.

The news broke to me just before seven o'clock on that Friday evening when an anxious parent rang to ask if I had seen the Channel 4 news flash of the sinking of the S.S. Jupiter. No one can prepare you for a moment like this. There is initial disbelief and a sense of the unreal. I calmed the parent, switched on the television and initiated the emergency contact procedure. This was the first difficulty – it was impossible to get through and then I was put on to somewhere else only to be told, we are not sure of the situation, but will keep in touch – a valiant not too successful promise. The local police rang mid evening to say that they would co-ordinate information as they had a link to the British Embassy in Athens. They were excellent and their re-assurance helped. The evening was spent by the telephone calming parents, promising things I was not totally sure that I could deliver, and watching the news as the first footage came in from Greece.

The nine o'clock news was informing us that everyone was safe and pictures were shown of pupils being brought ashore. It was nice to see two of our pupils among them. By mid evening I had made my first decision which was to remain at home by the telephone and not to go to school. The other two Walsall schools opened and parents came in. I felt that parents would feel better at home rather than in a confused anxious group and it also helped protect them from the media. This was to some less informed persons a controversial decision – but not to me or the parents of my pupils. I telephoned every parent and offered re-assuring words while wishing to myself that I knew more. At about ten o'clock, Kevin, my teacher in charge rang from Athens to say that 18 of our 20 pupils and the 3 adults were safe, but Debbie and Vivienne were missing. One hour later, Debbie was found in the local hospital, but no one had seen Vivienne.

The situation now became confused. I rang parents again and when I spoke to Richard Barley, Vivienne's Dad, he said do not worry as they had seen Vivienne on a news item coming ashore. The Chairman of Governors of Streetly School kept in regular contact during the early hours and was a source of strength throughout, by supporting my every decision and by offering encouraging words. It was now well after midnight and a long horrible wait. More phone calls occurred. Finally at 3.00a.m. I was telephoned with the news that Vivienne had not been found. I liaised with the police. Vivienne's Dad, Richard, was a police officer so with a police officer friend of his and a senior police officer, I went to the Barley home to break the news. Together the group of us went by police car to Central Television in Birmingham to check all the news footage to spot Vivienne coming ashore. Sadly, it was not Vivienne and our worst fears were realized.

I arrived home in Lichfield at 5.40am and briefly tried to sleep, but by seven o'clock the media were telephoning for information. The next day sped by, much of it in a blur, but fortunately there were practical tasks as the pupils' return had to be prepared for. The emergency services were excellent and the pupils were quickly brought home. I visited the Barley family and continued to reassure other parents, some of whom would not believe all was well until they were re-united with their children. There was our own staff to be informed and the very difficult task of handling the often unreasonable demands of the media. Plans for the pupils' return were made with privacy and protection being utmost in our minds and on Saturday evening, families were united, emotions shared and part one was effectively over. The real work was now to begin.

Managing the Crisis – Early Needs

By now, it was apparent that the school had a duty to meet a wide range of very different needs:

- pupils on the cruise
- staff on the cruise
- parents of the cruise pupils
- the Barley family and twelve-year-old brother, Alastair, still at the school
- close friends of Vivienne
- pupils and staff at the school
- the local community

For some of the above it was both emotional and practical support, for others it was information and re-assurance. Many wanted to help, but were often unsure how and yet needed to be given a chance to play a part without accidentally hindering a difficult process. Early practical steps were vital, even as simple as providing money to the families to replace clothes. Getting them shopping gave them something to do as a family which eased a few tensions. Many of the families found being together in the house with long spells of silence and tears and with little to do, very stressful.

Almost immediately, concerns began to surface that would require professional advice, and these included:

Cruise Pupils

- a range of emotions mostly new to thirteen- and fourteen-year-olds
- genuine trauma and bereavement
- why Vivienne, guilt – it should have been me?
- very poor sleep patterns including nightmares
- difficulties with their families, not being able to talk, feeling misunderstood
- lack of concentration, long spells of sitting with a wandering mind
- listlessness
- fear of water.

Cruise Staff

- deep sense of guilt at taking the trip
- personal emotions and the public need 'to be brave'
- not always easy to share problems
- strong sense of wrong by the male colleague because he did not have to enter the water and was rescued quite early in the operation.
- how would they handle their return to school?
- facing the Barley family.

Cruise Parents

- strong feeling of guilt at letting their children go
- the majority were not able to understand their children's emotions
- could not understand why their children could not talk to them about the tragedy
- much anger
- anger and sadness at what was a clear loss of childhood – 'he is no longer my little boy'

- no realization of the depth of the trauma and a belief that all would soon be well again; when in fact the reality is that things would never be the same again.

The Barley Family

- for Richard, Janet and Alastair there was all the emotion associated with the loss of Vivienne
- at first they refused to believe that Vivienne would not be found
- how to provide support and assist in the coming to terms with their loss
- the absence of a body. It was difficult for the family not to be able to have a funeral or have their loved one brought back. Later, they declined an offer to visit the sea area where the sinking took place, and this was perhaps linked to the lack of a body.

Vivienne's Friends

- they had to face the loss at a difficult adolescent age and were very emotional
- they felt guilty at either letting her go or at not being there
- those who were not on the cruise, but strong friends, felt a deep sense of isolation and exclusion
- they wanted almost immediately to do something public to show their affection and feelings
- they resented others who suddenly 'seemed to be friends of Vivienne'.

School Staff/Pupils and the Local Community

- they lacked information
- how do we 'control' or manage a genuine desire to help?
- there was much confusion as to how to respond. Everyone cared, but showing this was different in each case
- what questions can or should we ask? Fear of saying the wrong thing.

In facing these needs and concerns the school had several advantages. It was a happy, good community and people related well so there was a strong desire to help and to do it well. In a practical sense, there was the bonus of half-term. No one was back at school for a few days so time was available to plan and manage. During the half-term week, the Senior Management Team (Head, three Deputies, three Heads of School), met and with their own instincts and outside advice began to devise a strategy for managing the crisis, which they hoped would be sensible and sensitive.

Managing the Crisis – Strategies

While instinct and care had carried us through the first two days, it was vital to plan and to establish a mechanism for handling the crisis. The diagram that follows (see Figure 15.1) outlines the model chosen. It was established through our discussions and built on the relative strengths of the Senior Team and to some extent their involvement in the early hours of the tragedy.

Three important decisions were made:

(1) INFORM everyone

(2) Establish KEY WORKERS

(3) Keep the school running NORMALLY

In order to make these decisions work a number of strategies had to be implemented fairly urgently. The steps that we took were as follows:

A STAFF MEETING was held towards the end of half-term. All staff had been spoken to briefly following the tragedy, but it was felt vital that colleagues were brought together. This was to create a team bonding as it was important that everyone felt involved in some way. In dealing with tragedy in a community and while acting quickly under pressure it is all too easy to inadvertently miss someone out and create a sense of hurt.

The staff meeting was used to:

- Accurately inform everyone of the tragedy. Myths and rumours had to be dispelled.

- Explain the systems we were putting in place to care for the students.

- Establish guidelines so that not everyone was counselling, guiding and caring as this could lead to difficulties and confusion. Teachers are sensitive and the desire to help was strong, but it was important to realize the limits of our expertise and the danger of getting it wrong. In leading the staff meeting, I had to choose my words carefully as I was mindful of the hurt that I could do to some of my staff's feelings – but establishing the guidelines was crucial.

- Offer advice on what to do in practical terms as the cruise children would be in lessons next day. Tears, anger, lack of concentration would all surface and staff needed to be warned.

- It allowed the two teachers to meet their colleagues again. As I had explained much about the tragedy, it could be done gently.

- Stress the importance of normality. The school needed to be a busy, learning community. Work must go on for everyone and routines that are known would in themselves be supportive. Keeping students busy while being aware and sensitive was important.

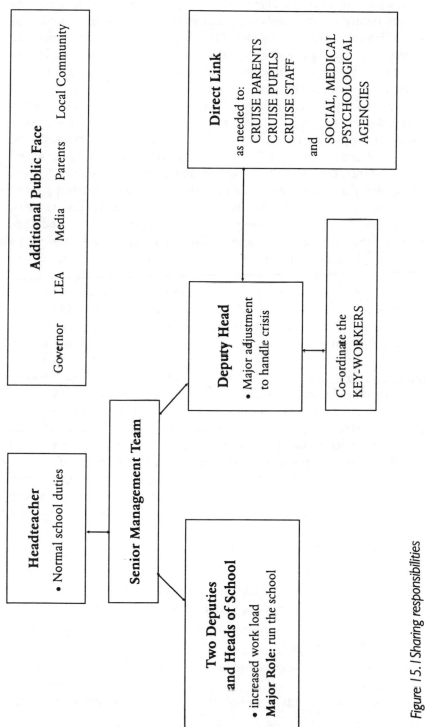

Figure 15.1 Sharing responsibilities

A PARENTS' MEETING was held on the same day and everyone came, even several who were separated. There was a strong bond generated here and one that lasted many months. Hands were held, fears and anxieties expressed, tears shed. The local education authority (LEA) had supplied a social worker, an educational psychologist and a clinical psychologist and these were able to support me in giving practical advice. It was interesting to note an early tension as these people were not known to the parents and there was some resentment as, in the first forty-eight hours of the crisis, the LEA had been slow to respond. Fortunately, the psychologists had warmth and humour and became sources of support for our parents. They tried to explain what was 'normal' in trauma and bereavement and to warn of difficulties that lay ahead. Their children would change and their lives would never be the same again and accepting that was both necessary and hard. Parents had to learn listening skills and to appreciate how important it was to let the children show emotion. They were given telephone numbers by the psychologists and encouraged to call as it would not be easy for them for some time to come. The psychologists also established a weekly clinic for parents and a number came to this and found mutual support.

An important decision was to try to keep the school functioning as it should as a learning environment. The Senior Team adjusted roles and took on new responsibilities so that the Head and a Deputy, Jenny Smedley, could have the time to manage the tragedy. The team had to be positive, public and prominent in seeing that school life was normal. Nothing was cancelled and a busy atmosphere was encouraged. Staff were excellent and everyone gave a great deal. Some who struggled with the emotional side, were able to help by doing more in running the school – they then felt that they had contributed.

On the day of the meetings, the pupils who were on the cruise and Vivienne's close friends were brought together. This was not easy as the three close friends who did not go felt excluded and not part of the group and yet their affection for Vivienne was very strong. One of their parents became a valuable go-between and by informing us of the feelings, helped us get the two groups together and build on the needs that had to be met. For those on the cruise, a strong bonding had already developed and it was to prove a valuable vehicle for recovery over the weeks ahead.

At the pupils' meeting they were told of:

- the Key Worker idea
- of the 'flat' – a room set aside for them to use whenever it was needed; it was a quiet, comfortable refuge.
- the sort of emotions and anxieties that they would experience and that this was normal
- the psychologist talked to them and tried to re-assure them as well as being honest about what lay ahead. They also arranged sessions of a practical nature. Advice was given on relaxation, on how to get back

to a regular sleep pattern, how to face water again, and approaches to school work. Over the weekend, pupils thought about and chose a key worker.

The success of our strategy and its role in the healing process was very dependent on the key worker. The pupils had to choose – it would have been inappropriate to assign them. The pupils needed teachers that they trusted, respected, were caring and warm. It says much for the quality of the staff at Streetly that this process worked, but it did have its difficulties. Two staff were oversubscribed! One, a young teacher, and form teacher of a number who went on the cruise was asked by six of the pupils to be their key-worker. She could not do it – she was very close to Vivienne and it was too emotional for her. She asked not to be involved as she feared she would fail the children. The children understood this and were able to choose someone else. For all the key-workers it was to be a demanding and very draining experience, especially as at the same time they were trying to run their teaching programme as well.

The essential requirement of the system in the early days and weeks was that the key worker must be instantly available. A system was set up for this and the flat occupied all day continuously. If a child came to it and asked for their key worker then the teacher in the flat fetched the key worker and covered their class while the short term difficulty was handled. Key workers would liaise daily with Mrs Smedley and decisions would then be taken as to whether to talk to other professionals, staff in the school, or parents. The overview was essential as ten staff going off in all sorts of directions could be difficult to manage. It allowed us to have a good picture and to tackle common problems jointly.

The flat – a safe haven – was vital. It was a fairly private room and part of our home economics suite. It was comfortable and we made it cosy, ensuring tea and coffee facilities were available. It was covered from 8.30am to 4.00pm non-stop. Early on, it was used heavily. The pupils needed space and privacy and to escape from the playground or crowded areas in the lunch hour. It was less used in lesson time and by some individuals much more than by others. It was not abused and once pupils had got through a bad spell they went back to lessons. The flat became a meeting place – almost a 'club' room for the cruise students where fears and anxieties could be shared. They talked of the sinking and of home, and of parents and how they did not understand. They often just wanted to be together. They needed much support and re-assurance and the role of helping each other was vital. Key workers found that they could sit in the background and help by being there – but talking was often done pupil to pupil. Key workers became skilled at moving in and out of the room, and of drifting gently in and out of conversations. Their listening ability meant that we could alert the psychologists and suggest where help was needed and what fears seemed most prevalent.

Back to School

The Monday after half-term brought the school back together again with other issues to be tackled. I decided to speak to all pupils and did so in a series of assemblies in the morning. The purpose of the assemblies were:

- to give accurate information. The media and rumours had created many myths about the sinking. It was important that everyone had the true picture. It also, we hoped, would mean that other children would not ask too many questions of the cruise pupils.

- to tell pupils of the need for sensitivity. They were briefed on asking questions and the value of talking to their friends about the disaster. They could help by being good listeners, by supporting when tears came and in practical ways over school work or by letting a teacher know if they noticed real problems. It was stressed that peer group support would be a very powerful tool in the healing process.

- to give permission to grieve. This was a tricky situation as pupils needed to know that it was normal to express their feelings, yet it was vital that this was 'controlled'. There is a fear that tears and feelings can overflow and be very disruptive. One saw the need for grieving but did not want it too widespread. It says much for the qualities of young people that they handled this well and they helped their friends enormously.

- to pray for Vivienne and the Barley family as well as give thanks for the safe return of the rest of the group.

- to allow the media an opportunity to take photographs and footage for the news. I deliberately stage managed this and gave them access to one assembly. I chose one with older pupils and containing few children that had been on the cruise. I was determined to protect the children as much as possible.

From the start of the cruise, the management of the media was difficult. Little can prepare you for the intrusion they make on your life and that of the school. They were often insensitive and uncaring, especially the national press. The local press were good as the school already had contacts and an excellent working relationship. At first, I was angry with the media and defiant in terms of refusing them access. I was not prepared to have them photograph upset children and ask totally insensitive questions. The police were helpful here and suggested a strategy that worked. Simply stage manage things for them so that they get information and photographs. If I did it, I could protect most of the children and prevent the unpleasant incidents – climbing into the school without permission, stopping other children at the gate, waiting outside homes. The demands of the media for interviews was excessive, but had to be tackled and was best done by the Head. I became skilled at choosing my words carefully and projecting the right image on television and radio. By being readily available, I protected my staff and parents from the media demands.

Little can prepare you for a crisis of this dimension and early on it is a lonely, lonely time. Fortunately, if that is the right word, there is so much to do and it is a little later that it hits you. Be prepared for your own emotional moments. It will put pressure on your family and you will feel tired, misunderstood and angry. In the middle of the half-term week when things seemed a little calm, I took two days out and went away. I left telephone numbers and was contactable. I needed my own space and above all I needed to re-charge my batteries as the first week back was bound to be very demanding. It is easy to neglect your own needs and pay a price later. While no one can tell you quite what to do, the support of phone calls and letters meant a lot. Many others have faced tragedy and quickly I realized that I was not alone and help was available.

After the Early Days:

Our management strategy meant a heavy investment in time, but in a caring community such as ours it was freely given. Staff willingly attended extra meetings and helped each other with work load. Clearly, in re-building the school in an emotional sense, there were no short cuts or quick solutions. Patience, affection and a lot of common-sense was important. Through November and on in to the New Year, the flat was heavily used and there were regular meetings for key workers with Jenny Smedley, the psychologists, the parents and the pupils.

The pupils' meetings were essential and they all attended for quite a few weeks. The psychologists who ran these deserve great credit. They were most skilful. Exercises were introduced, games played, talking and listening carried out – most with humour and warmth, so tension and anxiety was eased. By January some pupils had no real need of the weekly session and as their sleep patterns and concentration spans returned to normal began to attend less. Even so they came along because there was a sort of 'club' atmosphere and they were very close to each other and were able to provide mutual support.

By late Spring of 1989, some six months on, a clear pattern had emerged:

- Some children appeared to have 'mended'. Amazingly, from the very start two of the twenty appeared to have suffered no trauma. By March, about six seemed to be well on the road to recovery. They all naturally remained with the group and were supportive.

- Most of the cruise children had good spells and regression – a typical pattern, with moments of introspection, quiet, tears and despair. Conflict with parents was not unusual.

- The two teachers also had good spells and regression. Adolescents are very vulnerable, but so are adults and it was important not to miss the staff needs as these would be less obvious and rather private.

- Vivienne's friends found her loss hard to take while the family suffered great sadness. I continued to visit the Barley family regularly.

- Key workers were able to relax their involvement and they were only used occasionally. The flat was still a meeting place, but hardly ever needed as a refuge. It did not need to be staffed all the time.

Some eighteen months on and Streetly School was still providing support. The good spells were longer and the regression often short. But explosions and tears and lonely moments could surface. From the start, advice to us had been, be prepared for at least two years of trauma in some form or other. From our experience it was a little less than this. By the Spring of 1990, fifteen children appeared fine and no regression was noted. They appeared to be healthy, normal teenagers again. Vivienne's friends also seemed well. Three of the twenty pupils needed occasional help, but fairly infrequently.

The flat had ceased its role and the key workers were now rarely used. Two of the children had long term problems and on medical advice were receiving psychological support and counselling. While they had good spells, bouts of depression were still common. It is interesting to note that their parents found it very difficult to come to terms with the trauma. For a long time they found understanding the emotion difficult and one felt that they would not let their children grieve. They took the view that the children should snap out of it and quickly be right. For these two families, it was to be a long two years. While the school could not have done it, someone should have spotted the needs developing – but it is easy to be wise after the event.

In the months that followed the sinking, it was important to allow many children the opportunity to show emotion and feelings. Our aim was to try to manage it and to try to channel things into a positive response. Children want to help; they desperately need to show love and care. Memorials, tree-planting and the like can help. They provide a focus and divert energy from sadness into good. No formal service was held and with no body ever found, no funeral as such. Instead at the request of the family an evening of music and dance was held in the Town Hall. Vivienne was a keen singer and dancer. This enabled a lot of children and adults to be involved in a powerful, moving tribute, yet one that was positive and joyful. The memory of it will always remain with me and I was proud to have a place in it.

The musical was followed some months later by a small occasion in the school only for the cruise students, their parents and Vivienne's form and their parents. This was to be the form tribute to Vivienne. They had collected for and had made a plaque which was placed in the Hall. I spoke, as did the Streetly vicar and then bravely, Vivienne's best friend Martine read a tribute using the words attributed to Henry Scott Holland (Whitaker 1984):

> 'Death is nothing at all...I have only slipped away into the next room.
> I am I and you are you. Whatever we were to each other that we are

still. Call me by my old familiar name, speak to me in the easy way which you always used. Put no difference in your tone; wear no forced air of solemnity or sorrow. Laugh as we always laughed at the little jokes we enjoyed together. Play, smile, think of me, pray for me. Let my name be ever the household word that it always was. Let it be spoken without effort, without the ghost of a shadow on it. Life means all that it ever meant. It is the same as it ever was; there is absolutely unbroken continuity. Why should I be out of mind because I am out of sight? I am waiting for you for an interval, somewhere very near, just around the corner. All is well.' (p.86)

It was a dignified and moving experience and made me feel a little humble in the presence of such special young people.

Reflecting on the tragedy and its influence on the school the main lesson to learn is probably that of being prepared. Much that we did at Streetly was based on instinct and commonsense. Having a plan, a policy or a strategy in place could be most valuable. A plan would allow schools to think in advance on a range of issues such as:

- communication with the school
- who will be responsible for the media
- having a list available of organizations that exist to give support
- staff training in bereavement for those interested
- how the school will acknowledge death

One can never totally prepare for the unexpected…but you can be part way there.

Vivienne Barley lives on in the memory of Streetly School and even today I can see her lively personality and obvious energy as she chatted and walked the school corridors. She was a super young lady who is loved and missed. Yet despite the terrible sadness of her loss, the care that shone through the experience made Streetly School a stronger community, and I believe made better people of us all.

Suggested Reading

Blackburn, M. (1991) 'Bereaved children and their teachers.' *Bereavement Care 10*, 2, 19.

Capewell, E. (1994) 'Responding to children in trauma: a systems approach for schools.' *Bereavement Care 13*, 1, 2.

Johnson, J. (1989) 'Haunted by memories.' *Nursing Times 85*, 11, 56.

Pynoos, R. (1992) 'Grief and trauma in children and adolescents.' *Bereavement Care 11*, 1, 2.

Whitaker, A. (ed) (1984) *All the End is Harvest.* London: Darton, Longman and Todd.

CHAPTER 16

Voices from the Crowd
Stories from the Hillsborough Football Stadium Disaster

Paul Barnard and Maureen Kane

On the 15th April 1989, as the F.A. Cup semi-final between Liverpool and Nottingham Forest was starting at Sheffield's ground, Hillsborough, 95 people were crushed to death at the Leppings Lane end. Four years later the 96th victim died. Of those who did survive many suffered traumatic injuries; nobody left the stadium that day without being affected by the disaster that had happened there.

As the hugeness of the tragedy unfolded, many people felt an overwhelming sense of helplessness, from those who were at the match, to those who watched on TV or heard the news later. This left many people with a desire to do something, to find some way of expressing their personal grief and pain. People searched and found a million ways to express their feelings. Flowers and tributes covered the field at Anfield (Liverpool's football ground). Some people wrote down their thoughts, quite often for the first time. Poems appeared in the press and radio, were passed around pubs, stuck on walls around the City and nestled among flowers at Anfield.

Introduction

This chapter describes how Paul Barnard, a Children's Society Worker, came to be involved in the network of support following the Hillsborough Disaster. The account of his involvement includes stories which highlight issues for professionals who are working with children and young people after a disaster. Although these few stories do not contain all the answers, they do offer some meaning and may be able to help deepen our understanding of a situation which could otherwise appear to be meaningless and without hope.

The people named in this chapter have give permission for their stories to be used.

At the time of the Hillsborough Disaster, in April 1989, Paul was employed by the Children's Society as a Senior Residential Worker in one of their projects in Manchester. Previous to this Paul had a background of fifteen years working with children and young people in a variety of settings, and it was this experience which he was to draw on substantially during the early days of his involvement. In this first story, 'Barney's Story', Paul tells of how he came to be involved in the aftermath of the Hillsborough Disaster and its impact upon him.

Barney's Story

'On that day I was away from Liverpool, with the rest of my family celebrating our parents' Ruby Wedding. Alongside were my three brothers with whom I'd shared a lifetime of passionate involvement in sport; I can't recall a time when either together or apart we weren't to be found 'kicking around' a football. The previous Boxing Day had found us enacting our traditional, annual, combined family 'soccer and social' – over 20 years, unfailingly, in all weathers, family and friends had gathered, fortified to participate as player or spectator. This year my son had joined us. Touched with that same passion (and no little skill), he had adopted Liverpool as his team, influenced early by his uncle, a fanatical red. I had taken him on his first visit to Anfield (a rare event for me, an Evertonian); just as my Grandfather had taken me on that first magical day to watch his lowly but beloved Shrewsbury Town, as he introduced me to life on the terraces…where I was to be found at every opportunity throughout my early life. Then in 1981, I moved to Liverpool because of a career development. Once I was back in Liverpool I experienced a rekindling of the urge to play football again and was stimulated to return to the terraces of Goodison Park to witness Everton's triumphs of the early 1980s, Lineker *et al*. On my first day back in Liverpool, I had met Peter, who during the decade that followed was to become a close friend. The seats which my son and I had occupied during our first visit together to Anfield were a result of Peter lending us his season tickets.

Now, on the return journey home to Liverpool as the full extent of the tragedy was conveyed to us on the car radio, thoughts became focused and immediate. 'What of my friend Peter?' He was there, undoubtedly. A born and bred red, he had travelled Europe, lived through and suffered the trauma of the Heysel Football Stadium Disaster back in the mid-1980s; was he back home safe with Rachel and their two children Sarah and Jane?

Then we were through the Mersey Tunnel and home, the 'phone was ringing despite the midnight hour. My wife, Mary, had lived in

Liverpool all her life, born only a mile from our present house; no football supporter, but proud of her city, her people. Now a hospital social worker with the City Council she was to meet other hospital social workers first thing next morning, prepared to travel to Sheffield with others to do whatever was possible for as long as needed, in offering support to those bereaved and suffering. But before she left there was a personal dilemma to resolve.

'Ring Peter.'

'I can't. I'm too scared!'

I have to know. I ring. All's well...relatively so of course, but at least Peter is home safe. We'll talk some time, over a pint.

So Mary went off to Sheffield and the unknown. I set off to Manchester, to my work with young people. All thoughts are invaded as the local station on the car radio accompanies me on my journey; for Liverpool and its people there can be no other story that day, and for many days to come, than that of the tragic hours in a football stadium in Sheffield one sunlit afternoon. Facts, supposition, accusation, lament, acrimony, anger, pain, relief, appeals, music, prayer...words flood the airwaves. I felt a growing awareness of a need to do something, to act. I pick up the phone, speak to a colleague living and working in Liverpool. 'Surely we can do something, make some sort of contribution, after all that's what the Children's Society is about; being alongside people, communities...responding to need – well here in our region, where we live and work, many are crying out in need.' Other people act from similar instincts. In Liverpool colleagues respond to appeals by the voluntary sector and by the city, for support and resources. There were many more telephone calls including one to Brian Moore, the Children's Society Regional Director. He promptly responded by inviting all immediately concerned from the North-West Region of the Organisation to meet and formulate some response to the tragedy.

It was my feeling then, and still is today, that those who assembled in Brian's office that first week were representatives not just in action but also in spirit, of all our workers and supporters throughout the north-west and of many others associated with the Children's Society throughout the country. From the organization came a green light...just be there.

But how to be there?

The city was inundated with offers of help, immediate, numerous and of every variety imaginable (somewhere I still have the endless listings of 'offers of help' meticulously compiled over dedicated hours by the

Information Technology Department). Colleagues had attended country-wide meetings attempting to gauge how we could most usefully offer help. For myself I had instituted some information gathering, read a little of disasters; but overwhelmingly I was touched by the voices of colleagues and friends already involved in the first-line response, offering psychological and spiritual first-aid, initially in Sheffield, and then as the focus shifted to Liverpool, amongst the thousands who flocked to the great open-air cathedral that for a week was Anfield.'

That question 'How to be there?', has no easy answer.

In trying to find an answer, Paul remembers how he first started simply with 'a blank sheet of paper and a telephone'...the 'phone rang, he answered it! Thus began a long process of responding to 'phone calls, visiting people at home, sharing a cuppa (or a pint!), attending public meetings, going to the Inquiry, watching video footage, reading the words and above all listening to and hearing the voices from the crowd. Along with friends, neighbours, volunteers and professionals he attempted to get alongside people and try to understand their pain, their anger, their sadness, and their needs. He became involved in encouraging people to sit together, to share their experiences, and offered them support in telling their stories. What he heard influenced him in his practice; in making a beginning.

The listening process, the process of just being there, was underway. Paul felt it was important to be acclimatized to the language of the stories, to those voices; in order to enable him to stand alongside people in terms of culture, credibility, understanding, and trust.

However, as Paul listened he realized that much of what he was hearing was about adult voices and their needs, and there seemed to be precious little space at this stage for children and young people. He began to wonder about children and young people, and the particular concerns and questions that they may have when finding themselves confronted with such a large-scale disaster. So those were the next questions. 'What about the children in these situations? – Who are they and where are they to be found?'

As the weeks passed he found himself pondering on these same questions repeatedly. As a result of Paul making it clear to others that he had a particular interest in identifying the needs of children and young people, some evidence began to be revealed. Some youngsters began to relate their own personal stories to Paul, both verbally and in writing and the idea of a 'safe listening space' began to emerge. One particular story, in the form of a letter, which eventually arrived on his desk, was to make a particular impact and acted as a catalyst for the subsequent involvement with children, young people and their families. This letter, the next story, was later published in 'Interlink', a magazine set up by and for those affected by the Hillsborough Disaster. Written by Lisa, aged fourteen at the time, it clearly and powerfully describes the impact the Disaster had upon her.

Lisa's Letter

'The shock I faced was the death of my brother just a few short weeks ago. I have never experienced this kind of shock before in my life and I never want to again. Words cannot describe the feelings I had or still have as it changes all the time, never the same emotions.

Liverpool versus Nottingham Forest at Hillsborough (the ground of Sheffield Wednesday) was an ordinary football match where 95 people innocently died for the sake of SPORT. One of those 95 was my brother Colin.

Colin was just 19, a shy and hard-working lad. He had never been to an away match before because of his job as a barman in the Dockers Club. Colin left the Dockers Club because it was only a weekend job, and he had been promoted in his day job – as a TSB bank clerk. He was to celebrate leaving the dockers on Thursday but he never did because of the disaster.

On the Friday night before he died, whilst he was out, girls fought over him! So I left and said, "Bye, see you tomorrow".

I went home and left him to carry on enjoying the last night of his life. Those last words, "Bye, see you tomorrow" will always stay in my heart. But as the saying goes, "tomorrow never comes".

At 3.06 on the 15th April 1989 the football match was stopped, but it wasn't until 3.45 a.m. on the 16th April that the tragic news came to us via my brother Ian. Ian is my only brother now, but he has suffered the worst because he was more like a friend to Colin than a brother. Those twelve hours or so in between I felt numb. People have said before they felt like this, but I did not know what they meant until now, for there was little I could do except hope and pray that Colin would come back. Those hours were filled with sorrow and grief. I cried with pain, I cried with helplessness, but I also remembered all the time we had together. Colin did return, but not until Thursday 20th April 1989 and this was in a wooden box known as a coffin. Still the numbness never went. He had said the day before, "I'll come back home tomorrow and either get drunk with happiness if they win, or with sorrow if they lose." Neither happened. The pain and sorrow the players felt at that moment (three zero six p.m.) was practically the same as mine. They were not allowed to help, nor was I. They were not aware of what was going on, nor was I. There was little I could do, but much to hope for.

That Colin would come back.

That Colin would drive up in his car.

That mum and dad would comfort each other and release their grief.

That Ian would express his anger in some way.

That the other families who lost someone would comfort each other and manage.

That everyone in Liverpool would just be OK. It didn't matter what I felt as long as they were fine.

I am beginning to experience a lot of emotions like hurt from the tragedy, but unlike my family I cry in secret, just as Colin would have. I wouldn't want to hurt anyone, as Colin never did. I don't want to attract attention, as this was not Colin's style. Now my family are starting a fresh life, and trying to carry on from before 15th April 1989 because Colin has only died in body but never will in soul. He will always be in our thoughts and in our hearts. "Our" means family and friends because of the love, support and affection from everyone we know. SO REMEMBER "live today as if it were your last", for who knows it might just be. Colin didn't know that the party he was at the night before was going to be his last. God always takes the best first and there couldn't have been anyone better than our Col.'

This letter seemed to Paul to confirm his instincts – children and young people would have been affected by the disaster, and as a result would have their own particular and identifiable needs. Lisa had given a very personal account of the effect of the disaster upon her, and in doing so had communicated her needs in relation to such an unexpected and traumatic event in her life. This now left Paul wondering whether other children were experiencing similar feelings. He had to find out if this were myth or reality; the journey of exploration began. He spoke with some women from the Hillsborough Family Support Group; they too shared his concern about children and families. They had an idea: they would set up an activity which would involve children and their families – a family day out at the Camelot Theme Park! There was no doubt about the result – three coaches were needed for about 150 people responded to their invitation. All of them belonged to families who were involved with the Hillsborough Family Support Group, children, cousins, friends of families, and extended families.

The trip to Camelot was the first planned activity which involved children. Being around on the day and doing things together, queuing up for rides, going on rides, sitting down for a snack, listening to the children and listening to the adults talking about the children, it became obvious that many of them had not done anything like this since the disaster, maybe four or five months ago. Many adults expressed concern for themselves as a whole family; the events were still very close to them and they were still shocked and feeling anxious. They were honest in acknowledging that it was hard for them to pay attention to their children's needs, even though they recognized the importance of doing so.

Paul was now convinced that the process of trying to involve children and give them a voice should continue. He increased the opportunities to hear them, achieving this by inviting young people to join himself and other workers at a regular weekly meeting.

> 'Come tenpin bowling. Bring your friends along.'

or,

> 'Let's go to the pictures.'

The invitations weren't to meaningless activities, they were to something which was already part of their culture, part of the way they expressed themselves. As a result, an informal group of young people began to meet from time to time at places like the bowling alley, the cinema, or the swimming baths. These were all young people who were old enough to go out in the evening without their parents, and who were relating to each other as friends. Paul noticed that as adults tended to tell stories to each other, the young people tended to support one another in activity. However, in those shared times, there was also opportunity for shared experiences, short stories. A theme which Paul heard from a number of youngsters was about not knowing what was going on, not being given information at the time of the disaster. One commented that, 'People were coming in and out of the house but nobody told me what was going on'. Another said, 'That's strange, because the 'phone was going all the time, and nobody came up and told me that my brother was in hospital.'

It was obvious that there was a need to listen to the young people's stories and the way that they chose to tell them. To not allow them to express themselves would be to do them an injustice. A remarkable example of how young people in one particular community were helped to express themselves is shown in the next story, Pat's story. Pat Shields, at that time a Hillsborough worker for Halton Social Services, tells the story of the Castlefields Youth Day in April 1990, which marked for their community the first anniversary of the Hillsborough Disaster.

Pat's Story

'I want to share with you our story. It is about what happened in our community following the Hillsborough Disaster. It could easily happen in your community.

Four people died from the community of Runcorn.
Terence senior and Terence junior, age fourteen.
Anthony, age fourteen
Keith, age fifteen.

The three boys attended the two local secondary schools.

Terence junior and Keith lived in the same street.

All three boys were the eldest in each family.
Andrew and Gaynor lost their father and brother.
Philip lost his brother.
Lisa and Gareth lost their brother.
Jenny and Daniel lost their two uncles.
Matthew lost his two uncles and his best friend.
David and Jenny lost their best friend.
Sandra lost her boyfriend.
Tricia, Richard and Kate lost their favourite cousin.
The school football team lost one of its best players.

Anthony and Keith are buried alongside each other. Often you will see young people standing near their graves paying their respects. Mementos are left in the form of cards, poems and pictures of football heroes.

A number of young people in the area had been at the match themselves; some had sustained crushing injuries. Many more young people were exposed to the disaster via the television and media coverage. Immediately after the event the schools held services and later they planted trees in memory of the three boys. However, the schools rejected the need for outside help from Social Services; the feeling was – let's get on with the job at hand – Teaching!

Months later, Matthew, a usually model pupil, kept turning up for school late and not completing his homework. He was severely reprimanded. No-one seemed to understand this change of attitude until he broke down at home and his mother informed the school that Matthew's two uncles and his best friend had died.

I commenced work with Halton Social Services Department at the beginning of the year – my brief was that of full time Hillsborough worker. Much of the work, up until that time, had been with bereaved families. One of the reasons is that they are an easily identifiable group. However, all the literature on 'Post Traumatic Stress Disorder' (PTSD) (first described in *Diagnostic and Statistical Manual of Mental Disorders of the American Psychiatric Association* (DSM-III) 1980) suggests a 'ripple effect' – that psychological stress affects many people, following a disaster. I became acutely aware as I commenced my post that a large number of young people were still finding it difficult to come to terms with Hillsborough and what happened. Having identified this it was decided to provide a forum whereby the young people could come together to remember and pay their own personal tribute to the 95 whose lives were lost.

I got together with the youth and community worker and a worker from the voluntary sector and a number of adult survivors. Easter would soon be upon us, likewise the first anniversary of the Hillsborough Disaster. We decided, therefore, to hold our own Hillsborough Memorial, but we would call it a Hillsborough Young People's Day. The day would be held in the Easter holidays after the official memorial service at Anfield the previous Sunday.

This was as much as we planned. In order to make sure the day was a true representation of what the young people wanted, we held three planning meetings and invited any young people along who wanted to help us plan and take part in the day. The ages of the young people who attended the meetings ranged from ten to twenty. Everyone was able to make a valid contribution to the format of the day.

This would take the shape of:

(1) A short Memorial Service.

(2) A host of sports competitions and art and crafts.

(3) A disco in the evening.

The day arrived, as did a coach full of young people from Liverpool, a number of adult survivors and three of the bereaved families. The weather could not have been worse but in spite of the rain the turn out was phenomenal; 250 young people attended the day, possibly more.

Two of the local Ministers said a few words, some of the young people read poetry chosen by themselves from the *Words of Tribute* book, an anthology of 95 poems, written after the tragedy (Liverpool University Community Resource Unit 1989). The hymn chosen was 'Kum Ba Yah' (Words and Music: Spiritual),

> Kum ba yah, my Lord, kum ba yah,
> Kum ba yah, my Lord, kum ba
> Kum ba yah, my Lord, kum ba yah!
>   O Lord, Kum ba yah!

> Someone's crying Lord, kum ba yah,
> Someone's crying Lord, kum ba yah,
> Someone's crying Lord, kum ba yah,
>   O Lord, Kum ba yah!

Someone's singing Lord, kum ba yah,
Someone's singing Lord, kum ba yah,
Someone's singing Lord, kum ba yah,
 O Lord, Kum ba yah!

Someone's praying Lord, kum ba yah,
Someone's praying Lord, kum ba yah,
Someone's praying Lord, kum ba yah,
 O Lord, Kum ba yah!

Following the service the Youth Centre became a hive of activity. Everyone was busy signing up for the various sports competitions: five-a-side football, netball, pool and table tennis, but the 'It's a Knock-Out' was cancelled due to the weather. Also on the agenda was planning a Hillsborough Memorial Garden which was planted the following week by a group of young gardening enthusiasts. We made a football frieze of cartoon football players which the younger ones painted. The local art teacher designed a mural, depicting a football scene. Some of the survivors engaged the young people in making a banner for the youth centre which incorporated the names of the three boys who died.

Throughout the day the disco music blared out, thanks to one of the young people who volunteered his disco equipment and gave his time for the duration of the day. Everyone took turns at being DJ. Lessons in videoing were also given by our resident photographer who recently produced a video of the whole day. I think it would be fair to say that the event was a huge success. A follow up evening was arranged together with another disco. Again the young people from Liverpool came over. Certificates were given to all those who helped prepare the day and to those who won any of the competitions and to everyone for attending. One of my colleagues visited a family recently to find a certificate proudly framed and hung on the wall.

Our involvement with the young people did not end there. Periodically, a number of our young people met with others from Liverpool at various social functions – the last one being a night out ten-pin bowling. Paul Barnard took a group of young people to swim with Freddie the dolphin in the North Sea. A holiday was also planned for families. We have managed to involve other young people who have been bereaved, such as John, a fifteen-year-old boy whose brother hanged himself in a wood, and Anne a fifteen-year-old girl whose twin sister was killed in a road accident. This is the end of our story but it is not the end, because it is going to be a long time before the young people of Runcorn forget.'

The 'p.s.' to Pat's story is that not everybody saw the day as being a healthy expression of grief and sorrow. Some of the local adults were shocked at some of the activities of the day, especially the disco. It was difficult for them to understand what the young people were trying to express. Other adults went along intending only to stay for the Service at the beginning, but remained for the rest of the day chatting to each other and supporting the children's activities. Thus through the Children's Day it was also possible to reach out to some adults in a supportive way. The next story also shows how adults may be touched by the actions of the children around them.

The Natland Family Weekend

After that first year it became apparent that several families badly needed a break, to get away from it all, even for a few days. Paul planned a low-cost long weekend in the Lake District for several families together at the end of August 1990. Seven families went: thirteen adults and fourteen children plus Paul and other helpers, chiefly there to do the catering. The effect was amazing. The children quickly made friends with each other, bunking up together in their rooms. They helped to break down the barriers between the adults. Where families had been under immense strain and one partner was bottling up fear or anger, even eighteen months after the disaster, the interaction between the children and across family groups began to free some of the adults to talk. They shared their experiences of family life and inevitably of Hillsborough. The play and relaxation together released many tensions. While watching her daughters swimming with their Dad, one Mum told Paul that it was the first time she had seen him relaxing enough to come really close to the girls since the disaster. Up until then he had been too up-tight, afraid of getting close, keeping them at arms length. Yet now he was fooling around in the water, laughing, splashing and catching his girls in his arms. The family was being renewed.

The theme of renewal continues into the final story. Two young people and their friends are involved in a situation which is full of challenge and risk. From their friendship and shared achievement – swimming with Freddie the dolphin in the North Sea – the youngsters grow in confidence and begin to look to the future again.

Swimming with Freddie

In October 1990, Paul Barnard and Val Owen, the Outreach Worker for Liverpool's Alder Centre, took four teenage girls to Amble in Northumberland, to swim with Freddie, a wild free dolphin.

Two bereaved teenagers took their two friends. They were all keen strong swimmers and extra support was provided by an experienced diving couple. This was an opportunity to do something together away from it all, something adventurous and affirming and out of the ordinary. The weekend was a great success. Once in the North Sea with Freddie each young person had a different experience of him; for one he was playful – allowing her to stroke him, with another he was more gentle, even letting her hold his dorsal fin and ride with him, with a third Freddie did not come too close to alarm her. The fourth member of the group stayed in the boat enjoying everything that she saw.

The strength of the weekend lay in its thoughtful planning and the close rapport built up between the four young people, Paul and Val before they went away. They had met several times to discuss the weekend and to practice swimming in wet suits. There was trust within the group and the benefits were obvious. As soon as they returned to Liverpool, one of the young people wanted to play back the video recording of the swim with Freddie for her Mum and family straight away. They had just returned from the inquest into their other daughter's death. What they saw was their daughter smiling, and smiling all the time – a change that hardly seemed possible after just three days away. She had not smiled for months.

A few weeks later a social evening gave the four teenagers the chance to see the video again with friends and family, and to look at the photographs. Val and Paul did not need to say much, the young people spoke for themselves – they had taken important steps in moving on beginning to regain self-esteem and confidence.

A second dolphin expedition in 1991 worked well but did not have the impact of the first one. The second group was larger, included younger swimmers and there was not an equal mix of bereaved young people and their friends. The weekend was valuable, however, in helping some of them to move on after their grief and to achieve something away from the security of home and family, but it proved that there is nothing 'magical' in taking a group away to swim with a dolphin. In a way it reinforced the success of the first weekend.

These stories of action with children, young people, their families and their friends are interlaced with their own evidence and conclusions, which show the value of a simple but challenging strategy, that is one of setting up safe spaces for young people to tell their stories in their own way.

However, creating safe spaces is not just about being accessible to young people. Creating safe spaces means having to find out about and demonstrate an understanding of the young person's existing culture, network and support mechanisms – remembering to include their friends and family. It means taking time to listen to their stories and sometimes these will need to be listened to over and over again. It means dealing with the personal impact that listening to these stories will have, for this work is not without its costs. The workers need their own safe space to tell their own stories, so that they too may deal with their feelings.

Although no two disasters are the same, it is possible to apply the learning from one to another. These stories which relate to the response to one disaster, the Hillsborough Disaster, may help inform other future responses. The overwhelming piece of learning for those workers involved has been the need to listen and respond to the voice of the child, some of whom were calling from the crowd whilst others were in danger of being lost in that same crowd. Creating a safe space for them, offering them the opportunity to share stories may have helped them to become more than just survivors after a disaster, and to become more than just a voice in the crowd.

Acknowledgements

Our thanks to all those who shared their stories with us or worked with us in some way, thus making this chapter possible:

> the Team at the Hillsborough Centre and all those connected with the Centre, the Hillsborough Family Support Group,
>
> Lisa,
>
> Pat Shields,
>
> Karen Tonge (Youth Leader at Castlefields Youth Centre),
>
> Val Owen,
>
> the Team at the Alder Centre,
>
> Mandy Martin,
>
> and all those connected with the Liverpool Children's Project,
> especially the children, young people, and their families.

Finally we must acknowledge those who died at Hillsborough, their families and survivors, and all those who gave of themselves in listening and helping those who otherwise might just have become a voice in the crowd.

Suggested Reading

Alex, M. (1983) *Granpa and Me.* Lion.

Anders, R. *Look At Death.*

Anthony, E.J. *Child in his Family: Impact of Disease and Death.*

Gordon, A. *They Need to Know: Teaching Children About Dying.*

Grollman, E.A. (1990) *Talking About Death: A Dialogue Between Parent and Child.* Boston, MA: Beacon Press.

Hodgkinson, P.E. and Stewart, M. (1991) *Coping with Catastrophe.* London: Routledge.

Kubler-Ross, E. (1983) *On Children and Death.* London: Macmillan.

Liverpool University Community Resource Unit (1989) *Words of Tribute.* Litherland, Merseyside: Centaur Press.

Raphael, B. (1986) *When Disaster Strikes.* London: Unwin Hyman.

Torrie, A. (1978) *When Children Grieve.* Richmond, Surrey: Cruse.

Wynne Jones, P. (1985) *Children, Death and Bereavement.* London: Scripture Union.

CHAPTER 17

Making Memory Stores with Children and Families Affected by HIV

Ruth Neville

'The most important person in my life is Becky. I want her to know how much I love her. I want her to know the things about me and her, that only I can tell her.'

Four years ago, shortly after the birth of Becky, her only child, Carol was diagnosed as being HIV positive. Carol has not only had to come to terms with having a stigmatizing and as yet incurable fatal illness, she has had to confront what is perhaps one of the most painful issues for a parent – the likelihood that she will die before Becky reaches independence.

Carol is beginning to prepare for Becky's future without her. She is making a Memory Store. Created by Barnardos from their work with HIV positive parents, the Memory Store aims to help parents whose children face separation from them to gather and store the information and memories which will be so important in their children's future.

The Memory Store is a brightly coloured box. Inside are drawers where the special and precious memories of family life and childhood can be stored. Carol has made video recordings of family celebrations, birthdays, holidays and Christmas. With the help of her best friend, Sarah, she has made a video of 'A Day in the Life of Carol and Becky', showing the two of them doing the everyday things of their family life. She has taped herself singing the rhymes and songs she sang to Becky when she was a baby and has also taped her favourite records, including those which remind her of Becky's father, whom she has not seen since Becky was first born. She has put in acorns and fir cones from the woods they frequently walk in, shells from their trips to the seaside and a tiny plaited wrist band she made for Becky. There are locks of her and

Becky's hair, a soft scarf scented with her favourite perfume, plus an extra bottle of the perfume in case the smell wears off.

Carol spent many years in care. She remembers being moved in and out of foster families and residential homes until she was placed with Evelyn, the foster parent she still sees and who Becky calls 'Grandma'. She remembers how hard it was for her to have any sense of belonging or of being part of anything.

> 'I remember when Becky was born, feeling an overwhelming sense of protectiveness towards her. I would kill for her. Had my mum ever felt the same about me? I'll never know. The moment Becky was put into my arms I counted all her fingers and toes...we still play that now...I don't want her to forget.'

The most important and the most painful part of the Memory Store for Carol has been writing the Memory Book. This is a ring binder, with headed loose leaf sheets which help parents write down facts about their and their child's lives. Carol has used these pages to help her write as full a family history for Becky as she is able.

> 'It is difficult, there are lots of things I don't know about my parents and about my life. It's made me realize how much I want Becky to know about me and her.'

Carol has written about Becky's birth. Evelyn, Becky's 'Grandma' who was at the birth has also written her memories of the day (and night!). As well as the moving story of Becky's birth, Carol has recorded Becky's birth weight, the hospital she was born in and how she chose Becky's name. She has included the names and addresses of the special people in their lives and how Tabatha their cat ended up living with them.

It has been hard for Carol to write about her own background – there is so much she doesn't know or understand. She has written what she can remember about her own childhood and family, and has put in her own 'Life Story Book'.

> 'There's a lot in my book which makes me sad and angry. Why did I have to live in all those places? My book was written by Andrea (Carol's social worker). It's OK I suppose, but I'm glad I'm writing Becky's. It's like she'll have part of me...even when I'm dead.'

Carol has not only included factual information, she has also tried to describe herself; the things she enjoys doing, her likes and dislikes, the things she believes in and the things which excite and bore her. She knows that at the moment Becky can only see her as 'Mummy', but in the future Becky will need to know and understand what she was like as a person. She has taken great delight in recalling her times spent travelling abroad and the many adventures that happened to her.

Carol acknowledges it is unlikely she will live to support Becky through her teens. In common with many HIV positive parents, Carol does not want

Becky to know of her diagnosis until Becky is much older. She wants to protect Becky from the fear, hostility, prejudice and social ostracism which may arise if people knew of her mother's HIV status. Carol has written a letter for Becky to read when she gets older. She hopes that when Becky reads the letter, which explains about HIV and how Carol contracted the virus, it will help Becky have more understanding about her mother's illness and how deeply she was affected by it. Carol has also included a list of people who know of her diagnosis, and who she trusts will respond sensitively and openly to any concerns or questions Becky may have about HIV in the future.

Making the Memory Store is a long, painful but sometimes joyful ongoing process for Carol. She sees the Memory Store as a reflection of her life with Becky, a life she still has, and hopes will continue for years to come. Carol has now bought a chest to which she continues to add many symbols of their life together.

> 'You see the Memory Store is OK, but how can it fit in the many things I want to share with my child. I'm going to be around as long as possible for Becky, so I thought I'd better get something a bit bigger.'

In making the Memory Store Carol embarked upon a journey that involved her exploring and confronting deeply painful and traumatic events in her past, as well as many happy and joyful ones. This has helped her to begin to live very much in the present, and helped her to look towards the future. She has now made plans for Becky's future care, in the event of her illness or death.

It has been crucial that Carol has had absolute control in the making of her Memory Store. There have been times when she has hidden it away and not touched it for months. At times she chooses to work on it alone, at other times she involves trusted friends and workers who have all been asked to contribute towards it.

One of the joys of the Memory Store is that it can be adapted to meet the needs of families from widely differing lifestyles and cultures. Carol's box is overflowing with treasured poems, drawings, music and photos – the things that symbolize her and Becky's lives.

Monica, born in a small rural African village has filled her children's Memory Stores with tapes that describe her childhood in an African village. The tribal rituals, the food, songs, her community – echoing her rich cultural heritage of oral story telling.

Both Carol and Monica have chosen not to include their children in preparing the Memory Store, perhaps reflecting the difficulties and concerns many parents have in talking about their HIV status to their children. Some parents may choose to do it as a family activity, or to involve their children at a later stage when they have told them of their diagnosis. Susan chose to tell Mark when he was twelve about her positive diagnosis because she thought she was becoming unwell. Together they have made their family tree, gathered their family photographs in an album and talked about the many places they have lived in. However, Susan often works on the Memory Store alone, not quite ready to involve Mark fully in the making of it.

Carol, Monica and Susan want to invest in their children's future – they have created unique vibrant boxes which reflect the love, hopes, dreams and fears they hold for their children. They hope the Memory Stores will help the children cope with the profound inevitable loss they will one day experience. But perhaps more important than the completed beautiful Memory Stores are the journeys Carol, Monica and Susan have taken in making them. Finding their own way they have each begun to face their past. They have confronted and explored powerful events and feelings, and they are now looking to their and their children's future.

The process of making the Memory Store has led each one of them into making plans for their children's future care. Painful though this has been for each of them, they feel they can now get on with living their lives, confident in the knowledge their children will be cared for when they are unable to do so.

Living with a life threatening illness has meant Carol, Monica and Susan have shared many similar experiences as other parents the Barnardos Castle Project works with. The Project supports children and families whose lives are affected by serious illness.

Margaret, a mother of three young children found out she had cancer when she was thirty-two.

> 'Within ten minutes my whole life had been turned upside down. It was like the doctor had told me I was going to die there and then. All I could think about was my kids... I wouldn't see them on their birthdays or have another Christmas with them.'

Eight months later Margaret is still fighting her cancer but her life and the lives of her children have changed dramatically. She is able to explore her fears, uncertainty, grief and pain with trusted friends, relatives and workers. She is often physically and emotionally exhausted as a result of her illness and treatment but she has a rota of friends, neighbours and relatives who support her with the care of the children. One of her greatest worries is how her illness is affecting the children.

Beth, aged six, has withdrawn from her and recoils when she sees Margaret without her wig. Jonathon, eight, has become aggressive and disruptive at school and Neil, aged ten, is fiercely protective of her and is reluctant to leave her at any time. Margaret recognizes that she and the children need a great deal of support. She gets this from many areas – friends, relatives, school, neighbours and professional agencies – even the local pub have raised money for them all to go to Euro Disney when her treatment ends.

Her situation is not unique. It is very similar to that of Frances who was diagnosed as having a terminal illness two years ago. However, unlike Margaret, Frances is living in total isolation. She has not been able to tell any of her family, friends or neighbours she has a terminal illness. Frances has HIV. Her greatest fear is that people will find out and her children will be shunned, ostracized and terrorized. She fears the stigma of HIV and the discrimination and judgements that go with that.

She cannot tell family and friends because she fears their rejection. She cannot tell neighbours because she fears broken windows and arson attacks. She is worried about contacting helping agencies because she fears they will make ill-informed judgements about her ability to look after her children.

Frances and Margaret share many of the experiences and uncertainties of being in families where there is a life threatening illness. What they and their children need is a wide variety of care, support and acceptance. Because of the stigma attached to her illness these are the very things Frances feels she is denied. As she says:

> 'I can live with HIV. What I can't live with are peoples' attitudes. It's those that make my life unbearable.'

Memory Store Work with Children Affected by HIV

We have acknowledged how the experiences of families affected by serious chronic ill health can be similar, no matter what the condition is. Likewise the children we work with may be separated from people they love for many reasons…divorce, family breakdown, abuse, illness, or death and they may often experience similar feelings: anger, isolation, blame, guilt, fear, loneliness, confusion, loss of self-esteem. Children who are bereaved or separated from those they love because of HIV can experience the same range of feelings. The same methods we have developed to help other children in traumatic situations express their deep and painful feelings can be used to help children affected by HIV make sense of their situation and be more able to deal with it.

Memory Stores can not only be created with children, in preparation for a parent's death, they can be used to help children prepare for, or come to terms with divorce, moving countries, or the loss of a relative or friend. Workers are now using Memory Stores with children as an extension of Life Story Books.

The next part of this chapter looks at how Luke used the making of his Memory Store as an opportunity to explore his feelings and clarify some of his long held, deep misunderstandings.

Focused Work on Children's Past, Present and Future

Luke, who is now six, has been affected by HIV in devastating ways. His mother died two years ago as a result of AIDS, his father is now terminally ill, and his young brother Jack, who is three has also been diagnosed as HIV positive. Luke is the only one of his immediate family to be negative. Jack is being cared for by his grandparents; however, they are elderly and felt they would not be able to give Luke the long term care he needs. Since his mother's death, Luke has lived with two families who were relatives of his mother. Neither family was prepared for the impact of caring for a child who had experienced such intense loss and disruption. They found Luke's bedwetting, stealing, breaking of other children's toys, and nightmares too much to cope with. Luke is now living with a professional foster parent and is waiting for a suitable adoptive family to be found.

I was approached to see if I could work with Luke to help him express his feelings, so he might be more able to cope – with his past, his present and his future. After many months of non focused play, and the building of a warm trusting relationship, our work developed into helping Luke communicate his feelings and wishes about the new kind of family he needed and we began making his Memory Store.

Many of the focused play techniques I used with Luke were those I had used in the past with children who had experienced deeply unhappy and traumatic childhoods. Some of the ones I describe will be familiar in some shape or form to many workers. None of them is unique or special to working with children affected by HIV. It can be so easy to feel out of our depth and de-skilled when confronted with the issues that surround children and HIV. It is important to remember we have developed many skills and resources in communicating with troubled and unhappy children and perhaps our best resource is being able to accept and respond, openly and genuinely, to the things children are trying to show and tell us.

Luke immediately took to the brightly coloured box, with the drawers that were able to keep his 'special things'. We worked in our 'special' playroom, and almost inevitably, Luke began calling the Memory Store 'my special box'. Luke, in fact, highlighted one of the difficulties with the Memory Stores. Each box has MEMORY STORE written on it. Luke's response on realizing this was to say:

> 'I don't know why it's got Memory Store written on – it's my "special box" isn't it?.'

Exploring the Past

Photographs and Special People

Before we began to make the Memory Store, his grandparents gave me lots of information about Luke, Jack, and their mum and dad. They found old photographs, including ones of Luke's parents when they were children. Our first few sessions were spent helping Luke remember his early childhood. These sessions gave him an opportunity to identify the people and events that were particularly important to him. This time also helped Luke to build a more positive self-image and identity, and restored some of his self-esteem. When we put the photographs in an album he had chosen, he saw how much he looked like his mummy and daddy. The album became his alone as he wrote the names of each person underneath their photograph. He had his definite favourite photo, one that showed his mother cuddling him when he was a toddler, and would hold it and say with an air of total amazement 'My mummy used to cuddle me'. The photo album was the first of Luke's treasures to go in his special box, and was added to throughout the whole time we were making his Memory Store. We also used the following techniques.

I Remember a Time

This was a very simple adaptation of the game *All About Me* (Hemmings 1991), which helped Luke identify and talk about some of his early experiences. I made individual cards, each with a sentence about remembering something which Luke could then complete; for example, 'I remember getting…for my birthday', 'I remember playing with…' 'I remember feeling sad when…' 'I remember Daddy doing…' 'Mummy saying…'

Luke was able to use these cards to help him rebuild his picture of his short but complex life. His completed cards, and the drawings he did of some of his memories again went into his 'special' box.

The Life Snake and the Germ

Luke had begun to explore his memories of past events and this had highlighted a number of painful and frightening misunderstandings 'I remember my daddy telling me off. He went to work and stayed there. He never came home. He was cross because I was naughty.' To help Luke build upon his memories and to clarify other misunderstandings he might have, we began to make Luke's Life Snake. This is similar to the many techniques often used in beginning to make Life Story Books with children. Flow charts are sometimes used with drawings which represent people and places. Road Maps are sometimes helpful with older children, using signs that symbolically represent stages in the child's life, for example crossroads, road blocks, one way signs, traffic lights, speed limits. They are all tools which can be adapted and used creatively with children to help them build the picture of their life. What is much more important than the end result is the process the child goes through in making them. This is vividly illustrated by Luke's Life Snake.

Luke had a passion for jungle animals, so together we drew a snake on a huge piece of paper. Starting at the top of the snake we drew simple figures of the people who were in his family when he was first born. At the side we drew faces to show how Luke felt or might have felt at the time. We got to the point where Luke's mum had been taken into hospital and had died. Luke and his brother Jack were not taken to see their mother in hospital. This was our conversation when Luke began to tell me about when his mum died.

'My mummy died.'

'Your Mummy died. I wonder how you felt when mummy died?.'

At this point Luke scrunched up his face, made a growling noise and began throwing things around the room.

'It looks to me like you might have been very frightened, angry and upset'.

'My mummy died because she coughed and sneezed.'

'You think Mummy died because she coughed and sneezed? I wonder how you feel when you cough and sneeze?.'

'I'm going to die too, aren't I, Ruth?.'

'You think you're going to die like Mummy?'

(Luke nodded his head)

'Mummy had a very unusual germ, different to most germs. It made her very, very poorly. It was that germ that made Mummy die. Do you remember when the doctor took some blood out of your arm? That was to see whether you had got the germ when you were in Mummy's tummy; they would be able to see if it was in your blood. It wasn't there. That means you aren't going to die like Mummy.'

'Yes Ruth, but what if the germ was in my other arm?'

Luke's clear childlike logic brought me up with such a jolt. I had tried to clarify his misunderstanding and reassure him. In fact Luke had lived with the fear he would die whenever he coughed and sneezed for so long, that a simple explanation from me was not going to make much difference to him immediately.

Over the following weeks and months we talked about the germ many times. Luke found a donor card in my office and wanted to know what it was for. He wanted to know what the heart and lungs did. When he asked what do livers do, I had to admit I wasn't sure.

'I'm not sure about that. I think it helps our bodies get rid of the things that aren't too good for it...but I don't know for sure.'

'I have things that aren't too good for me inside my body.'

'You think you have things that aren't good for you inside your body. I wonder what those things might be?.'

'You know Ruth, it's the germ, I've got the germ from Jack'.

I told him that Jack did have the germ which was why he went to the hospital so often, so the doctors could make sure Jack stayed as well as possible for as long as possible. We talked about how there are strong germs which can easily get into your body, but once they are in your body they only make you a little bit poorly and you can easily get better. We talked about germs that can only live deep inside someone's body, and how it is hard for them to get past the suits of armour we all have – our skin. So even though Jack had the germ it couldn't get out of Jack's body into Luke's.

'Even if I hit him on the head with an iron bar?'

Luke drew pictures of the germ trying to get into his body and being stopped by his own suit of armour. We played games where I pretended to be the germ and couldn't find a way past Luke's skin.

Special People

It took us many weeks to complete Luke's Life Snake.

There were many things that had happened to him that he didn't understand or had caused him great pain. He would often need to leave the focused work and spend part of the session in therapeutic play. Luke's Life Snake had helped him identify the important people in his life, many of whom he no longer saw, or saw infrequently. Luke had many things he wanted to give, ask, or say to these people but had no opportunity or way of doing this.

To help Luke we began by making Luke's 'Love Tree'. We drew a large tree and Luke drew hearts, writing on each the name of someone he loved and stuck these onto his tree. The following week he wanted to do the same; this time we drew flowers for each person, and made these into his garden of flowers. Each of these pictures went into his Special Box.

Luke loved making hearts for people and writing messages on them. Luke wrote lots of messages for his Mummy, and said 'I really want to tell Mummy that I love her, but she's died and I can't'. We talked about the fact that even though somebody had died we sometimes still wanted to be able to say things to them.

Luke loved balloons and we often have them at work. They can make instant puppets or masks to hide behind, they can be blown up and burst when children feel angry or want to make loud noises. Luke wrote the message he really wanted to give to his mum on a small piece of paper. We rolled this up, and put it inside a balloon Luke had chosen, blew the balloon up, tied some string around it and set off to the park where Luke had played with his mum. When we were in the park I asked Luke if he could think of the message he wanted his mum to have, and to think of it as he let his balloon go. As his balloon went soaring upwards, Luke turned to me and said 'I think she'll get that', and went off to play on the swings.

Feelings

Not only can it be hard for children to articulate their feelings, it can be hard for them to identify what their feelings are. They may not have the language and, even if they have, they may well have learnt that adults do not want them to talk about, or show their feelings. If a child is to regain the self-esteem and sense of belonging that is so often broken or damaged through loss, it is crucial they have the opportunity to express and have their feelings acknowledged. So often children express these feelings in similar ways to Luke – bedwetting, stealing, nightmares. Other children may simply become withdrawn, anxious or over-protective.

When Susan told her son, Mark, she was HIV positive, she thought she was seriously ill. Her illness in fact was unrelated to HIV, and she is still asymptomatic. Having told Mark about her diagnosis she then felt unable to talk to him about it further, assuring him she would be well for a long time. For Mark, now aged thirteen, the fear of his mother's illness remained constantly with him. He often played truant from school, would not go out with friends and stayed in his room. His anxiety about his mother overwhelmed him.

We met and had our talking sessions high on the hills above his town. He would speak movingly about his fears, 'Every time my mum tells me she has a cold I don't believe her. I think she's going to die'.

Mark told me of the isolation he felt, a common feeling in children who are living with traumatic experiences. His sense of isolation was added to by the stigma and prejudice he knew surrounded HIV.

> 'There's a boy at my school who's mum has cancer. He can tell everyone about her, and the teachers all feel sorry for him. I can't tell anyone about my mum, they'd call her a slag or a druggie, and I won't have anyone saying that about my mum.'

Mark was living in a world of uncertainty and stress, just like his mother. When she had been diagnosed seven years ago, she had been told she had AIDS and that she would probably live for another two years. As management and treatment of HIV becomes more advanced people's life expectancy increases and often, so too does the uncertainty of people living with the infection. Mark's mother remained well, and it was too painful for her to consider the possibility she may die before Mark reached independence. When Mark had once asked her who he would live with if she died, she had told him, 'Don't be silly, I'm not going to die'.

His mother had wanted to reassure Mark, but her response did not take away his fears. They increased. He learnt to deal with his fears in isolation, creating his own understanding of the things that were happening and may happen to him. He felt alone and totally out of control. He felt he could not ask his mum the things he wanted to know because he was frightened of hurting and upsetting her. He did not want to see his friends any more, scared that they would guess his mum was HIV positive. He was even more scared that he would one day tell them and the prejudice he and his mum may then experience would be his fault.

Mark's feeling he might not be able to control who knew what about his situation reminded me of the children I had worked with who had been sexually abused. They had lived under enforced secrecy for so long, their bodies, space, and self-esteem had been so violated and invaded, that once they told people of the abuse and were believed it could sometimes be hard for them to stop talking about it. It was difficult for them to rebuild the boundaries they needed to ensure they could talk about their abuse in safe and appropriate environments. I used an exercise sometimes within groups which helps children identify the information they are willing to share. It gives them the powerful message they can be in control of their information in a positive way, and reinforces the idea they can make decisions about what to tell and to whom.

I brought along an envelope and piece of paper to one of our sessions. I asked Mark to write on the outside of the envelope what he would be prepared to share with anyone. On the inside flap of the envelope, I asked him to write what he might be prepared to share later with someone if he trusted them. The piece of paper was to go inside the sealed envelope. On this he could write the thing he might never want to share, or that he would only share if he had a really good reason to do so. Mark could decide what he wanted to do with his envelope. Maybe he could keep it himself, I could lock it unopened in our safe at work, or he could destroy it, perhaps burning it or tearing it up. Mark decided to take his envelope home to keep in his bedroom. He knew his mother would never look through his things.

Mark shared with me the things that were on his envelope, but chose to keep the information he had written on his paper private. Doing this exercise helped Mark identify that he wanted to be able to tell his mum he was worried about her, and he wanted her to be able to talk honestly to him. He wanted to be able to talk to someone his own age, but only if they had a mum or dad who was HIV positive. Mark acknowledged he wasn't prepared to tell his friends about his mum, but that he did have control over this.

When we were making Luke's Memory Store we had to make lots of space and opportunities for him to confront and express these feelings. Mark was more articulate and could identify and express his feelings. It was much harder for Luke. Sometimes he simply did not know what his feelings were, or how to put them into words. Simple faces looking sad, angry, happy or frightened drawn on cards can help children identify and express their feelings (Jewett 1984).

Feelings Wheel

The 'Feelings Wheel' helped Luke identify and face some of the many conflicting feelings he had. To make a Feelings Wheel, draw a circle on a large piece of paper, and divide it into segments so that it looks like a wheel. In each segment draw a face that shows a feeling: happy, sad, lonely, frightened, confused, silly, angry, worried, excited.

We used the Feelings Wheel in many different ways. Sometimes we would play games with the Feelings Wheel; we would place the wheel on the floor, put a bottle on it and spin the bottle. Whichever face the bottle landed on we would act how we might look if we were feeling that way. We were then able to talk about the times Luke had felt like that, and the things that had happened which made him feel that way. When we began exploring the kind of family Luke wanted to live in until he was a man, I wrote out cards with different situations on them, and Luke would point to the wheel to show how he might feel in that situation. I drew a life-size outline of Luke and he coloured all the feelings he had inside his body. We would make feeling models out of clay — angry ones, sad ones, frightened ones, happy ones, and cuddly ones. All these continued to go in his 'Special Box'.

Looking to the Future

Luke's 'Special Box' was beginning to grow. In his box he had information about his mum and dad, the things they liked doing, where they had gone to school and worked. His grandparents had written about his parents' wedding and the first house they lived in together. We had written and drawn the things that Luke was good at, the things that made him happy and sad.

Luke had completed his Life Snake, and pages of his Memory Book had been written by relatives, previous carers, his present foster parent, and the two of us in our sessions together.

He had photographs, birthday cards, videos of him and Jack playing together, treasured toys and a list of people he could contact when he got older. Luke had confronted and faced his past and was ready to look towards his future.

The Bulb

To help Luke think about his future and the kind of family he needed to live with we planted bulbs – quick growing gladioli. As he planted each bulb in its container I asked Luke what a bulb needed to grow into a big, strong and healthy plant.

'It needs a plant pot.'

'It needs a plant pot…somewhere to live.'

'It needs to have soil.'

'It needs to have soil...for food'.

'It needs to have water to drink. I'm going to give my bulbs to... *(here he named several significant people in his life)* They can look after them and make sure burglars don't get them.'

'You're going to give your bulbs to special people to make sure they look after them. Your bulbs need lots of things to make sure they grow big and strong. Maybe next week we can think about what boys need so they can grow into big men?'

Luke left one of his bulbs at work and each week after that the first thing he did was to look to see how his bulb was doing. In the following weeks we were able to think about what boys needed and then what Luke himself needed to grow into a man.

Guided Fantasy

To help Luke explore more about what he wanted in his future he had his 'special story' – a guided fantasy. Even young children can participate in guided fantasies, particularly if it leads straight on from *sleeping lions*. Sleeping lions is a game many children are familiar with. You ask the children to lie as still as they can on the floor; they must try to make sure they do not move any part of their body. I have found this to be a non-threatening way of helping children to relax. Once the children are relaxed you can begin to tell them they are going to hear a special story, one that they will help to make up.

'You are lying on a beach and you've had a lovely day with your friends. You think you'd like a little bit of quiet, so you decide to do some exploring on your own... You walk a little way up the beach, and you see a house on the cliff that looks very nice and friendly, but you notice that it's empty.

You think this would be a good house to explore. You climb up to the house and walk through – right away you like the house. You go upstairs and you see a door...and you're really surprised because the door has got your name on it. Right away you know this is your room and inside the room is everything that belongs to you, and everything you want in the future. You have a good look around and when you come out you can draw your very own room.'

Luke drew a picture of his room, in fact he drew a garden where he was playing with a man and woman, a baby and a small child. Luke described his picture 'This is my new mum and dad, I'll live with them until I'm a big man. This is my new baby brother. Jack has come to have his tea with us'.

Luke's ABC

Luke had got to the age where he loved using his newly acquired reading and writing skills.

We made Luke's Own ABC poster, a large piece of paper divided into squares, each with a letter of the alphabet in it. Luke then thought of things or people that were important to him, things that described him, and things he wanted from his new family. Luke filled all his squares with great enthusiasm; X was for the kisses he wanted from his new mummy, and N was nee, 'I want to be able to sit on her nee'. J was for Jack, and G was for Grandma 'I want to see them like I do now'. But perhaps most important of all was Luke's L and S 'I'm LUKE, and I'm SPECIAL'.

Luke's Memory Store (or Special Box), like Carol's, Monica's, and Susan's reflects his complex, painful and sometimes joyful life. It contains his deepest fears and longed for hopes. Like the women, in making his Special Box Luke has made a journey of exploration and discovery.

Conclusion

It can be very easy to feel de-skilled when we are confronted with the issues and feelings that surround children who are affected by HIV. Many of the social taboos – death, sex and sexuality, come sharply to the surface with this illness. We may worry about what we think children will ask us and how we will find the words to respond. It may mean we have to explore and confront some of our own deeply held attitudes and values, so that we do not compound the pain, confusion and isolation the children and their parents may feel. None of these are new fears or demands for workers. It is very important to remember that above anything else they are children who may be experiencing intense and profound loss and uncertainty, things which, sadly, many children, in many situations experience. To help them express and cope with their pain, and so look forward to their futures with less fear and uncertainty, we can draw upon many skills and play methods that have evolved from other areas of work with troubled children. As always, the best resource children can have is our warmth, sincerity and acceptance of themselves and their feelings.

Acknowledgements

This chapter is largely based on 'The Memory Store: A Review' Ruth Neville, which first appeared in *Adoption and Fostering* Vol 18, No. 3. Autumn edition 1994.

The author would like to thank British Agencies for Adoption and Fostering for their permission in reproducing it in this article.

Resources

Memory Stores and accompanying guide to using them are available from Barnardos Publications, Barnardos Trading Estate, Paycocke Road, Basildon, Essex, SS14 3DR. Price £27.00 plus postage and packing, telephone (01268) 520224.

Hemmings, P. (1991) *All About Me.* Available from Barnardos Publications, Barnardos Trading Estate, Paycocke Road, Basildon, Essex, SS14 3DR.

Jewett, C. (1984) *Helping Children Cope with Separation and Loss.* London: Batsford/British Adoption and Fostering.

Part Five

Projects in the USA

CHAPTER 18

Embracing Fears and Sharing Tears
Working with Grieving Children

Jennifer Levine
with Debra Noell

Introduction

'My man left me...' sang eight-year-old Ellen[1] as she shared a special song in group that her mom had taught her. Ellen's two younger brothers also sang their 'special songs'. The group was their safe place to talk about Mom as they were not permitted to sing or talk about her at home. The children's parents had separated before their Mom's death, and Dad had a girlfriend they were instructed to call 'mom'. My heart ached for these three children who were being taught not to feel and not to share. To make matters worse, the minister at the funeral told these children their mother was a sinner and went to hell! Thank goodness they had one open and loving aunt who fought their father to bring them to the Children's Bereavement Group.

Why are grief groups important? I believe they are important for a number of reasons. One is that they create a safe place for children to remember and share and hurt and then begin to heal. Another is it seems to be most effective for grieving children to be with other grieving children. It makes their sense of isolation and feeling different seem less intense, and allows them to be a part of a group experience that validates the difficulties they are experiencing and assures them of finding help.

---

1   The children's names have been changed to protect their privacy.

Pre-Group Work

Referrals to our children's grief groups come from many sources, including school counselors, ministers, psychologists, and parents of children who have been in previous groups. Our groups are not seen as therapy, but as support and education about the grief process. When I receive a referral, I send out a registration packet that includes a brochure about the group, an intake form requesting basic information (see Figure 18.1), and a handout discussing the importance of helping grieving children, which supports the parents/caregivers decision to enroll them in the group. After the parents/caregivers return the intake form, I schedule a pre-group interview with the children.

Date: . . . .

Child's Name:. . . . . Date of Birth: . . . .

Address: . . . . Zip: . . . .

School: . . . . Grade: . . . . . Sex: . . . .

Your Name:. . . . . How Related: . . . .

Home Phone: . . . . Work Phone: . . . .

Person Who Died: . . . . Date of Death:. . . . .

Relation to Child:. . . . .

Cause of Death: . . . .

In one sentence, describe the relationship between the deceased and this child:. . . . .

. . . .

Is this the first death your child has experienced? . . . .

If 'no', please explain:. . . . .

List any special concerns you have regarding your child and the death: . . . . .

. . . .

How did you hear about this group? . . . .

I give permission for (child's name):. . . . .

to attend this 8 week program on grief (your name):. . . . .

© Copyright 1992 Jennifer Levine

Figure 18.1 Children's Bereavement Group Intake

Experience is a wonderful teacher – especially of unpleasant experiences. I learned the importance of doing pre-group interviews from a girl named Abbey, age five, who was referred to me by her school counselor. Her mother described her as a 'challenging' child who was having difficulty dealing with the sudden death of her father. At the first group, I thought her behavior was due to first-night jitters, but I realized during our second group that something was wrong. Abbey grew more disruptive, pinching the other children, taking her shoes off and throwing things. I quickly realized she was not ready for a group experience but in dire need of one-to-one assistance. Had I done a pre-group interview, I would have known better than to place her in the group and, since then, I interview all the children before accepting them into the program. The interview also serves another purpose. It allows the children to meet me, so that when they come to their first group meeting, they will recognize at least one face – mine.

During the pre-group interview, I ask the parent/caregiver to wait while I meet with their children. I introduce myself and ask the children if they know why they are here – most do not. I encourage them to tell me their story about who died and what they understand, as this allows me to assess their level of information and comprehension. I then ask them to fill in a drawing of their support people (see Figure 18.2). This helps me identify their awareness of support, and enables me to determine their ability to follow directions and work at a task that involves thinking and printing or drawing. For children who do not know how to print, I encourage them to draw pictures of their support people, and I help them in printing names. If they can follow simple instructions, converse even minimally with me, and work on the support people design, I accept them into the group.

When I began the groups in Fort Wayne, Indiana, USA, there were no other services available for grieving children, so I allowed a wide age span in the groups – from four to eighteen years. One group with such a wide range of ages went quite well; most did not. A four-year-old and an eighteen-year-old have very different concepts of death and very different needs. Now there are other services available through other agencies and non-profit groups. Due to these other programs, I have adjusted my age range from five to twelve years.

Before the group begins, I schedule a parent/caregiver education night. This meeting is for parents/caregivers only and generally lasts about two hours. To be effective with grieving children, we must educate their parents/caregivers about the grieving process and how it differs for children. It is especially important for them to have an understanding of what is 'normal' in their children. Consider Alan, age six, whose mother was murdered. His parents were divorced and his father had remarried, so after his mother was murdered Alan went to live with his father and stepmother. Alan began to act out both at home and at school – picking fights and defying authority. He created difficulties with his siblings and his classmates. He was quickly becoming labelled a bully

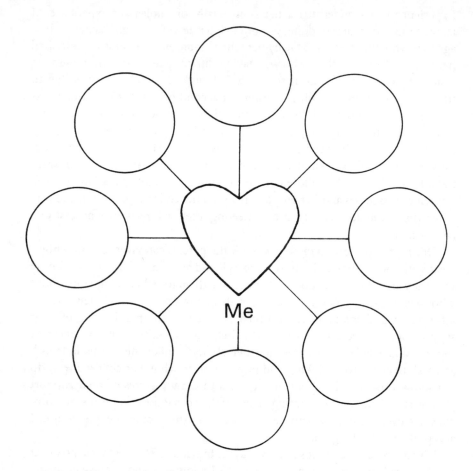

Figure 18.2 My support people

and troublemaker. Due to his stepmother's inexperience with grief, she did not realize his behaviours were his way of demonstrating how very awful he felt about his mother's murder, and therefore disciplined him harshly, telling him he was a bad boy. She did not realize the feelings behind his behaviour were intense anger, hurt, fear, worry and guilt. Because we cover these feelings and behaviors in the orientation, she and her husband were greatly relieved to learn he was 'normal'. I helped them develop alternative ways to discipline him, such as teaching him the Styrofoam cup stomp (explained in detail below).

During the orientation, I give out printed copies of the material we discuss so they can refer back to it if needed. We talk about what is normal in grieving children and look at a developmental chart that illustrates children's under-

Figure 18.3 Developmental Death Awareness (Copyright © 1992 Jennifer Levine)

Age	Developmental stage	Erikson's stages	Death Awareness	Questions
Birth–1 year	Early Infancy	Basic Trust vs. Mistrust • am I being cared for? • or, are people non-caring?	• Does not understand concept of death • Notices the separation	'Where's Mom?'
1–3 years	Later Infancy (toddlers)	Autonomy vs. Shame and Doubt • is it OK to explore or am I told not to as it isn't safe? • wants to 'hide' inadequacies.	same	same
4–5 years	Early Childhood	Initiative vs. Guilt • can I do things on my own? • or, will my parents disapprove if I am independent?	• Thinks everyone sees things as he/she does • Magical thinking • Fear of separation • Death seen as accidental rather than unavoidable • Death seen as punishment bad behaviour • Assumes it won't happen to him/her • Death is reversible and temporary • Boogeymen	'How will Mom eat... go to the bathroom... breathe?'
6–11 years	Middle Childhood	Industry vs. Inferiority • can be successful or mediocre or failure	• Death is final • Can neither deny nor accept death in his/her life • Magical thinking • Personifies death (monsters, boogeymen) • Greatest level of death anxiety • Mutilation anxiety • Death seen as punishment for bad behaviour • Can understand facts	Speaks of death loss often Wants detailed information regarding the death and bodies: 'What happens to the eyeballs; do the fingernails still grow?' Other biological questions.
12–20 years	Puberty and Adolescence	Identity vs. Role Diffusion • exploring self of staying confused and self-conscious • or, staying merged with parents to avoid dealing with identity issues	• Adult concept of death • Focuses on body • May reject funeral customs to avoid reality of death • Worries about pain and suffering • May push self to limits to defy death	'Do we live just to die?'

standing of death (see Figure 18.3). We talk about what helps and what hinders children in their mourning process and we view an informative video by Dr Alan Wolfelt (1991) called 'A Child's View of Grief'. We also review and discuss the workbook which we will use in the group called *When Someone Very Special Dies* (Heegaard 1991), and then we end with a question and answer period. A common question has to do with parents'/caregivers' hesitancy to allow their children to see their tears and deep sadness. I tell them it is OK because it gives the children permission to share their tears and sadness.

Meeting with the parents/caregivers gives me a clearer picture of what the children are experiencing and often offers insight into problems or potential problem areas. Frequently parents/caregivers are tearful, exhausted, and/or worried that they have done irreparable damage to their children. Learning how to respond to their children can lessen their burden during an already difficult time.

Group Program

When I originally began these groups, I based them on a six week design. It did not take long to realize that more time was needed to cover effectively all I wanted to at least touch upon. I decided to increase the program to eight weeks, meeting every Monday night from 7 to 8:30 p.m. Once registration was full (no more than ten children), any further requests were placed on a waiting list for the next group. Generally, I would wait at least two weeks after one group ended before beginning another. Our first week's focus is on getting to know each other and learning about changes we all experience in our lives everyday. The second week we begin to address the different causes of death and the specific cause of death of their loved one. Week three we look at funerals and unanswered questions. Week four introduces feelings and learning to name what we feel in our bodies. We talk about sad feelings and if it seems appropriate, we mention suicide. Week five addresses specific feelings like anger and feeling scared and worried. We try to do a little on basic problem solving here also. Week six addresses how they were told about the death and what they would change about that if they could. We also touch upon guilt feelings. Week seven is quite popular with the children as we talk about remembering and create memory boxes, which I explain in more detail later in this chapter. In our last week we talk about our support people and end with a closing ceremony.

Techniques

A number of years ago, while working with children who had cancer, I developed the Listen With Your Heart Game (LWYH). I discovered by using a game to discuss a difficult topic, the children were less threatened and I am continually surprised at the success this simple game has with children in crisis. The game includes a handmade toss toy (bean bag) shaped like a heart and a stack of cards with questions on them (see Figure 18.4). The toss toy is made out of brightly coloured material and has eyes, a nose, a mouth and big yellow ears sewn onto it. There is a small pocket on the back that closes with velcro. This is where the music button (a gadget that when pushed, plays music) is placed – that way you can continually change the tune if you want.

We start each group meeting by pressing the musical trinket in the back of the toss toy and tossing it around the group. Whoever has it when the music stops draws a card and answers the question printed on it. Not only do they have fun doing this, they actually try to figure a way to make sure they get to answer the questions! Some wonderful discussions are generated in this manner. For example, Bill age nine, got the card that said: 'Something I'd like to say to my special person who died is...' This gave him permission to say he was angry about his brother's drinking that led to his fatal accident.

- Tell what's different about you since your special person died.
- Tell why we have funerals.
- Something I'd like to tell my special person who died is. . . . . .
- If I could create a special memorial plaque for my special person who died, it would say . . . .
- Tell why talking about your feelings is important.
- What happens to the physical body when someone dies?
- One way to show someone I love them is . . . .
- Something I have learned about grief is. . . . .
- Something I still don't understand about death and dying is. . .
- The feeling I have that gives me the most trouble is. . . . . Tell why.
- Since my special person died, I still worry about . . . .
- Describe your feelings when you learned your special person had died.
- My special person who died taught me about . . . .
- My favourite memory of my special person who died is . . . . .
- One thing I hated the most about the funeral was . . . .
- Someone I can always go to to talk about feelings is . . . .

Figure 18.4 Grief questions for listen with your heart game

I am an educator at heart. The foundation of my work is the belief that helping others understand the dynamics of their experience is part of helping them heal. When dealing with children and grief, I believe it helps to define words they may be hearing but do not understand, words like grief or cancer. Teaching them what is normal and what other children experience is also helpful. Using a workbook offers a structure that is familiar to most children [as in school] and because the normal grief process can be chaotic and disruptive, the structure is generally reassuring.

I selected *When Someone Very Special Dies* (1991) because it has a simple easy-to-follow format. Marge Eaton Heegaard does a wonderful job of taking us through the normal process of grief while weaving in the many facets we need to discuss. She begins with looking at change and generally addresses feelings.

While we use the workbook, it is not our only tool. We make use of art, books, games, and music – whatever seems to be most effective with that particular group. Often we improvise, depending on the mood. We might hand out a balloon to the children and ask them to write on the deflated balloon the feeling that most troubles them. We then instruct them to blow up the balloon to the size of that feeling. Then, one by one, we ask them to tell a story about the feeling and then release the balloon and watch it fly. This exercise is quite symbolic of the pressure we feel when we keep our feelings stuffed inside, and the wonder of release when we feel safe enough to share them. Another popular balloon activity is the balloon stomp. We put questions inside all the balloons, blow them up and tie them, throw them on the floor, and the children take turns stomping a balloon and answering the question inside.

Helping children find appropriate ways to express their feelings is most important. We address sadness, fear, worry, and anger, but not all children naturally know how to express these feelings in safe ways. Children learn by watching the adults around them, and sadly, not all adults know safe ways to express feelings either. Therefore we believe it is beneficial to give children safe options of expression.

Drawing pictures of sadness is helpful to children. Sally, age nine, drew a heart broken in two with tears flowing from it to illustrate her feelings about her father's death. We may also encourage them to draw their family as animals, then talk about what they drew. Using animals as the family characters allows for distance from the actual family members and also offers us a symbol that reflects how they see each person. For example, we've seen pigs, bears, cats, dogs, tigers, gorillas, and many others. Each presents its own picture of a personality.

The use of stories is another tool that can prompt discussion. The second week of group we introduce the story *Aarvy Aardvark Finds Hope* (O'Toole 1988) and each of the following six weeks we read a chapter at the beginning of the group. This is a delightful story that addresses feelings of loss and grief in the animals' lives. It complements the sections we work on in the workbook during that same time. *The Hurt* (Doleski 1983) is a good story to illustrate the importance of sharing our feelings and not stuffing them inside. When we discuss sadness, we may also talk about people who experience extreme sadness that can sometimes lead to suicide. We use this as an opportunity to do some education related to suicide. In one of our groups we had a five-year-old child whose father committed suicide. When we were talking about sadness, he said sometimes people get too sad and want to be with their dads and have a plan to get there. We immediately asked him what that plan might be. He said a little boy would find the tallest building in town and jump from it. We asked what it would take for this little boy not to do it, and he said for someone to stop him. We asked him to tell the little boy we would miss him more than all the stars in the universe and hoped very much that he would not do that. After the group, we spoke with him and got his permission to talk with his mother and therapist. As children often speak metaphorically or allow their behaviors to tell their story, we need to remember they may not have the words to tell us how they feel.

Frequently, the children in the group experience fears. A common fear is that someone else in their family will die; some fear that the person who died will come back and haunt them. The most intense fear we have seen is in children who have had a loved one murdered, especially if the perpetrator has not been apprehended. They fear the murderer will return and kill them too. One technique we use in dealing with fear (especially at bedtime) is to teach the children about the pink bubble. We tell them to close their eyes and imagine a pink bubble around them. No one and nothing can penetrate the bubble because it is created from special magical material. We balance this imaginary exercise with practical suggestions, such as knowing who to go to for help and what to do in an emergency. Most grieving children worry about something. When talking about worries we teach them problem solving techniques. We have them identify their worries and choose one worry that is or could become a problem, like worrying they will cry at school. We then brainstorm solutions. We may also read a silly story like *How to Get Rid of Bad Dreams* (Hazbry and Condy 1983), which is about nightmares and offers creative solutions to child-like crises.

Children, like many adults, need help in learning appropriate ways to express their anger. Our favorite anger tool is the Styrofoam cup stomp, and we have yet to find a child who did not relish doing this. We take Styrofoam (polystyrene) coffee cups and turn them upside down on the floor (does not work on carpet), then we have them think about what makes them really angry. We ask them to move their anger into their foot, and on the count of three, they stomp! And, boy do they stomp!! One little girl whose mother was terminally ill came in for an individual session one day and proudly announced she had used her cups. She said her cousin hit her and she was very angry because her grandmother would not let her hit back. So, she took an entire bag of cups, lined them down a long sidewalk, and proceeded to stomp every one of them! She said she was feeling very angry when she started, but laughing a lot when she finished. Other activities, such as blowing up paper bags and popping them, are also effective. It is important for us to teach children safe and effective ways to express their anger. *When Emily Woke Up Angry* (Duncan 1989) is a children's story that illustrates how each of us choose different ways to deal with our anger. My personal favorite is throwing eggs at trees. Generally, I teach this one to adults. It's not too expensive, is ecologically sound, and does it feel good!

One of our most popular activities in the group is the night we discuss the importance of remembering and the creation of memory boxes. We invite the parents into the group for the last half hour to assist. We decorate cardboard pencil boxes with a variety of construction paper (thick paper in various colours) shiny wrapping paper, stickers and glitter. It is touching to watch them show their love as they put together their special box for memories and keepsakes about their loved one who died. Some of the children take their boxes to school to share for show and tell (a special time in the classroom where they share special things with their classmates). One little girl designed hers and put her grandmother's eyelash curler and lipstick in it. Another whose baby brother died from cancer tried to put all his toys in her box. There is something very important about having a special place to keep their memories.

Another activity we have used and seen remarkable results with is writing good-bye letters. We do this when we talk about how their loved one died. It worked wonders with a six-year-old boy whose father died suddenly of a heart attack. He was very quiet and somewhat difficult to understand, and his mother was concerned about a nervous tic in one eye which he developed after the death of his father. In his good-bye letter he wrote, 'Dear Dad, I miss you. I miss playing with you. I love you'. His mother later reported he eagerly shared his letter with her and his tic disappeared!

Closing Ceremony

Heegaard (1988) suggests the importance of closure. We incorporated some of her suggestions and added some of our own in our closing ceremony. We also end each weekly group with a closing activity. The one activity most children want is the group hug. Usually one or two will yell they want to be in the middle of our hug where we all gather together in a circle, count to three, and squeeze. The ones in the middle get extra 'squished'. The children make sure we remember the hug.

We have a closing ceremony at the last meeting. We tie a balloon to each child's chair that says something like 'You Are Special'. We have a sweet treat (usually cupcakes with special decorative things on top). We put a candle in each of the children's cupcakes and one by one light them saying: 'The light in me recognizes the light in you'. The parents/caregivers are invited to the closing ceremony and are asked to write a few things on a circular piece of paper about their children. For example, 'Missy is a sensitive little girl who cares for everyone'. It is their chance to validate their children in front of their peers. The children write something positive about each other on squares and write how they feel about their parents/caregivers on triangles. The triangles are then taped onto their parents/caregivers – often in strange places!! We have each child stand one at a time, and we tape all the circles and squares onto their clothes as they are read to the group. This is symbolic of having them own that which is shared. We end by taking group pictures that are later mailed to the children for their memory boxes.

Conclusion

It is essential to educate grieving children about the process of grief, the importance of allowing them expression, of children supporting children and of remembering fun and play even during very serious times. When Ellen and her brothers sang their special country western songs again at our closing ceremony, they sang with deep feeling and bright eyes. Although they knew talking and sharing about Mom was off limits at home, they also knew there were other people in the world who wanted to hear what they had to say and would listen willingly. It is my belief that as we give children the gift of listening to them, they gift us with their honesty and undisguised pain. We have much to teach and learn from each other. When we are open and honest with our grief we can experience a process of transformation – one that changes us dramatically as we eventually reach a 'new normal' in our lives.

References

Doleski, T. (1983) *The Hurt*. Mahwah, NJ: Paulist Press.

Duncan, R. (1989) *When Emily Woke Up Angry*. New York, NY: Barron's Educational Series, Inc.

Hazbry, N. and Condy, R. (1983) *How to Get Rid of Bad Dreams*. New York, NY: Scholastic, Inc.

Heegaard, M. (1988) *Facilitator Guide for: When Someone Very Special Dies*. Minneapolis, MN: Woodland Press.

Heegaard, M. (1991) *When Someone Very Special Dies*. Minneapolis, MN: Woodland Press.

O'Toole, D. (1988) *Aarvy Aardvark Finds Hope*. Burnsville, NC: Mountain Rainbow Publications.

Wolfelt, Dr. A. (1991) *A Child's View of Grief*. (videotape) Fort Collins, CO: Center for Loss & Life Transition.

CHAPTER 19

Group Interventions with Bereaved Children Five to Seventeen Years of Age
From a Medical Center-Based Young Person's Grief Support Program

Ben Wolfe

Introduction

You have probably heard the story of the 'shattered glass'. The story describes a window that is broken and the realization that no matter how hard one tries, after being glued back together the glass will never be the same again. We also know that of our lives. We know when significant events take place in our lives, we too can never be who we were before. Major transition points shatter the glass. Some individuals think they can quickly find all the pieces and glue them back together as they were previously for either themselves, other members of their family or friends. Others learn some of the glass will always be blurred. Transitions are not always negative, but are 'windows in time'. They are the events that reshape us. They remind us that although we want predictability and control in our lives, neither is guaranteed. Life changing events challenge our coping skills and force us to re-examine our priorities.

Youngsters who have experienced the death of a family member, relative or close friend have an entirely different perspective on what the 'glass' looks like today compared to youngsters who have not had similar experiences. They are changed because of the death. They are different from who they were before and will, at various stages throughout their lives, revisit the old 'window'. The difficulty will be, after the glass is shattered, that lives do move on and the glass as they once knew it will never be the same. How then, can youngsters be helped who are grieving the death of a significant person in their lives?

The goal of this chapter is to share what we at St Mary's Medical Center's Grief Support Center have found useful over the past eleven years when working with five- to seventeen-year-old youngsters in children and adolescent bereavement support groups. Having had over 600 youngsters participate in the Young Person's Grief Support Program (YPGSP) we continue to remind ourselves of the need for flexibility, and the need to help youngsters develop coping skills to deal not only with the short-term issues identified upon entering one of the groups, but also with how to continue the coping patterns in the long term. We believe strongly in the concept of bereavement support groups for youngsters and believe that such groups can and do facilitate children's healthy adjustment to the death of a parent, sibling, grandparent, relative or friend. We also continue to recognize that not all youngsters and their families do well in groups ... some are just not 'groupies'. As facilitators we have learned a great deal throughout the years, and believe our facilitative role is to help youngsters and their families make informed decisions on how to cope, and to empower the youngsters to integrate a death into their lives, move on and feel better after leaving the group than when they entered.

There is a fine line between support groups and therapy groups, and we at the Grief Support Center believe youngsters who participate in bereavement groups, and the persons who refer them, are seeking *support*, not therapy. The youngsters are not trying directly to change their behaviour, nor are they trying to analyse what happened; rather, they are now trying to find the tools to cope with the 'shattered glass'. Most youngsters do not enter the groups because they are clinically depressed or suicidal as a result of the death, they are there to learn how to cope with the changes death brings, both internally and externally. Although grief is personal and each 'shattered glass' is unique, most young people do experience common feelings when coping with a death.

An umbrella for various support programs and services, St Mary's Grief Support Center (GSC) is located within the Social Services Department at St Mary's Medical Center in Duluth, Minnesota, USA. The GSC provides a comprehensive program of counselling, support, advocacy, education, and research for individuals who are dealing with, or affected by, an impending death or who are bereaved. Programs and services are not only for adults, parents, and children throughout the region, but also for health and educational institutions, community members and specialized groups in northern sections of Minnesota, Wisconsin, and Michigan.

Originally developed in January 1985 as an extension of St Mary's Medical Center's mission and services, the GSC serves not only the needs of the Center's staff, patients and their families, but has developed a reputation as a program that serves the entire region and provides consultation on bereavement issues to churches, hospitals, hospice programs, physicians, schools and universities, and a host of professional and commercial organizations throughout the United States, Canada and overseas.

The GSC's Young Person's Grief Support Program, originally developed in 1983, has been replicated in numerous locations in the United States, Canada, Great Britain and Australia. The bereavement groups are young person focused and I see the role of our facilitators as advocating for the youngster, yet providing the adult who makes the referral with as much support as needed.

History and Structure of the Medical Center-Based Young Person's Grief Support Program

Originally designed for youngsters nine to thirteen years of age and their families, the Grief Support Center's YPGSP was implemented in November, 1983. Prior to the beginning of the program, a large number of requests by doctors, nurses, school counsellors, other professionals, parents, relatives, clergy, and the juvenile court system were received by the Medical Center regarding some type of assistance for young persons who were suffering the effects of grief as a result of a death (Wolfe 1987).

Table 19.1 Total number of Young Person's Grief Support Programs (St Mary's Grief Support Center, Duluth, MN) (offered between November 1983 – May 1994)

Total programs offered over 11-year period	86
Total participants that were signed-up	633
Total number that never attended even one session although they were signed-up, interviewed, and we thought they would be attending	29
Number of individuals that dropped out of programs after attending one or more sessions	68
Total number of youngsters that completed all 86 programs	536
Average number signed-up per session 7.4	
Average number that completed each session after subtracting 'no shows' 6.2	
Completion Rate: Not counting the 29 'No Shows'	89%

In the summer of 1983, programs in our community for this type of youngster did not exist. When we checked throughout the State of Minnesota we found that only two groups related to grief existed for children on a continual, programmatic basis, and these were being held at two children's hospitals, one in Minneapolis and one in St Paul. These groups were only for young cancer patients and their siblings at one hospital, and at the other hospital only for bereaved siblings whose brother or sister had died from any type of injury, illness, or disease.

Duluth does not have the large population of Minneapolis and St Paul; therefore, we thought that we needed a program for youngsters who were bereaved from any type of death. In addition, we believed that as long as the youngster needed assistance, the person who died did not have to be a sibling but, in fact, could be anyone. We also thought that recently bereaved youngsters would probably be inappropriate for the program until further into their grief work, but decided that we would not have any 'absolute time rules' regarding entry into the program. The common denominator was that all participants would have experienced the death of someone close to them. This is still the case and this criterion works extremely well. Over the eleven years the program has been operational, we have had individuals join groups in time spans ranging from one week after a death to three, four, five years previously. A number of youngsters have experienced deaths ten years ago but were never allowed to grieve and had not dealt with issues related to the loss. Over the years we have had parents, due to the impending death of a family member or friend, put their child or children on the 'next group list' – just to be certain that they got in. Most youngsters have joined a group between two months to one year after the death. The groups are only for bereaved youngsters and we do not allow friends to come for moral support if they were not close to or did not know the person that died.

Originally, the Young Person's Grief Support Programs were conducted in seven week sessions and operated on fall, winter, and spring schedules. Six weeks were for the young persons and the seventh week for their parents and/or guardians. As a result of parents contacting us in the fall of 1984, it was becoming very clear that groups were needed for ages younger and older than our nine to thirteen age group. The program was then revised for the following winter and spring sessions in order to accommodate five to nine year olds and ten to fifteen year olds. For the past nine years, the groups have been offered for five to eight, nine to thirteen, and fourteen to seventeen and the youngsters now participate for seven straight weeks. The eighth week involves their parents and/or guardians where they share observations, evaluate the program and learn behaviours which lend more support to their children. Parents continue to comment on the confidential evaluations that they feel the parent get-togethers are very beneficial. Programs still operate on fall, winter, and spring schedules and we continue to have youngsters younger and older than the age groups listed. The groups are offered on separate days of each week with each group meeting at the Medical Center from 3:30 to 5:00 p.m. where the sessions are held in a very comfortable room equipped with couches and armchairs.

Cookies, milk, and lemonade are available for the two younger age groups and coffee is added to that list for the older attendees. The food is always eaten and facilitates participation in a 'loosening-up time' for conversation. At the conclusion of the program, certificates are distributed as well as names, addresses, and telephone numbers of each group member and both facilitators.

Table 19.2 Ages of 633 young people who took part in the Young Person's Grief Support Program (86 programs) (November 1983 to May 1994)

Age	Number of young people	Percentage of total number of young people		
4	9	1%		
5	39	6%	190 young people	
6	35	6%	in this age group	30%
7	62	10%	Average age 6.5 years	
8	45	7%		
9	46	7%		
10	58	9%	259 young people	
11	46	7%	in this age group	41%
12	57	9%	Average age 11 years	
13	52	8%		
14	44	7%		
15	59	9%	184 young people	
16	36	6%	in this age group	29%
17	3	5%	Average age 15.6 years	
18	9	1%		
19	4	1%		
20	1	0.2%		

Average age of 633 young people 11 years

Of the 536 youngsters who completed YPGSP:

Sex	Number of young people	Percentage of total number of young people
Girls	298	56%
Boys	238	44%

Each group was, and still is, intended to consist of no more than eight nor less than four participants. Only on two occasions have we had fewer than four participants out of the 86 times we have offered the program. Quite a few times we have had more than eight youngsters per group.

The biggest complaint by group participants over the years has been that sessions should be a few weeks longer. However, we would rather keep the program at seven weeks in duration and have them leave feeling positive about group than walk away thinking that it was too long. In addition, the youngsters have worked through a sufficient number of issues in their groups to make us believe that it is time to 'cut the strings'.

Over the first three years, on-going support groups for those that 'graduated' from the program were offered after the initial grief support program was completed. Three months after their group was finished, program graduates, and their parents or guardians came back to the Medical Center and met with their original facilitators and their group, and did the same after every six months. The young people and their parents continued to meet separately. The goal was to see how the youngsters were managing, from their personal perspective and the observations of their parents. After the three month 're-union graduate group', they were then invited to participate with the larger group. This consisted of all of the young people their age that had also 'graduated' from previous groups in the program. Parents were also invited.

Each group offered has two professional facilitators. Our experience has demonstrated that a female and male are best, rather than two females or two males as leaders, but that is our bias. It would obviously depend more on the facilitators' personalities and their ability to deal with young people, than their gender. Facilitators over the past eleven years have consisted of medical social workers, bereavement counsellors, medical students, and university undergraduate and graduate students in psychology or social work.

The major component of the program which we have included from the beginning and feel strongly about is the need to interview each child, and at least one parent or guardian if possible, in their own home before group participation begins. The purpose of the home visit is not as a screening process, but a way of getting to know the youngster, their role in the family, and their home environment. This also provides the youngsters with the opportunity to get to know a little about the facilitators.

For those children who live beyond 25 miles from the Medical Center, we meet with the youngsters in our office prior to the first session. For the first few years we tried to have both facilitators of each of the groups do the interviews, and we still try to do that, but due to time constraints, it is not always possible. Consequently, only one facilitator does the home interview. This has not been a problem as long as the youngsters are familiar with one person when they arrive at group.

Registration for the program is only accepted from the parent or guardian. At the time of registration, usually by telephone, information about the youngster is recorded. Part of the intake information gathered about youngsters is whether or not they will be able accurately to tell the story of how the person(s) died and describe who told them the information. We have on numerous occasions experienced situations where parents have only told the truth about how the person died on the day before youngsters attended their first session. These parents thought that it would be too painful for the youngsters to know the truth before sessions began. Truth is important and needs to be strongly encouraged before the child attends a bereavement group. It is NOT the role of the facilitators to tell the story or tell the truth about what happened; that role is for the parent(s) or guardian(s). Facilitators can help parents by sharing with them approaches to consider when talking to their youngster or when correcting the story from what was once considered the truth.

Why Have Youngsters Been Referred to the YPGSP

'She was afraid I was going to die. She was afraid to go to sleep at night. She wouldn't go to school as she was afraid to leave me and wouldn't spend nights away from home. I had to make her take showers where before she would do it on a daily basis. After group she was more relaxed, back to "normal" and started to go to school again. She is even staying at friends houses again now which she couldn't do one year ago.' (*mother of an eleven-year-old girl*)

'After the sessions were finished he wasn't mad anymore. He didn't blame himself for his dad's death, his grades improved, his truancy improved and he got better at listening and minding and accepting responsibility.' (*mother of a thirteen-year-old boy who was court ordered to group*)

'A complete change. Little by little I watched her bloom. Her personality changed with her acceptance of the death. Also, the mystery of death was cleared up for her. After two years I would now say, even about a teenager, that she is now normal. We've filled out questionnaires together and cried together. We could not have done this two years ago. Shows you how far both of us have come.' (*mother of a fifteen-year-old girl*)

'Her grades went down and she was not as cheerful, she was sad. She wouldn't want to be away from me and was mad at her dad. She started to steal and said she always thought about NaNa and got this feeling and would then steal. It hasn't happened since group finished. She's a lot more confident now and knows her feelings are real and okay. She's started to lighten up. Compared to one year ago she is 100% better.' (*mother of a nine-year-old girl*)

'The groups have opened our family communication, helped me deal with my sons better and forced me to take care of my own grief in a positive way.' (*mother of three boys aged fourteen, nine and six that participated in two different groups*)

How Do We, Through the YPGSP, Help Bereaved Youngsters?

The following section describes our eight week YPGSP sessions and demonstrates how various techniques have been helpful with youngsters of five to seventeen years of age.

Session 1

This is clearly the most important session and must connect youngsters to the group, allow them to feel safe and secure, and help them recognize the importance of what will happen through the group process. This session should provide the glue that will keep them wanting to return for session two and beyond. As facilitators, we have learned if we can encourage children to return for session number two, they will most likely attend all of the sessions.

During this first session, we explain the program history and go over rules of the group. For the five- to eight-year-old age group, the rules we have are that no siblings should sit next to each other, no interrupting others when they are talking, speak loud, and tell us if you have to go to the bathroom (we've learned our lesson here!!!) We share with the youngsters that if they are in the same school with other children in the group it would not feel real good if they told other children about who is in the group and what they are talking about. We strongly encourage them to share with their parents concerns and issues that are discussed in the group and through 'homework' assignments encourage family interaction.

The only two 'rules' that truly exist for the older age groups focus on confidentiality and mandatory reporting by the facilitators if we are concerned about the safety of the participants. We explain to the youngsters that after talking with them first we will contact their parents or guardians if we are concerned about their safety. We inform them that the group is theirs and that each member is not only valued, but encouraged to participate to the extent that they feel comfortable. We do encourage the youngsters to share with their parents or guardians whatever information they wish about the group, leaving the content up to them.

After each facilitator introduces him or herself, group members then introduce themselves as a way of getting to know each other and as a way to 'loosen up'. Only later in the session do they describe in detail, who died and all the circumstances surrounding the death(s). It is important to remember that

Table 19.3 The relationship of the person who died to the participants in
the Young Person's Grief Support Program (November 1983 to May 1994)
(738 deaths are represented for 633 youngsters)

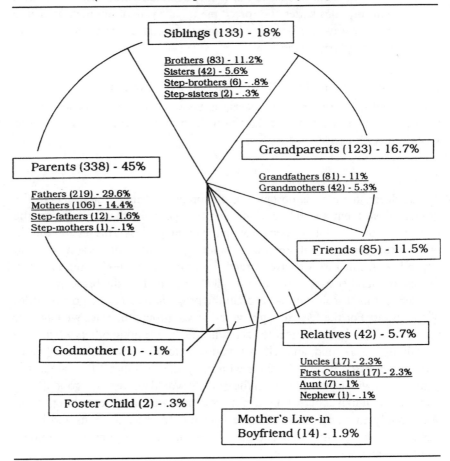

many of us as facilitators have experienced our own 'shattered glass' and
experience our own grief, some of which comes back quietly and may
unexpectedly be aroused by the group process. We feel disclosure by facilitators
of their thoughts and feelings, if used appropriately, serves as a model and adds
to the group process.

Youngsters in this first session, regardless of which age group they are in,
learn to appreciate that other young people also experience similar feelings and
concerns after a death. During this session we also provide the youngster with
the opportunity to share his or her story about the death with the group. This

Table 19.4 Young people on the Young Person's Grief Support Program
(November 1983 to May 1994) explain the cause of death of the person
who died (738 deaths are represented for 633 youngsters)

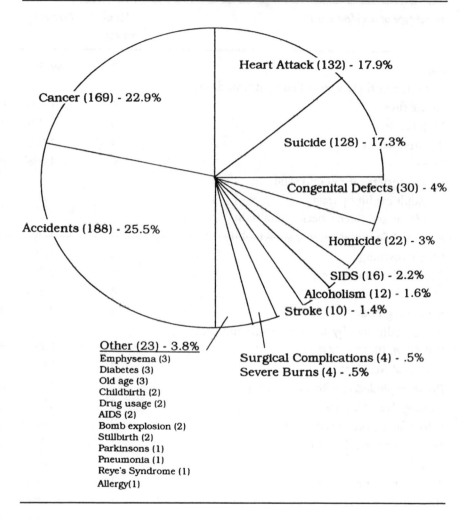

first session can be very emotional and may produce tears, although that is never
our goal, and tissues are always available.

We have learned that humour is as important as tears. The group sessions
need to be as 'light' as they are emotional. A balance is needed to avoid
overwhelming a youngster who is not used to sharing intimate stories. Youngsters may ask themselves, 'If session number one was this heavy, do I really want
to come back for more?' We do not want to challenge a fragile youngster but
rather have them appreciate our facilitative role as guides who help them explore

Table 19.5 In deaths caused by accidents, young people in the Young Person's Grief Support Program (86 Programs, November 1983 to May 1994) explain the types of accident (188 deaths – 25.5% of 738 deaths)

What type of accident was it?	Total number	Percentage
Car	93	49.5%
(Some of these were killed by drunk drivers)		
House fires	14	7.4%
Motorcycle	10	5.3%
2 seater plane crash	9	4.8%
Train	9	4.8%
Youngsters car ran into train 4		
Adult car hit by train 3		
Motorized three wheeler hit a train 2		
Snowmobile hit by another snowmobile	6	3.2%
Lake Drowning	6	3.2%
Snowmobile hit by a car	5	2.7%
Skiing	4	2.1%
Swimming pool	4	2.1%
Accidentally shot by another person and died	4	2.1%
Fell down flight of stairs	3	1.6%
Industrial Accident	2	1%
Bomb exploded at military building	2	1%
Cutting Tree/tree fell	2	1%
Self-inflicted firearm accident	2	1%
Major airline crash victim	1	.5%
Bicycle	1	.5%
Three wheeler accident	1	.5%
Boat fire	1	.5%
Lightning	1	.5%
Carbon monoxide accidental poisoning	1	.5%
Homemade bomb exploded	1	.5%
Lawn mower explosion	1	.5%
Sledding	1	.5%
School bus	1	.5%
Electrocuted	1	.5%
Hunting Accident (gun fell)	1	.5%
Lifting barbells and they fell	1	.5%

their feelings and thoughts, learn new information, find out what choices are available to them and empower them to work through their grief. Youngsters who feel defensive will not come back!

As facilitators we hope we are sensitive to each youngster, but also feel it is our role to ask probing questions and seek out information, some of which may not have been shared with others prior to attending the group.

Case Example – Corky

Corky, age six, came to session number one seven weeks after her sister died from Sudden Infant Death Syndrome. When it was time to share her story concerning the circumstances of the death, Corky hesitated, then clearly stated, 'Mommy killed the baby!' After asking her what she meant, Corky told the group, 'Mommy killed the baby. She killed Jill because I saw her beating on Jill's chest.' Corky then went on to tell us how the fire department came to the house and took the baby away. Corky did not attend the visitation or the funeral, and up to this point thought her baby sister was still somewhere at the fire station, only a few blocks from their house. Corky also drove by the fire station each day while on the school bus going to and from school. Up to this point she had not told anyone else that her mother 'killed' her baby sister, Jill.

We asked Corky to find out exactly what happened to Jill and share it with us at the next session. After she discussed the circumstances of the death with her mother and father, Corky was able to tell us that her mother, a nurse, was actually attempting to resuscitate Jill, and told us that Jill's body was buried in the ground at a cemetery and not at the fire station as she had thought.

Corky's parents clearly thought they were protecting her by not telling her everything that happened, and also, by not providing her the opportunity to participate in the various family rituals after Jill's death.

ACTIVITY: JOURNAL KEEPING

Throughout the program we remind the middle age and older youngsters that keeping a journal as a tool can be an excellent opportunity to reflect and write and can be extremely helpful. In this first session, we inform them that journaling is personal and is useful when ideas, feelings or thoughts surface and the youngsters feel comfortable jotting them down. Grammar and sentence structure is not important and journal entries can often be just words or thoughts. Journals can be kept in a notebook, on blank pages, or in a 'special blank pages book' given to the youngster. The journal should not be a diary nor should it be time consuming or take the place of 'listening ears' if available. Journaling provides an opportunity for personal awareness and a way to explore how a person processes the experience internally. Journals are very personal and can be shared with the group, with only the facilitators, or with no one.

Case example... Excerpts from a youngster's journal in a YPGSP nine-to-thirteen-year-old age group

Wednesday: 'Nobody knows how it feels when a parent dies unless you've gone through it. I mean people say I know how it is my grandma died. That's different; when someone says their grandparents died, you'll probably believe it. But parents, no way.

They just don't. I remember the feelings I had before mom died, they were, "I wish mom would just hurry up and die," it's hard waiting, hoping and knowing what's going to happen. I felt kind of guilty today for feeling that way. I'm not sure if I should feel that way or not. Sometimes, I can't believe mom is really gone, and sometimes I'll come home and shout out ... mom ... I hear dead silence. That hurts.'

Sunday: 'My family went out to the cabin today. This is the first time since mother's death. It was hard. Something was missing. Her pep, her love, her caring ... everything our family used to do ... singing together by the fire in our yard. Mom would play the guitar. We didn't do that this time ... something was missing.'

Sunday (same day but later in the afternoon): 'I was baby-sitting today and a little boy asked me where my mother was buried. I know before I started this class two weeks ago, I probably would have started to cry, but instead I told him, without feeling any hurt. I think I'm dealing with it, or at least starting to.'

During this first session we hand out to the five-to-eight-year-old group coloured folders and have them write their names and draw a picture on the front of the folder with crayons provided. We explain to them that each week, starting session two, we will have various handouts and worksheets which they will need to put into their folders. We remind them to bring the folder back each week when they come to group. We do not utilize folders for the middle or older age groups as we have learned that the majority do not bring them back to group.

During this first session we start to 'terminate' each of the groups by informing participants that the group they are in is only seven sessions long and each week their attendance is important.

Session 2

The five-to-eight-year-old group reviews the rules and shares how their previous week went. After, we ask them to describe briefly a little about another person in the group and who their relative or friend was that died and how they died. After this is done we go on to the next activity.

ACTIVITY FOR THE 5–8 YEAR OLD GROUP: DRAW THE FIRST THING THAT COMES TO YOUR MIND WHEN YOU HEAR THE WORD *DEATH*

We hand out a piece of paper which has on the top of it the sentence, 'Draw the first thing that comes to your mind when you hear the word *death*'. The group members are separated from one another during this exercise so that each youngster's drawing is unique ... if not, you will find the drawings often have a very similar flavour!! When the drawings are completed, they share them with the entire group. Discussion by the group at that time revolves around what the drawings were and issues brought up through the drawings.

ACTIVITY FOR THE MIDDLE AND OLDER AGE GROUPS: WHAT WORDS COME TO YOUR MIND WHEN YOU HEAR THE WORD *DEATH*?

This exercise is done with pencil and paper. Each youngster is asked to write down at least four words that come to mind when they hear the word *death*. They can extend that list if they wish. After this is done, they are asked to share the words with the group, to select the one word which has the most significance to them and talk about it. Despite the fact that many of the words are similar for each of them, they are still asked to share the reason why they selected the words.

BRAINSTORMING ACTIVITY: WHAT IS GRIEF?

After the previous activity is completed by each of the age groups, the concept of grief is discussed along with how youngsters and their families have changed since the person(s) died. A flip chart or white board is used for this exercise. Brainstorming is used to describe the variety of thoughts, feelings, physical symptoms and behaviours that took place shortly after the death and may still be taking place. After this is completed, each of the youngsters is asked to identify those areas where they have been affected most. As an extension of this exercise they are then asked to identify the same areas for their parents and/or guardians and describe how their reactions may be affecting the youngster. During this process they are reminded that bereavement needs to be seen as a period of crisis or life transition.

The five-to-eight-year-old group, in particular, needs to have a gentle approach, discussing what the word *feelings* means. This group generally responds quickly with words like mad, sad, glad and angry, and shortly after they continue to brainstorm additional words that clearly describe what they have gone through since the death(s). It is reassuring for youngsters, especially the younger children, to visualize on a flip chart and discuss what they, and the others in the group are or have been experiencing as a result of their 'shattered glass'. As facilitators, one of our roles is constantly to summarize what we are hearing and try to connect each youngster's comments to others in the group.

We try to normalize the grief process as much as we can, indicating that each person will grieve differently for different periods of time and be influenced by cultural considerations and other factors. We remind the group that grief is an on-going process, and throughout their lives there will be different 'windows of grief' that may open, requiring each youngster to revisit the death and their relationship with the dead person.

Shuchter (1986), Glick, Weiss and Parkes (1974), have found that bereaved individuals continued to show signs of internal attachment long after the death and, in fact, the ability to maintain an internal attachment to the person who has died may be a sign of healthy recovery, not of pathology. We believe that as facilitators it is our role to help the youngsters develop 'a new relationship with the person who has died,' help them hold onto the emotional connection with that person and integrate the loss into their lives. This is one of the key goals for the group that we continually stress. Throughout the sessions we also remind the group that grief is not 'fixed' in a seven week program but it can provide an extremely healthy start to regaining control of their lives.

The youngsters in each of the age groups are asked to bring photos of the person(s) who died for the next sessions and are also asked to write a short biography of the person(s) who died on paper provided, and, like the pictures, have it ready for the next session. The five- to eight-year-olds generally have an adult at home help them with the biography. One 'light' question asked on the five- to eight-year-old biography sheets is, 'If the person who died caught you taking cookies out of the cookie jar, what would they say?' This always brings a lot of fun remarks!

Session 3
ACTIVITY: BIOGRAPHY OF THE PERSON WHO DIED

A biography of the person who died is read, often just prior to when the photos are circulated to other members of the group.

One thirteen-year-old wrote

'My mom was born on January 12, 1942, in Minnesota. She had a brother who was eleven years younger than her and she had a mother and father. Some of her many hobbies were cooking, sewing, gardening, skiing, bike riding and singing. She was always an optimist and all her friends say she changed their lives because after all her illnesses she still had a positive attitude. Her motto in life was "live each day to the fullest and let tomorrow take care of itself". She had few dislikes but some of them were camping, cabbage and complainers. Of all the people my mother knew, I have never known one who didn't like her. She was married in 1965. She then had two children. In 1981 my mom found out she had a brain tumor. She then got spinal meningitis and was in a coma for three weeks. She then was blind, but overcame blindness in a few months. One year later she was diagnosed with breast cancer. She had a mastectomy. She had chemotherapy for about one year. Then she had uterine cancer and had her uterus removed. Then she was diagnosed with lung cancer. She tried to hold on, but she was so sick. She went around in a wheelchair and was in and out of the hospital for weeks. But she got worse. On September 21, 1984, my mom died. I think that everyone who knew her will never forget her.'

ACTIVITY: SHARING PHOTOS OF THOSE WHO HAVE DIED

Each person shares his or her photos with the group they are in describing when the photos were taken and what significance the photos have for them. It is important to have them only bring a few favourite photos of the person(s) who have died, otherwise they will bring quite a few along and you'll never get time to finish this session.

ACTIVITY FIVE- TO EIGHT-YEAR-OLDS: DRAW A FAVOURITE TIME DOING SOMETHING WITH THE PERSON(S) WHO DIED

The five-to-eight-year-old group is given paper which has written on top of it, 'Draw a favourite time doing something with the person(s) who has died'. The crayons are handed out and each youngster then draws whatever comes to his or her mind and this is then discussed with the group. Again, it is always important to separate the youngsters to get different drawings! The purpose of this activity is to identify how involved the dead person was with the youngster and have them 'relive' those times and tell a 'story' about that time or event. Stories range from sliding to fishing, from reading stories, cooking and camping, to being hugged and tickling one another. Most youngsters this age do have good things to say about the person who has died, which is different from some of the middle or older ages.

ACTIVITY FOR MIDDLE AND OLDER AGE GROUPS: LIST THE THINGS YOU LIKED ABOUT THE PERSON WHO DIED

Each group member in the middle and older age groups is given a sheet of paper and asked to identify at least four things they liked about the person who died. The members usually find this easy to do and list many more than four items. We then discuss the 'likes' regarding the person who is now dead. In some cases it is difficult for the young person to find positive things to say about the person who has died and this is discussed.

Case example – Joe

Joe was ten years old when he entered the group, two months after his step-father had shot himself in the alley behind their home in front of Joe, his two sisters and his mother. Joe was not close to his step-father and would continually find negative things to talk about regarding his step-father during the group. He could not find anything positive to say when this exercise was started. By the conclusion of the activity he was able to identify a few positive things his step-father had done or said, and this was helpful to him. When Joe could not find positive things to say, it was interesting to observe the other youngsters in the group who began to place more value on the 'little things' in their own relationships with the person who died they had not really perceived as important or meaningful prior to Joe's comments. Although Joe's relationship with his step-father was not what he had hoped it would be, he was not glad his step-father was dead. However, at this phase in Joe's life, it was easier for him not to have his step-father in the home.

ACTIVITY FOR FIVE- TO EIGHT-YEAR-OLDS: DRAW A PICTURE OF A SAD TIME THAT YOU CAN REMEMBER HAVING TO DO WITH THE PERSON WHO DIED

This activity is similar to the previous one. Each youngster is given crayons and a sheet of paper with the sentence, 'Draw a picture of a sad time that you can remember having to do with the person who died'. Sometimes the youngsters find this hard, but generally they draw a picture of some activity that the dead person is not there to participate in. These drawings are generally 'activity focused', times that the dead person should have been a part of the family activity or part of the child's own world.

When there are youngsters in any of the age groups who are there because of a baby's death, this activity may need to take on a different focus. Some dislikes may be harder to find until issues such as 'more time was spent with the baby', or, 'everyone was asking about the baby and not about me', start to surface in the discussion.

ACTIVITY FOR MIDDLE AND OLDER AGE GROUPS: LIST THE THINGS YOU DISLIKED ABOUT THE PERSON WHO DIED

Each middle and older group member, in a process similar to the previous activity, is given a sheet of paper and asked to identify at least four things they disliked about the person who died. The members find this much more difficult than listing four things they liked. We discuss these dislikes and why it is difficult to share them with others. Youngsters grapple with the question of 'loyalty to the dead'.

This activity is important as it allows youngsters to discuss openly why it is acceptable and important to have a 'total view' of the person who died and not just a view of a 'perfect person'.

Case example – Debbie

Debbie, age seventeen, was still extremely mad and angry at her boyfriend who on Christmas day killed himself with a rifle while talking on the telephone with her after she had recently broken up with him. John had been drinking alcohol at the time and was having a difficult time coping with not having Debbie in his life. Debbie tried talking with John about not doing anything that would hurt him or his family, and during the middle of the conversation he said, 'Listen to this,' and shot himself with her on the other end of the telephone.

She was traumatized by the incident, but gradually was able to separate John's action from what she needed to do, and that was to break off the relationship with John and not 'take him back'. She was angry that he could not live without her and that he had been drinking at the time of his suicide. John's brother was in the house when he killed himself and his parents were visiting relatives two-and-a-half hours' drive away at the time.

Other members in Debbie's group were also there as a result of suicides of parents, or friends, and reinforced that it was natural and healthy to be angry at John's actions.

ACTIVITY FOR MIDDLE AND OLDER AGE GROUPS: QUALITY OF THE RELATIONSHIP

Each group member in the middle and older age groups is given another piece of paper and asked to mark down the numbers 1, 2, 3, 4 and 5. They are then asked to write the name of the person who has died next to number 1. After they do this they are asked to list the four most important people in your entire world next to the remaining four numbers, with only one name on each line. Some youngsters can do this quickly, while others find it hard to list even two important or close people. When they do so their parents' names may be excluded.

At this stage of the group process, participants are asked to draw a circle and think of it as a pie. They are then asked to look at the five names they have listed and cut the pie into pieces based on 'how important these people are to you'. The first name was the person who died, and they are asked to think of how large a piece was this person when they were alive. After the pieces are cut and a percentage is given to each one, the facilitators discuss with the youngsters what makes people important in our lives and what happens to us when that piece is not there.

The various activities completed during this session continue to help each of the youngsters appreciate the changes death brings. Exploring the relationship with the person who has died brings with it all the gratifying, ambivalent, and disappointing aspects of that relationship. This session also focuses on reorganizing the children's sense of identity and reviewing the significant relationships that now exist in their lives.

Group members are asked to bring a material possession that belonged to the person who has died for the next session.

Session 4

ACTIVITY FOR ALL AGE GROUPS: MATERIAL POSSESSIONS

Material possessions that once belonged to the person who is now dead are brought to the group and shared with group members. Each person tells how they received the possession and what makes it important to them. One of the group facilitators, at any given point in the 'possession sharing time', interrupts the discussion and offers to buy for $5, $10, or even $20 the possession that is being shared. The facilitator tries to buy the item by stating, 'It really isn't worth very much financially so why not sell it and make some money on the deal'. Some group members take the facilitator up on the deal, take the money and hand over the possession. SOON AFTER these same people ALWAYS say they want the possession back and will return the money. The facilitators says, 'A deal is a deal', and argues about buying it 'fair and square'. This always produces great discussion about the value of a possession. The relationship to the possession and the meaning behind having something that belonged to the dead person is then discussed further.

> ### Case example – Joe
>
> Joe, who was mentioned previously, brought his step-father's expensive leather cowboy hat to the group for the sharing of material possessions. When the facilitator pulled out a $20 bill and offered to buy the hat Joe jumped at the deal. His twelve-year-old sister who was also in the group hollered out, 'Mom will kill you if she ever finds out you sold dad's hat!' Joe appeared not to care and was really excited to have the $20. The rest of the young people in the group wondered how could he sell the hat, but also saw $20 as a lot of money.
>
> As the group finished for the day after a lively discussion, Joe wanted to get his step-father's hat back in exchange for the $20. The facilitator, who had now been wearing the hat for the past hour, continued to give reasons why 'A deal is a deal' and why Joe should have thought about its value when he first sold the hat. All the other group members were wondering what would happen if he did not get the hat back. Would his mother really kill him as his sister indicated previously? For your information, the facilitator did return the hat and received his $20 back.

Additional discussion points during this session include:

(1) How did the school respond after the death? What should they have done, or could still do differently to support you?

(2) How have your friends and other support systems helped, or have they abandoned you after the death?

(3)   What changes have happened at home since the person died? How have grandparents and other relatives dealt with the death?

(4)   What new roles or expectations now exist? (If siblings are in the same group this question is generally lively!)

(5)   Should a parent date or remarry, or enter into a new relationship after one parent dies?

(6)   Who would you live with if something happened to your parents, or if your surviving parent died?

(7)   Where does religion or spirituality fit into your grief process?

(8)   What do group members think that, 'developing a new relationship with the person who has died', means?

Session 5

This session is intended to review what happened to the body after the death. It focuses on any involvement the youngsters had in decisions regarding matters such as: organ or tissue donation; embalming, burying or cremating the body; their involvement in preparing the body or helping with such things as dressing or fixing the hair of the deceased; their role in the visitation or wake and the casket or urn selection; involvement in any way during the funeral or memorial service; any assistance given in respect to poster displays, music, flowers, and arranging of objects for the service itself; attendance at the cemetery for interment after the service; the lowering of the casket while they were at the cemetery; placing or throwing objects into the grave; and the time after the cemetery – did they go back to a special place for something to eat? Additional questions deal with whether the people the youngsters wanted around them during those first few days were present or not and whether the church/synagogue provided what the young person had hoped would be 'a meaningful service for the person who had died'?

ACTIVITY FOR FIVE- TO EIGHT-YEAR-OLDS: DRAW A PICTURE OF WHAT YOU REMEMBER OF THE VISITATION (WAKE), THE FUNERAL OR MEMORIAL SERVICE

A sheet of paper is given to each youngster and they are asked to draw a picture of what they remember of either the visitation, the funeral or memorial service. After the youngsters draw what they remember, they share this with the group, explaining in great detail everything that took place. The facilitator's role here is to find out what the children know took place and if they know why these different rituals were done. Also, similar to what the middle and older age groups are discussing (they do not draw the visitation, funeral or memorial service, but discuss it openly with other members of the group), how involved were the children in the planning and implementation of the various rituals.

Youngsters in the five- to eight-year-old age group who did not attend either the visitation or the funeral, are asked to draw what *they think it may have looked like*. Many children have not been part of the visitation or funeral process and their imagination needs to be put on paper to see 'where they are coming from'. If they have no idea what actually took place, they are asked to come to the next session with a drawing by their parent(s) of what actually did take place and who was there, and so forth. Similar to Corky's story shared in Session One, not all youngsters are provided with the opportunity to participate in family rituals.

This session for all age groups concludes with other questions or concerns regarding the funeral/memorial service and questions the youngsters may want answered next week when each of the groups goes on a field trip to a local funeral home.

Session 6
ACTIVITY FOR ALL AGE GROUPS: FUNERAL HOME VISIT

When we do the home interview and the initial assessment, we inform the adult and youngster that we will be going on a 'field trip' to a local funeral home only a ten minute walk from the Medical Center. The purpose of this one-hour visit is to allow the youngsters to ask questions of a funeral director and explore the funeral home when they are not emotionally involved. They *DO NOT* see a dead body. Parents of the younger and middle age groups are also invited to join the groups on the tour if they wish. We have learned over the years that the older adolescents do not want their parents coming along and, as a result, we do not invite them to join us. We do, however, provide the opportunity and make arrangements for any parent or guardian who would like to tour the funeral home.

When we arrive at the funeral home we usually discuss the role of funeral home personnel, discuss how they do their work and answer questions. We then go into a casket room and look, touch and ask questions about caskets. In addition to adult caskets, we also are able to see caskets used for infants and children. They are able to look inside the caskets with the mattresses lifted up, are able to hold different types of urns and examine full-size vaults that caskets are placed in at certain cemeteries. For many years, we would then go into the prep room to see the embalming table, embalming tank, and other equipment, but recently due to government safety regulations, we are no longer able to do this. Instead, we use slides to 'show' the prep room and discuss what takes place. Cosmetics are then demonstrated and explained, and if we have time we inspect the limousines and the hearses.

The five- to eight-year-olds love the caskets, cosmetics and the 'big cars', and always ask the most questions of any of the age groups! The questions from the youngest children range from, 'How do you lift a dead body?' to 'What do you do with the dead person's legs after you cut them off?' Many parents have questions answered that they themselves never knew or were never in a position to ask. The middle age group has the second highest amount of questions asked and the lowest group for asking questions, generally, is the fourteen-to-seventeen-year-old adolescent group.

ACTIVITY FOR THE FIVE- TO EIGHT-YEAR-OLD GROUP: DRAW A PICTURE OF WHAT YOU LIKED BEST ABOUT OUR VISIT TO THE FUNERAL HOME

After the tour each of the groups return to the Medical Center for 'munchies' and discuss what the tour was like, answering any additional questions that children or their parents may have.

The five-to-eight-year-olds are each given a piece of paper and crayons and they are asked to draw what they liked best about their visit to the funeral home. Without exception, the majority of the children in this age group have indicated their favourite part of the visit was the different types of caskets and they draw the caskets (at least they try … with some similarities!).

Session 7

This final session includes a major emphasis on: developing a new relationship with the deceased, reorganizing their lives, investing in new relationships, integrating the death into their daily living and appreciating the grief process as on-going.

To start the session, we discuss issues that the group may still need to explore along with various rituals that may be considered for anniversary dates, holidays or birthdays, or other important times. Throughout the sessions there are always some holidays, birthdays or anniversary dates, and we discuss with each age group how the members dealt with that event, or if it was important for them to do anything at all.

Case example – Diane

Diane was ten years old when she entered the nine-to-thirteen-year-old age group. Almost one year before, her fifteen-year-old brother had shot himself in the house while the entire family was at home. Diane was the first one to find her brother. When the planning for the visitation and funeral was in process, Diane was invited, but not encouraged by the family, to participate in all of the events. In group, Diane shared how angry she was that her older high school sister received all the attention from friends after the death and had read a short reading at the service. Diane thought that now she wanted to do something also, even though it was almost a year since her brother's death.

Since her brother's one year anniversary date was approaching, she realized in the group that she could still do something meaningful which would help her in her grief. She decided she would write a short poem and read it at his grave when the family and friends went out there on the anniversary.

In the next group session after the anniversary she talked openly about how she read her poem at the gravesite and how she felt better for being treated as an equal to her sister in their grief.

During this session we also ask the middle and older youngsters to consider the concerns of their parents, guardians, or themselves seven weeks ago when they entered the group and discuss views of their progress? Depending on the maturity level of the five-to-eight-year-old group, we may also ask them how they are different now from when they started the group and what they learned by being part of the group.

ACTIVITY FOR FIVE- TO EIGHT-YEAR-OLDS: ROLE PLAY – HOW WOULD YOU NOW HELP A FRIEND SHORTLY AFTER SOMEONE THEY KNEW DIED?

We ask the five- to eight-year-olds to role play what they have learned in group about helping someone else who has also experienced the death of a loved one or friend. The idea of this activity is to transfer what the youngsters learned to the 'real world'.

In closing, this final session allows the youngsters in all age groups the opportunity to share what they learned in group and how they can help someone else.

The following comments were made by some of the young people after they had completed the program:

'It was like after the group I could start a new life.' ... ten year old.

'Group helped me learn that other people had the same problems I did and that they grieve too.' ... ten year old.

'I learned to open up and say what I was feeling. The grieving process is a long hard one but with people at group it really helps.' ... twelve year old.

'I still miss my dad, but after sharing with other kids a weight has been lifted off me.' ... ten year old.

'It's different now because now I can go away from home and not be scared.' ... ten year old.

We explore what the participants liked and disliked about the group and what would they like us to discuss with their parents and/or guardians next week at the parent meeting. We remind them of our need to protect their confidentiality and assure them that we are not going to tell parents or guardians all the secrets.

Various activities over the years have been used to close the program, at which time certificates are distributed as well as names, addresses, and telephone numbers of each group member and both facilitators.

Session 8

During this session, parents and guardians from each of the groups are asked to introduce themselves and share information about who they had in the group. We ask them to describe why they wanted their youngster to participate and what changes they have seen over the seven weeks. Since one of the rules is confidentiality, we remind the parents we will not tell everything about the youngsters. We do, however, 'stretch' the confidentiality issue quite a bit with the five- to eight-year-olds' parents/guardians if we feel the information is important enough to be shared.

> **Parents have, like their children, been positive about meeting at the Medical Center and made the following comments about meeting with other parents as part of the program:**
>
> 'Was good as we had a chance to ask questions about unsettled questions.'
>
> 'Was good to hear other parents talk about their relationship with their kids.'
>
> 'Most beneficial as we found out the kids reactions and they were most enlightening.'
>
> 'It also helps the affected parent realize the problems are not only theirs, but many are shared by others. It also gives one ideas how to cope with their problems.'

Conclusion

Offshoots of the program over the past eleven years have included hundreds of presentations on grief, loss and the development of children, adolescent and adult support groups at the local, regional, state, national and international levels. Additional programs for young people offered by the Grief Support Center have also been operating as a result of the Young Person's Grief Support Program. These include Sibling's Day, an annual one day workshop for siblings five-to-thirteen years of age whose brothers or sisters are chronically or terminally ill, or have special needs, and a program called Kids Can Cope, for ages nine to sixteen, who have a family member, relative or friend that currently has cancer or any serious medical condition.

In conclusion, the death of a loved one is a transition point and the beginning of an on-going grief process. When death affects a family member, close relative or friend, we will be changed forever. We will not be the person we once were. To expect youngsters to be unchanged by the death, and not to feel different in any way, is unrealistic. As facilitators, we are constantly reminding ourselves that youngsters are part of a larger family unit. It is *not* our role to fill or take over the supportive role of parents or guardians, but to support them in that role.

It is my hope this chapter will provide a map to guide you in your work with bereaved five- to seventeen-year-olds. We have learned a great deal at the Grief Support Center over the years from those who are bereaved and this chapter has been written from the perspective of what has and has not worked. I would like to thank the youngsters and their families for the privilege of allowing us to enter their lives and share their stories.

References

Glick, I.O., Weiss, I.O. & Parkes, C.M. (1974) *The First Year of Bereavement.* New York, NY: Wiley-Interscience.

Shuchter, S.R. (1986) *Dimensions of Grief: Adjusting to the Death of a Spouse.* San Francisco, CA: Jossey-Bass.

Wolfe, B. (1987) 'Children Grieve Too: A Four Year Hospital-Based Young Person's Grief Support Program.' In J. Morgan (ed), *Bereavement: Helping the Survivors.* London, Ontario: King's College, 89–104.

CHAPTER 20

The Use of Art Therapy and Group Process with Grieving Children

Clifford B. Davis

Introduction

The purpose of this paper is to present the healing potential of art therapy and group process in the lives of grieving children. The paper documents my grief education work with children and their families. Portions of this paper are contained in my Report and Analysis entitled 'A Grief Education Program With Older Children And Their Parents' at Midwestern Baptist Theological Seminary (Davis 1988a). Since that time, I have continued to apply these methods in groups and with individual children to help facilitate their grief.

Children in Grief: A Theoretical Perspective

The place children hold in the family system is often overlooked. Children are not included in many of the major decisions and are not allowed to share family information except in a limited way. We want to protect them so we do not tell them the truth or the facts. This is particularly true of crisis experiences such as divorce or the death of a loved one. Elisabeth Kubler-Ross (1969) points out the experience of a child on the occasion of a death when she speaks of:

> ' ... a society in which death is viewed as taboo, discussion of it is regarded as morbid, and children are excluded with the presumption and pretext that it would be "too much" for them. They are then sent off to relatives often accompanied by some unconvincing lies of "mother has gone on a long trip" or other unbelievable stories. The child senses that something is wrong, and his distrust of adults will only multiply if other relatives add new variations of the story, avoid

his questions or suspicions, or shower him with gifts as a meager substitute for a loss he is not permitted to deal with. Sooner or later the child will become aware of the changed family situation and, depending on the age and personality of the child, will have an unresolved grief and regard this incident as a frightening, mysterious, in any case traumatic experience with untrustworthy grownups, which he has no way to cope with.' (pp.6–7)

In my 10 years of pastoral ministry, and more specifically during the last four years of crisis counselling, I have been amazed at how certain children have survived and coped during their time of crisis. As a whole, they have not received permission to feel the expected feelings of grief and have often been misinformed or not informed at all as to what has actually happened to them and to their family.

As my guide to the grief work needed by my clients, children or adults, I followed the four tasks of mourning that J. William Worden has presented: to accept the reality of the loss; to experience the pain of grief; to adjust to an environment in which the deceased is missing; and to withdraw emotional energy and reinvest it in another relationship (Worden 1982, pp. 11–16). He also states that the same tasks of grieving apply to both adults and children, with modifications relevant to the child's cognitive, personal, social, and emotional development (p. 103). It is possible to make a dramatic difference in the life of a child who is allowed to grieve in a healthy way. I heartily agree with Andrew Lester when he refers to the critical importance of intervening in children's crises, due to the long-range effects their understanding at that point may have on their development (Lester 1985, pp. 48–49).

The family unit itself also plays a significant role. We do not suffer a loss alone, and in order for a healing experience to take place, we need our support system to be firmly in place. Charles Gerkin suggests that how we experience a crisis will depend on whether there is a network of relationships surrounding us that gives support, understanding, and encouragement (Gerkin 1979, p. 59).

This network of support serves to encourage and elicit our feelings as we grieve our loss. There is a very real potential for healing within the family unit upon which the members can draw. Bessel van der Kolk speaks of the importance to traumatized individuals for the recreation of this sense of human interdependence and community (van der Kolk 1987, p. 115). Andrew Puckett emphasizes that children facing grief need stability, need to be included, need to be curious, and they need to express their feelings. He states that all children need permission to cry, to be angry, to talk about feelings of guilt, to hurt, and to express any other feelings they may have (Lester 1987, p. 87).

The family provides an appropriate setting in which this permission can be expressed. Parents encouraging their children to express their feelings, and to be heard, can often bring healing to a child and to a family. The counsellor, as well, brings a sense of authority to this experience in much the same way that the parents do. With this authority, the counsellor, too, gives permission to the children and parents to share their feelings of grief.

The author of *Psychological Trauma*, Bessel A. van der Kolk, lists six factors that affect the duration and severity of our response to trauma. These include the severity of the stressor, any genetic predisposition, our developmental phase, a person's social support system, any prior traumatization, and our preexisting personality. He emphasizes that the lack of support during a traumatic experience may leave lasting marks on later adjustment and functioning (pp. 10–12). Howard Clinebell (1984) also points to the importance of this support:

> 'All human crises are essentially interpersonal events. Both the causes and the potential resources for constructive coping are derived, to a considerable degree, from one's interpersonal support system, and nuclear families who do not have close relationships with their extended families (or its equivalent in a network of close friends) are acutely vulnerable to crises of all types. It behooves the pastor, therefore, to use the family systems perspective in approaching all crisis counseling; especially family crises.' (p.298)

Scott Sullender (1985, p. 136) certainly sees grief as a family affair. He explains that community begins with our immediate family. Of all the people available to support us as we grieve, our immediate family is the first and closest. The nuclear family, parents and children, is the closest community in which we live. We look to this community first in a time of crisis.

The family system perspective has provided a very basic and firm foundation for working with families in crisis. Virginia Satir, the most noted author in the area of family systems, has seen a very consistent pattern in healthy families. This includes high self-worth; direct, clear, specific, and honest communication; rules that are flexible, human, appropriate, and subject to change; and an open and hopeful link to society. In troubled families, she has found the following to be true: low self-worth; indirect, vague, and dishonest communication; rigid, inhuman, nonnegotiable, and everlasting rules; and fearful, placating, and blaming link to society (Satir 1972, p. 4).

Normal L. Paul has based his approach with grieving families on his 'corrective mourning experience'. He assists the family to *relive* their grief and to finish their fixated grief process. While doing this, they learn to share pain. He has suggested that a part of the family pathology lies in its inability first of all, to be empathic with one another, and secondly, to share painful feelings (Paul and Grosser 1965; Sullender 1985, p. 137).

Historically, death education and counselling is a relatively new area of research. Such individuals as Elisabeth Kubler-Ross, Rabbi Earl Grollman, and John Bowlby have written extensively of the losses we experience. Bowlby even notes the predictable behaviour of two- or three-year-olds when their mothers leave them. He has found three phases that they experience – protest, despair, and detachment (Bowlby 1965, pp. 27–29). Others disagree and say that we do not grieve until our cognitive development allows us to understand our loss. It is between the ages of six and twelve that children move into this phase of cognitive development (Biehler 1976, p. 474). Struggling with what is real, they are curious and want to learn more about themselves and their world. Their experience and learning about death and its impact may certainly shape their future coping abilities and outlook in life.

Using the Group Process

I chose several vehicles that I felt to be appropriate for facilitating this catharsis. The group settings within my doctoral work and with the hospice have been intended to move beyond the level of a support group. Support is extremely important, but another step needs to be taken. Andrew Lester suggests that 'one important goal for caring for children in crisis is that of providing an opportunity for them to express the emotive content of their trauma. We can provide a safe context for feelings to be described, felt, and discussed without fear of disapproval' (1985, p. 62). This support holds true for children as well as their parents.

One mode for the emotional release of their grief was in the group experience. Mutual sharing may result in positive strokes being received and intense feelings being touched and expressed. The group setting provided a natural setting for the development of trust and the taking of risks. Jared Pingleton (1985) affirms that, 'though group psycho-therapy is definitely not easy or simple, it could become a potent resource to meet the parishioners' counseling needs'. This certainly applies to the children's lives we touch as they struggle with death.

Using Art Therapy

A second method that I have chosen includes the use of art therapy. The objectives of art therapy are fourfold: awareness; expression of energy and feelings; working through a problem; and spontaneity, creativity and joy. Art uses active methods to experience or cathect feelings. It also allows destructive energy to be expressed and sublimated into a constructive channel. We may discover new ways of responding to the world and develop the ability to create new situations in which we try out our new decisions and feelings. Art can be used to focus on well-being and wholeness, as well as to help develop and build new skills. The use of art also facilitates self-nurturing and promotes healing (Davis 1987).

Andrew Lester places great value on art therapy. Art therapists are adept at using art for diagnostic purposes. They also use art as a therapeutic medium to help children work through emotional conflicts (Lester 1985, p. 99).

The use of art therapy in a group setting has been increasing. Harriet Wadeson, in her book *Art Psychotherapy* (1980), refers to the family systems perspective and highlights the use of art with families:

> 'Although parents are often more articulate verbally than their young children, in art activity the children are usually on an equal footing with the adults. Children often feel quite comfortable with the media and find a way of making themselves 'heard' within the family that may not be possible for them in their regular family interactions.' (p.281)

It is evident that children readily engage in art, and I have chosen to use art in this context in response to the comfort that they feel with various forms of art.

Figure 20.1. 'Broken ghetto blaster', drawn by a six-year-old girl after the death of her grandfather.

Drawing

A second method that I have chosen includes the use of art, specifically drawing. This will encourage the children and the parents to express their feelings in a tangible way. The book of drawings presents an ongoing story for each child. They serve as the children's journal of our experience together. From the first picture to the last 'kinetic family drawing', the children work on putting their ideas and images related to loss into a concrete form with which they could then deal. Next to the success of the puppets, these drawings have been a major tool through which the children express themselves.

Figure 20.1 illustrates how powerful a child's drawing can be. This six-year-old girl drew this picture after her grandfather's death. The mother was concerned about the casket she thought the child had drawn. I knew this child and the family quite well and I asked the child to tell me about her drawing. She explained that 'this is my ghetto blaster, I dropped it and it broke'. This drawing was completed the week of her grandfather's funeral. We spoke about brokenness and how sad she appears in the picture. (Permission has been given by family to use these drawings.) One week later she spontaneously drew her grandfather's funeral (Figure 20.2). It was very important to her to cover him

Figure 20.2. A six-year-old girl's depiction of her grandfather's funeral (this same child drew the 'ghetto blaster' in Figure 20.1).

up in the casket. With this drawing she could identify the loss and the rituals surrounding the loss. Her drawings made this death very concrete and real for her. We took time to process her feelings and questions concerning the funeral, burial, and her intense feelings.

The book of drawings I ask the children to create involves a number of drawings that focus on their particular losses. I begin by requesting a self-portrait that includes a description of themselves using words or phrases that best fit them. I also ask them to complete a drawing of their family in action. This is known as the 'kinetic family drawing test' and serves well to indicate family relationships, feelings, and potential issues or themes. As a group or with individual children, I ask them to draw 'feeling faces' to identify and begin expressing the various feelings related to the grief. A ten-year-old girl attempting to identify her various feelings completed the drawing in Figure 20.3. After completing the various faces, I ask them to draw this most recent death-related loss to show how they feel.

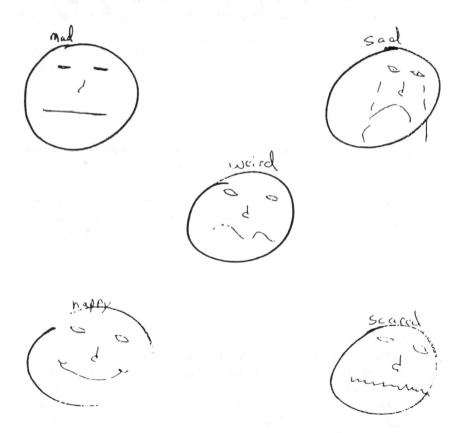

Figure 20.3. A ten-year-old's visualizations of her various feelings of grief.

The children also complete a letter saying good-bye to this person. This opportunity allows the child to say anything they need to say or did not get to say to the deceased. I follow this letter with a creative drawing of their choice granting the children the opportunity to relax and simply doodle thereby temporarily distracting themselves from the heaviness of their losses. The children compete a second kinetic family drawing by the end of the group or by the fifth or sixth session. This helps to evaluate their progress. The children decorate their books as they see fit and the books are theirs to keep after the group concludes.

Puppets

Another vehicle for the emotional catharsis of the participants was play and the use of puppets. Lester (1985, p. 85) states that play is to children what talk and work are to adults. Erik Erikson understands play as 'a function of the ego, an attempt to synchronize the bodily and the social processes of the self' (1963, p. 211). It is easy to understand and appreciate the importance of play in a child's development.

I chose to use puppets as a form of play for the children because through a puppet, a child can distance himself or herself sufficiently from their feelings or a difficult topic in order to achieve a sense of safety. A child will project a personality, a history, and significant feelings onto a puppet. In this way, the child expresses himself or herself without being threatened. It is important to understand the developmental stage in which these fourth through sixth graders are engaged. Erikson's key phrase here is 'industry versus inferiority'. A child this age would say, 'I am what I learn'. The child wants to 'get busy with something and to be busy with others' (Erikson 1980, p.87). My overall goal is grief education for older children and their parents. This focus would facilitate the building of new coping skills and foster supportive exchanges between their peers and within their families. The practical aspect of this counselling was to lay a solid foundation for a shared grief experience to become reality. The puppets provide a channel for the expression of their feelings and energy. Children connect with their puppets even as they are making them. The puppets begin acting and talking for the children as they come to life in the children's hands. The children work hard on their puppets and take great pride in what they have made.

In evaluating the role of the puppets, I am convinced that they play a successful part throughout the sessions. They give each child a safe and comfortable way of looking at our subject matter and expressing what they are feeling. The puppets release an enormous amount of energy for the children and become a definite part of who they are within our experience together.

Storytelling

Another form of expression for children is storytelling. Andrew Lester devotes an entire chapter of his book to emphasizing the importance of storytelling as a tool for reaching children. The grief process involves telling our stories and any method of expression which facilitates their experience may be helpful. I use *Thumpy's Story* (Dodge 1984) or another of the excellent books already written for children. The children may also write their own stories or act out what they have experienced through drama or role playing.

Clay

Clay is another excellent art therapy tool. Several art therapists use clay identified as 'mad clay', which is reserved for the expression of anger. Clay itself can be a powerful catalyst to prompt feelings. Simply touching and manipulating the clay will elicit a feeling response. In a group session, close supervision will be necessary when working with clay.

A Word of Caution

We, as therapists or counsellors, must realize that with any drawing or work of art, we are making only possible suggestions as to what they may mean. Only the person who actually did the drawing can understand what it really means. Their pictures or artwork are very personal for each of the children. Any connection that I would make between what a child has drawn or created, and the personality and development of that child, has come only after getting to know that particular child and having observed them as they drew.

Implications

Art therapy is a relatively new form of expressive therapy. Many of us who are engaged in art therapy know of its success and healing potential. Anyone who is involved with grieving individuals, children or adults, can use drawings and puppets to facilitate grief work in a very simple manner. As we increase our use of art and various types of artwork, additional supervision and training in art therapy are highly advised.

Another extremely important and practical use of art therapy is for the health care professional. There is such an alarmingly high rate of burnout among health care workers. An excellent outlet for me is to use art as my stress release. I draw when I am grieving. I work in clay for my own relaxation. This has proven to be extremely healing, and a great stress reducer for me as well. My own personal use of art has also served to encourage my creativity and to keep me engaged in grief education and counselling. I encourage each of us to use art therapy for our families as well as for ourselves. It is now an integral part of my own self-care.

I also raise the issue of a family's resistance to dealing with a child's grief. Dr. Lester (Davis 1988b) has responded by saying:

> 'Many parents and adults do want to protect the children from emotion because there is a kind of a popular grass roots perception that if children get upset, it will do damage to them. So that, by and large, adults want to keep children calm from seeing anything, or feeling anything, or saying anything that will get them upset. They do not want them to go to funerals, or hear the bad news, etcetera. So one of the reasons for that resistance is the fear that if my child gets upset then that will do harm to the child.'

Another reason for resistance is the idea that children do not pay attention to death and divorce. They are able to go on playing and being happy in such a way that parents or other adults may believe that the children do not care about or are not aware of the loss. Dr. Lester further suggested that parents and adults try to protect themselves from having to hurt for the child and in effect are really protecting their own emotional responses (Davis 1988b).

Conclusion

This chapter has presented numerous methods and theories for working with grieving children and their families. It is encouraging for each of us to know of the growing interest in death education and counselling for children. The impact we have on a children's first losses stays with them for the rest of their lives and influences each loss thereafter. Art therapy in a group setting is an excellent resource for children struggling with a loss.

References
Biehler, R.F. (1976) *Child Development: An Introduction.* Boston: Houghton Mifflin.

Bowlby, J. (1969) *Attachment.* 'Attachment and Loss' series, Volume 1. New York, NY: Basic Books.

Clinebell, H. (1984) *Basic Types of Pastoral Care and Counseling.* Nashville, TN: Abingdon Press.

Davis, C.B. (1987) Notes taken in class taught by J. Vogt: 'Communication through art'. University of Missouri at Kansas City, MO, Winter.

Davis, C.B. (1988a) 'A grief education program for older children and their parents.' Unpublished report and analysis completed for Midwestern Baptist Theological Seminary, Kansas City, MO.

Davis, C.B. (1988b) Interview with Dr. Andrew D. Lester, Professor of Psychology of Religion, Southern Baptist Theological Seminary, Louisville, KY.

Dodge, N.C. (1984) *Thumpy's Story.* Springfield, IL: Prairie Lark Press.

Erikson, E.H. (1963) *Childhood and Society.* New York, NY: W.W. Norton.

Erikson, E.H. (1980) *Identity and the Life Cycle.* New York, NY: W.W. Norton.

Gerkin, C.V. (1979) *Crisis Experience in Modern Life.* Nashville, TN: Abingdon Press.

Kubler-Ross, E. (1969) *On Death and Dying.* New York, NY: Macmillan.

Lester, A.D. (1985) *Pastoral Care with Children in Crisis.* Philadelphia, PA: Westminster Press.

Lester, A.D. (ed) (1987) *When Children Suffer.* Philadelphia, PA: Westminster Press.

Paul, N.L. and Grosser, G.H. (1965) 'Operational mourning and its role in conjoint family therapy.' *Community Mental Health Journal 1,* 339–345. (Quoted in R.S. Sullender 1985, op cit., p. 137.)

Pingleton, J. (1985) 'Group counseling in the church: An integrative theoretical and practical analysis.' *Psychology and Theology 13,* 27.

Satir, V. (1972) *Peoplemaking.* Palo Alto, CA: Science and Behavior Books.

Sullender, R.S. (1985) *Grief and Growth.* New York, NY: Paulist Press.

van der Kolk, B.A. (1987) *Psychological Trauma.* Washington, DC: American Psychiatric Press.

Wadeson, H. (1980) *Art Psychotherapy.* New York, NY: John Wiley.

Worden, W.J. (1982) *Grief Counseling and Grief Therapy.* New York, NY: Springer Publishing.

Acknowledgement

This chapter was originally published in *Issues in Comprehensive Pediatric Nursing 12,* 4, pp.269–80, Taylor and Francis, Washington, DC. Reproduced with permission. All rights reserved.

About the Authors

Paul Barnard is a Project Leader with the Children's Society. Paul has a background and training in education and social work, and for the past twenty years has worked with children, young people and their families in a wide range of situations and circumstances within the statutory and voluntary sectors. As a result of Paul's involvement with children and young people in the aftermath of the Hillsborough Football Stadium Disaster of 1989, he established Liverpool Children's Project which addresses the needs of children and young people who have experienced bereavement and trauma.

Jenny Baulkwill, BA, CQSW, has been a Principal Social Worker at St Christopher's Hospice since April 1990. She has a degree in Social Studies and a Diploma in Psychiatric Social Work. After qualifying in 1983 she worked in an area mental health team in Norwich for three years. Following this she moved to London to work in a district mental health team based at St Mary's Hospital, Paddington.

Jo Carroll BA, MSc, CQSW, after qualifying as a social worker in 1974, she worked as a probation officer in Surrey and in 1983 joined the Swindon Child and Family Guidance Service. In 1987 she completed a course on Therapeutic Communication with Children and in 1990 became an independent play therapist, offering therapy to children, and consultation and training to other practitioners.

Penny Casdagli has worked extensively for over twenty-six years as an actress, writer and director. In 1987, she won the British Drama Award for the Best Young People's Play, and founded the Neti-Neti Theatre Company of which she was Artistic Director until 1994. She is the author of several works on loss and bereavement, bullying and self-esteem. Through Willow Productions she now works as a freelance drama consultant, writer and director, both in the UK and internationally, most recently in Bangladesh, Singapore, Thailand and Hungary.

Diana Crossley, BSc(Hons), DipClin Psych, is a Macmillan Child Psychologist working with Winston's Wish, a grief support programme for children, based in Gloucestershire. She undertook her clinical psychology training in Cardiff and in her final year specialised in palliative care. During this time she helped develop the Winston's Wish Programme. She coordinates the children's service for Winston's Wish, and provides individual help for bereaved children, for children facing an expected death and their families.

Ann Couldrick, RGN, HV Cert, Cert Couns, originally trained as a health visitor and MacMillan Nurse but is currently a bereavement counsellor at Sir Michael Sobell House, Churchill Hospital, Oxford where she has worked for fifteen years. Ann is also a counsellor in a general practice and a freelance trainer in bereavement and psycho-social issues in palliative care. She has published booklets on grief and bereavement and has a special interest in working with the parent who has lost a partner.

Sally Curnick, SRN, RSCN, NDN, DipHum Psy, is employed by the Cancer and Leukaemia in Childhood Trust and has been a domicilary care nurse since 1987. Prior to this Sally worked for two years in paediatric terminal care. She currently works with Anne Harris in the bereaved siblings groups.

Dr Clifford B. Davis, DMin, is the coordinator of pastoral and grief services at the Hospice of The Independence Regional Health Center, Independence, Missouri USA. He was Director and Chaplin of the Spiritual Life programme at the Gillis Centre for Children in Kansas City, Missouri, USA. Dr Davis has published several papers on grief related issues and currently teaches at Park College, Missouri.

Dr Jess Gordon, MB, ChB (Edin), MRC Psych, is a Consultant in Child and Family Psychiatry with the Northampton Child and Family Consultation Service. She is Hon. Advisor to the NSPCC and until recently, advisor to the Northampton branch of CRUSE – Bereavement Care. She has over twenty years' experience in working with children and families following bereavement and other losses. She was widowed when her three sons were in late adolescence.

Anne Harris, RGN, RSCN, CQSW, originally trained as a nurse and worked for a time in London before undertaking her CQSW in Newcastle Upon Tyne. She is currently the Malcolm Sargent Cancer Fund Social Worker at Bristol Children's Hospital where she has worked since 1987.

Peta Hemmings, BA(Hons), CQSW, is Senior Practitioner with Barnardo's Orchard Project specializing in working with families where problems arise from serious illness or bereavement. She is currently involved in Doctoral Research at York University analysing methods of social work intervention with young bereaved children. Peta also lectures and organizes training for a wide variety of agencies.

Maureen Hitcham, CQSW, began in social work in 1974, then between 1980–90 she developed direct work techniques for work with sexually abused children. In 1990 she joined the Malcolm Sargent Cancer Fund Team at the Royal Victoria Infirmary in Newcastle, where she continued to develop ways of communicating with children. Maureen has published papers and produced a Video and Handbook on this subject.

Maureen Kane, Cert Ed, is a freelance consultant and trainer who works with professionals from a number of different disciplines, including child care, medical, educational, and youth services. Her own background is in education, having taught for twelve years in mainstream and residential settings with young people with special needs. Her work now mainly centres around the issues raised for staff and adults by their experiences, and young people's experiences of trauma, separation and loss.

Jennifer Levine, MA, Reg. Nurse, has many years experience in mental health, working with children who have cancer and their families and with grieving children. She has been a bereavement services co-ordinator for a visiting Hospice Service in Fort Wayne, Indiana, USA where she lives. She has also been in private practice as a counsellor and group leader but is currently working on new books for children on grief-related topics following the success of two earlier publications.

Barbara Monroe, BA, BPhil, CQSW, has been a social worker for over twenty years in a variety of settings including the probation service, child protection and community health. She worked in a specialist neurology/neurosurgery unit for five years with a particular interest in paediatrics. She has spent the last six years at St Christopher's Hospice, latterly as Director of Social Work and the Bereavement Service, where a special interest has been the development of services for bereaved children. She is married with two teenage children.

Ruth Neville, MSW, CQSW, is a senior practioner with Barnardos Castle Project in Leeds. She largely works with children and parents who are affected by HIV. Ruth has also worked with Family Service Units and The Childrens Society working with children and young people living in unhappy or abusive families. Before qualifying as a social worker at York University in 1987, Ruth was a play worker.

Debra Noell worked as a volunteer worker with Jennifer Levine's children's grief group. She is a journalist and has published throughout the USA regarding health, women's issues and grief and is currently working for the Journal *Gazette* in Fort Wayne, Indiana, USA, where she lives.

Sister Margaret Pennells, MA (Social Work), CQSW, has been a social worker with the Child and Family Consultation Service, Northampton for the past six years, before which she worked as a psychiatric social worker in the Schools Psychological Service, Merseyside. Along with Sue Smith, she has pioneered a structured group work programme for bereaved children and adolescents and has developed a video training package for which they received the Social Work Today Award 1991. Sister Margaret also works for CRUSE as a trainer and volunteer bereavement counsellor and has been involved extensively in training professionals in bereavement work both locally and nationally. She is a member of the Good Shepherd Congregation.

Judy Sanderson, BA, CQSW, is a community link worker at the Acorn's Children's Hospice with a special interest in training. Previously, Judy ran a bereavement service for families and she has also worked with children in foster and adoptive placements, helping them cope with the separation and loss of their birth families.

John Shears, BSc (Econ), PGCE, is currently Headteacher at Redruth Community School, Cornwall. He has taught in Coventry, was Head of Middle School, Oxon (1974–79), Deputy Headteacher, Shropshire (1979–85) and Headteacher at the Streetly School, West Midlands (1985–91). He is married with two daughters.

Sue Smith, CQSW, Dip Couns, works as the co-ordinator for CRUSE – bereavement care, Birmingham South, and was previously a social worker at the General Hospital, Northampton. Before this she worked in a child care team as a social worker. Along with Sister Margaret, she has been involved in pioneering the group work programme for bereaved children and adolescents and in developing the training package with videos, for which they obtained the Social Work Today Award for 1991. She has also been involved in training professionals both locally and nationally, and is the volunteer co-ordinator for GAP, a Northampton voluntary organization for loss and bereavement counselling.

Julie Stokes, BSc, MSc, CPsychol is a principal clinical psychologist with the department of Health Psychology based at Gloucestershire Royal Hospital and has worked for five years in a Palliative Care Team. She has studied at a variety of centres in North America which have developed child bereavement programmes and 'Winston's Wish', a grief support programme, was subsequently developed. Julie is currently the Programme Director and is also involved with children whose parents have HIV/AIDS.

David A. Waskett, Dip Psy-Soc Pall Care, RMN, RNMS, CQSW, has worked as a charge nurse, as a social worker in an Intake Team, Mansfield, then with the Cambridge Psychiatric Rehabilitation Service and finally as a principal social worker at a hospice in Essex, running the bereavement service. At present he has a part-time post in a Community Care Team, otherwise he is self-employed as a trainer, counsellor and consultant in bereavement and loss. He is an accredited assistant tutor with the Clinical Theology Association.

Jan Wilby, MEd, Dip Couns, is a trained teacher and has previously worked as a youth and community leader. She is currently Head of Social Science and Head of Guidance and Support in a multi-cultural comprehensive school. Jan has studied Transcultural Bereavement Counselling as a specific issue.

Ben Wolfe, MEd, is an independent clinical social worker and Director of St Mary's Grief Support Center in Duluth, Minnesota, USA. He is a death educator and grief counsellor and runs grief support groups for young people. Ben also teaches graduate courses on dying and death at the University of Wisconsin, and on life threatening illness at the University of Minnesota. He has presented over 900 workshops and training programmes in the USA and internationally.

Christine Wood, MA, CQSW, read history at the University of Glasgow followed by a post-graduate qualification in social work. Over the past twenty-five years she has held several social work posts in hospital and General Practice settings. From July 1989–1994 she was Principal Social Worker at St. Christopher's Hospice.

Subject Index

Author Index